Glenn Gould, Music and Mind

To Eve, my favourite musician, on her birthday, 1983

xo

John

GLENN GOULD
Music & Mind

GEOFFREY PAYZANT

VNR

Van Nostrand Reinhold Ltd. Toronto
New York   Cincinnati   London   Melbourne

Design by Brant Cowie/Artplus
Typesetting by Swift-o-type Limited
Printed and bound by The Hunter Rose Company Limited

Library of Congress Catalogue Number 77-94211

CANADIAN CATALOGUING IN PUBLICATION DATA

Payzant, Geoffrey, 1926-
  Glenn Gould, music and mind

Bibliography: p.
ISBN 0-442-29802-1

1. Gould, Glenn. 2. Music — philosophy and aesthetics. 3. Sound — recording and reproducing. I. Title.

| ML417.G69P39 | 786.1'0924 | C78-001013-2 |

Grateful acknowledgement is made to those who have given permission for the use of previously copyrighted material in this book. Every reasonable care has been taken to correctly acknowledge copyright ownership. The author and publisher would welcome information that will enable them to rectify any errors or omissions in succeeding printings. Please see pages 184 to 186 for a complete list of acknowledgements.

79 80 81 82 83 7 6 5 4 3 2

Printed and bound in Canada

To Mary Lou

Contents

Preface

This book is not like other books about pianists. How could it be? Gould is not like other pianists. Paderewski was a pianist who took time away from the piano to be Prime Minister of Poland. Hofmann was a pianist who in his spare time worked on mechanical inventions. Gould is not a pianist who takes time away from the piano to think. He is a musical thinker who makes use of all available means to thought, including the piano. That the world thinks of him only as a pianist does not mean that he is under some kind of obligation to be what the world thinks he is, and do as the world expects. And of course he does not.

Perhaps Gould is garrulous, and sometimes ponderous or facetious. Whatever the reason, his musical thought has not been widely or seriously discussed; hence this book. In it I have collated his most important writings, and have tried to explain them (in the few instances where they are not self-explanatory) and to comment upon them. Many of his writings have appeared in out-of-the-way places, and some of the most informative originally appeared in radio and television programs which now exist only in archives and private collections. I have had access to nearly all of these, going back to the mid-1950s when Gould's renown as performer and writer expanded from his native Canada to the international arena.

Where possible I have quoted him directly and sometimes at considerable length, because he is his own best expositor. At the top of his form, and when not being defensive, Gould is an accomplished literary artist, particularly in the dialogue-essay form which he has used in several articles and scripts. I have, therefore, tried to keep Gould himself in the foreground throughout, with my own comments and those of other people providing continuity. And I have kept references to academic philosophers to a minimum, using them mainly for clarification, because I did not want to force Gould's thought into theoretical contexts which it might not fit, and in which the immense benefit to his readers of his unique experience as a working musician might become lost.

Top-ranking musical performers who are also eminent as writers are exceedingly rare; in English-speaking North America I can think of only two who can be compared with Glenn Gould: Charles Rosen and Leonard Bernstein. In my view, Gould is the most original and profound musical thinker of the three. And surprisingly, he is the most prolific. Charles Rosen, as cerebral a pianist as Gould but not as famous, has written a large book and a small one and some articles, all erudite in ways that most of Gould's writings are not. But Rosen does not write about such philosophical problems as the composer-performer-audience relationships, music and morality, music and technology, the mode of existence of a work of musical art, and matters connected with these, as Gould does. Neither does Leonard Bernstein, with his big-budget films for television, and the books and talk discs which have been spun off them, revealing the analytical insights of a giant musical intelligence.

In sheer number of words, if we include his scripts for radio, television, film and talk disc, along with his published articles and liner notes, Gould has written more about music than either Rosen or Bernstein. His writings are philosophically more probing (and hence more disturbing) than even Bernstein's in his 1973 Charles Eliot Norton Lectures, although in these Bernstein shows that he has a first-hand knowledge of the philosophical tradition in musical aesthetics, as Gould apparently has not.

The evidence of Gould's writings, recordings and actions could, of course, be interpreted otherwise than I have done. One alternative would be to assume that Gould has all along been playing a secret game with us, and at some level does not intend to be taken seriously. In this book I have done the opposite, as a consequence of having brought all his writings together and examined them as a unified whole. Despite his terrible puns, extended jokes and lapses into literary opulence, his aesthetics is a complex but very clear pattern of ideas, remarkably consistent and steady in its aim since his youth. While we can be excused for questioning the seriousness of his intent in many individual utterances, they must in total be taken very seriously, for Gould is talking about the salvation of humankind.

Often he is naive, and sometimes cute; and he will stop at nothing to get our attention. But frivolous and disingenuous he is not. We should not be misled by the fact that many of his writings appear in pop-culture media. Of his readers no less than of his listeners he has high expectations. He credits us with intelligence and perspicuity beyond the ordinary.

Perhaps the author of the second book on Glenn Gould will attempt a "conventional" biography. He will fail. Gould has protected his private life from public scrutiny, firmly but courteously, as no other celebrity among artists in our time has done. Moreover, unless I am much in error, his private life is in fact austere and unremarkable. A book on his life and times would be brief and boring, unless it were (as Gould himself once said it would have to be) a work of fiction, something like a biography of Sherlock Holmes or Horatio Hornblower.

He has, however, lived an exciting inner life, a life of the mind, and has been telling us about it for decades. This is the *real* life of Glenn Gould, and it is the subject of this book.

Many people have helped in a variety of ways with the making of this book, and I am grateful to them all. There are some without whose help it could never have come into being, or without whose advice its shortcomings would have been more distressingly evident. They are: David Barnett, Susan Bolotin, Steven Bucher, John Robert Colombo, Jonathan Cott, Richard Coulter, James Creighton, Gordon Epperson, Barbara Finn, Eva Friede, Hans Friede, R. A. Greene, Myrtle Guerrero, Gail Herstein, Helmut Kallmann, Michael Koerner, Jean Lavender, Douglas Lloyd, Keith MacMillan, Robert McRae, Harvey Olnick, David Oppenheim, Godfrey Ridout, Paul Robinson, Wolfgang Siegel, Janet Somerville, Francis Sparshott, A.M. Wall, Morris Wayman, Susan Wilson, Robin Woods, Arthur Younger, and, most particularly, John Beckwith.

I am also grateful for the help of CBS Records, CJRT-FM in Toronto, the T. Eaton Company Ltd., Encyclopedia of Music in Canada, General Gramophone Publications Limited, the Music

Committee of Hart House (University of Toronto), *High Fidelity Magazine*, the National Film Board of Canada, the National Library of Canada (Music Division), Random House, Inc., University of Toronto Media Centre.

Special acknowledgement is due to the Canadian Broadcasting Corporation, and particularly to the Program Archives, Music Library, Photograph Library, Record Library, and Reference Library.

This book has been published with the help of a grant from the Humanities Research Council of Canada, using funds provided by the Canada Council.

G.P.
Toronto
March 28, 1978

Un sage était autrefois un philosophe,
un poète, un musicien. Ces talents ont
dégénéré en se séparant. — DIDEROT

CHAPTER 1

Beginnings

Glenn Gould was born in Toronto on September 25, 1932. He is the only child of parents both of whom were musical: his mother played piano and organ and in her youth she aspired to a career in music; his father is an amateur violinist.

Gould tells of his maternal grandmother, who lived in "rural Canada," as he puts it (meaning Uxbridge, Ontario) and was devoted to "those indefatigable anthem-composers of the English Victorian tradition, whose works she kept stacked on the console of her reed organ, and to the greater glories of whose Mendelssohnian euphony she would pump furiously at the bellows pedals, convinced that with each scrupulous avoidance of parallel fifths the devil was given his comeuppance, and responding to the inevitable compression of a tonal answer at a cadential stretto as an article of faith."[1] Edvard Grieg was a first cousin of his mother's grandfather.[2]

The boy's early years were spent in a comfortable and supportive family environment, with a modest house in Toronto on a hilly, quiet street with many trees, not far from the shore of Lake Ontario. The family also owned a winterized cottage at Uptergrove on Lake Simcoe, ninety miles north of Toronto.

When Gould was three years old it became evident that he possessed exceptional musical abilities, including absolute pitch and some ability to read staff notation. His mother helped him at the piano, and was his only music teacher until he was ten.

At five he decided to become a composer, and was playing his own little compositions for family and friends. A lady of advanced years gives an eyewitness account of an occasion when he came with his mother to perform some of these pieces at a meeting of the Women's Missionary Society at Emmanuel Presbyterian Church, a few blocks from the Gould house. The lady remembers that Glenn was attired in a white satin suit with short pants and charmed the ladies. Perhaps the sartorial details in this recollection are a survival from those sickly-sweet stories about Sepperl Haydn and Wolferl Mozart which were read to unsuspecting children of an earlier generation, out of semi-popular music magazines.

When he was six Glenn was taken for the first time to hear a live musical performance by a celebrated soloist.

It was Hofmann. It was, I think, his last performance in Toronto, and it was a staggering impression. The only thing I can really remember is that, when I was being brought home in the car, I was in that wonderful state of half-awakeness in which you hear all sorts of incredible sounds going through your mind. They were all *orchestral* sounds, but I was playing them all, and suddenly I was Hofmann. I was enchanted.[3]

Here is a similar recollection, probably from a few years later:

I remember, when I was a kid, I always associated the New York Philharmonic broadcasts, which we used to hear on Sunday afternoons, with great, vast fields of snow—white and grey. We used to go up north to the country for weekends and, about four o'clock in the afternoon, the Philharmonic would be on when we were on our way back to Toronto. And, in wintertime, it was usually grey—a sort of endless vista of snow, frozen lake, horizon, this sort of thing — and Beethoven never sounded so good.[4]

Glenn had his early formal education at Williamson Road Public School, a high-ceilinged, three-storey, mostly brick building with an unwelcoming facade. For young Gould it was half a block down the hill, turn right, and another half-block, to terrors both real and imagined, and boredom.

I found going to school a most unhappy experience and got along miserably with most of my teachers and all of my fellow students.[5]

Gould tells a story of his first and only fishing expedition. His father was an ardent fly-fisherman and not much interested in trolling from a boat, so it was a neighbour at Uptergrove who took his own children and Glenn out to fish. This was in the summer of 1939; Gould was six years old:

We went out in the boat and I was the first to catch a fish. And when the little perch came up and started wiggling about, I suddenly saw this thing entirely from the fish's point of view — it was such a powerful experience I picked up my fish, and said I was going to throw it back. At that moment — this has remained with me as a sort of block against people who exert influence over children — the father suddenly pushed me back into my seat, probably for the sensible reason that I was rocking the boat.

Then he took the fish out of my reach, at which I went into a tantrum and started jumping up and down, stamping my feet and pulling my hair and stuff like that. And I kept it up until we got into shore. I refused to speak to those children for the rest of the summer, of course, and I immediately went to work on my father to convince him he should abandon fishing. It took me ten years, but this is probably the greatest thing I have ever done.[6]

In later life Gould's anti-fishing views developed into an active campaign, according to a description in Alfred Bester's 1964 article in *Holiday*:

Howard Scott, Gould's former producer at Columbia, says that at Gould's summer home at Lake Simcoe, Glenn goes out in his power boat every morning and evening and roars around the lake, weaving among the fishermen to spook the fish and save them from their doom. Scott says it's quite a sight to watch the fishermen in bathing suits hollering at Gould, and Gould in overcoat and cap yelling back.[7]

Robert Fulford, a distinguished Canadian author and editor, is a few months older than Glenn Gould. He wrote:

Glenn was a remarkable kid. I met him in the third grade when we were nine years old. We lived next door to each other in the east end of Toronto. Even as a child Glenn was isolated because he was working like hell to be a great man. He had a tremendous feeling and loving affection for music. . . . It was an utter, complete feeling. He knew who he was and where he was going.[8]

At age ten years Gould began lessons at the Toronto Conservatory of Music.† (It was later renamed The Royal Conservatory of Music of Toronto, and will be so called hereinafter to avoid confusion.) Alberto Guerrero was his piano teacher; he had organ lessons from Frederick C. Silvester, and theory from Leo Smith. Gould says:

I didn't become very serious until I was perhaps ten or eleven, when I really began to work with the idea of a career. It was something to sit and think about when I was bored with the [school] teacher, as I always was; and it was also a wonderful escape from my fellow students, whom I was always getting in wrong with.[9]

His organ studies continued, on and off, for about six years, and he considers them to be the basis of both his keyboard technique and his love for the music of J.S. Bach. He took a contemptuous view of

---

†*See* Appendix — Glenn Gould from Ten to Twenty: A Chronology.

pianists who performed transcriptions of Bach's organ works, and he refused to learn Mozart's Piano Sonata in A Major, K.331 because everyone else was playing it. Indeed he resisted all of Mozart's music with one exception: the Fugue in C Major, K.394, a particularly un-Mozartean piece.

By the time he was ten he could play all of Book I of J.S. Bach's *The Well-Tempered Clavier*; at twelve and thirteen he was learning the Partitas (among other things). A newspaper photograph of him at age thirteen shows him at his piano with a budgerigar on a perch held in his hand.[10] Book I of *The Well-Tempered Clavier* and a volume of the Partitas, both in the G. Schirmer edition, are on the piano. (The bird's name was Mozart, according to the caption.)

The young Gould had many pets, including goldfish named Bach, Beethoven, Chopin and Haydn. His succession of dogs included Sinbad, Sir Nickolson of Garelocheed, and Banquo. He had rabbits, turtles and a non-deodorized skunk, but their names are not on record. It would not surprise me to learn that the skunk's name was Stravinsky.

The annual Kiwanis Music Festival (about which there is more to come) was first held in Toronto in February, 1944. Glenn Gould competed in it and on February 15 won the "Piano trophy competition," apparently after a playoff between winners of the various piano classes. He again played on February 16 in the Festival's "Grand Finale Concert." So far as I have been able to discover, the earliest newspaper reports of his piano playing appeared at this time. An unnamed reporter wrote: "Among good talent probably young Glenn Gould stood out by his modest piano performance. Many people younger have been thrust on the concert stage to play more ambitious things, but young Gould took hold with that sort of commanding intelligence and responsibility which indicate an ability worth watching."[11] Augustus Bridle, a regular local critic of the day, wrote: "Glen Gould (Lady Kemp Sch.) played like a young Mozart classic."[12] "Lady Kemp Sch." refers to the Lady Kemp Scholarship of $200 which Gould had won in the piano trophy competition the day before. What "a young Mozart classic" was intended to mean I cannot guess.

A contingent of senior students at the Royal Conservatory signed up for this first Kiwanis Festival. "Just for the experience," they solemnly told each other, to make it clear that they were above being concerned about winning and losing. Among them were several highly accomplished musicians who subsequently became well known as performers. At the Festival they were devastated when this child of eleven, seeming even younger than his years, walked confidently on stage in short pants (Sepperl and Wolferl again?) and scored highest of them all.

Gould almost immediately became a celebrity, although at first in a small and local way. Young musicians fabricate stories about each other no less than do their seniors, and the Gould apocrypha·have been accumulating ever since. Many tales have been told, some by Gould himself; most of them have been refuted by him or by someone who claimed to be close to him or to the event. This has, of course, contributed to Gould's success in protecting his privacy, and in achieving the isolation without which he believes he could not survive as an artist.

Gould frequently protests that he was not a child prodigy, but of course the evidence goes against this disclaimer. In 1945 he passed the associateship examination as a solo performer in piano at the Royal Conservatory of Music of Toronto; this is considered a professional level of attainment. In 1946 he passed the music theory examinations, and was awarded the Associate diploma of the Conservatory with highest honours.

He continued piano lessons with Alberto Guerrero until 1952, and the two musicians remained friends until the latter's death in 1959. Guerrero was never convinced that Gould's extravagant gestures and his singing were indispensible adjuncts to his playing on the piano.

John Beckwith, the well-known Canadian musician, has said of Guerrero, who was his own teacher:

Unusually gifted himself as a child, Guerrero was especially successful with talented younger students. He felt that if physical efficiency could be developed by the early teens the individual temperament would have a vehicle for whatever it had to say.[13]

Gould received his secondary school education at Malvern Collegiate Institute, not far from his home, from 1945 to 1951, but he did not complete the requirements for matriculation. Like his neighbour Robert Fulford, who had dropped out some time before, he has managed to get by with something less than a full high school education. There are no former Malvern students more illustrious than Fulford and Gould.

Fulford has placed on record three reasons for his own dropping out of school. The official reason is that he was "a creative individual in rebellion against a repressive environment." The unofficial reason is that he "was lousy in school."[14] The truth, he says, is not that he was dropping out of school, but that he was dropping out of the neighbourhood (known as "the Beach"), of which he said:

For an adolescent it was a closed, deadening Wasp world, a suspicious and narrow and clique-ish little compartment in which we all worked hard to avoid knowing both ourselves and our neighbors. A Beach boy was emotionally fixated at age sixteen or less, bound to a code of athletic good-guyism that admitted the existence of no emotional, spiritual, or intellectual ambiguities.[15]

Glenn Gould stayed the full term at Malvern. He was on a special program of studies designed to give him the time he needed for practice and the study of music, and this is why he finished with less than the matriculation requirements.

Undoubtedly the most significant influence upon Gould in his teens was Artur Schnabel. He never heard Schnabel in person, but he has said:

When I was in my teens (which is the only time when one has idols, I guess) I really had only one—speaking of performers—and that was Schnabel, on whose Beethoven, and to a lesser extent Schubert and Brahms, I was brought up. I think, in part, it was because Schnabel seemed to be a person who didn't really care very much about the piano as an instrument. The piano was a means to an end, for him, and the end was to approach Beethoven.[16]

A conflict is evident in this description of Schnabel as a person who did not really care very much for the piano as an instrument. It is a major and recurring theme in Gould's writings about music, and has caused him anguish at climactic moments in his career. The conflict is between the physical characteristics of specific musical instruments or types of instruments (such as the piano) on the one hand, and purely cerebral music, as it might exist in the imagination, or in unspecified open score, on the other. A piano is a device for producing physical (that is, acoustical) events: configurations made up of audible tones of various frequencies, wave-forms, and intensities. Gould rightly believes that a piece of music is not merely a collection of acoustical events. In common with everyone else who has tried to think seriously about these matters, he encounters difficulty in trying to formulate a statement of what music really is. Whatever music might be, Gould apparently thinks it is more mental than physical, more a form of cognition than of sensation; he has thought this since early youth.

Among the other significant influences upon Gould in his teenage years was *Tristan und Isolde*, which he said made him weep when he first heard it at the age of fifteen.[17] Also at about this age he first encountered Rosalyn Tureck's recordings of the music of Bach, and in them found powerful support for his own ideas of how this music might be played—ideas which were at odds with those of his teacher, Alberto Guerrero. Gould says that the models for Guerrero's generation of teachers were Casals, Landowska and Edwin Fischer, who played with what Gould considers excessive rubato. By contrast, he found Tureck's playing "upright," with "a sense of repose, and I don't mean languor, I mean positiveness. . . ." He was influenced by Tureck, but not by the other three, he says.[18]

By his eighteenth year Gould had developed particular admiration for the conducting of Leopold Stokowski. Of Stokowski Gould said:

He was, and is, for want of a better word, an *ecstatic*. Stokowski is involved with the notes, the tempo marks, the dynamic indications of the score, to the same extent that a film-maker is involved with the original book or source which supplies the impetus, the idea, of his film. So Stokowski's performances, then, stand or fall by the degree to which he can infuse them with a sense of his own commitment to the project at hand.[19]

This passage deserves careful rereading and some extra thought, for it contains the germ of Glenn Gould's musical aesthetics, and tells us of one of its sources. The point is that a film-maker is *not* bound to follow the original book, word for word, and in its original sequence of events; neither should a performer be bound to follow every detail of the composer's score.[20]†

Of his teenage composing activities Gould has said little. A piano sonata of 1948 is mentioned in an article about Gould published in 1956, but there is no evidence that the sonata has been performed in public; it has not been published. He wrote a set of piano pieces when he was sixteen; they were intended to be incidental music to Shakespeare's *Twelfth Night*. He played them during the intermission of a performance of that play at Malvern Collegiate Institute. The pieces were titled: "Regal Atmosphere," "Elizabethan Gaiety," "Whimsical Nonsense," and "Nocturne." Of his composing he says:

I went through a twelve-tone period in my late teens and early twenties, and the works of that era—not because they are twelve-tone but simply because

---

† Glenn Gould is a dedicated film buff, and has provided the music for two commercial films, *Slaughterhouse Five* and *The Terminal Man*. (See Filmography).

I was not particularly convinced with what I did with the idiom — are now put into mothballs.[21]

Two compositions of this period, however, were performed in a student concert at the Royal Conservatory of Music in January 1951: a twelve-tone sonata for bassoon and piano, and a set of five piano pieces ("influenced by Webern's Opus 5," Gould said). Gould played the piano and the bassoonist was Nicholas Kilburn.

Gould's public performances during his teen years were few, which indicates that his parents stood firm against suggestions that he be pushed into the limelight. Nevertheless, there was no hiding away such a talent, so his performances received much attention in the Toronto newspapers. Some of the reviewers were puzzled, as might have been expected. But some were remarkably perceptive.

Gould's performing debut was not as a pianist but as an organist. It took place on December 12, 1945 at Eaton Auditorium† in Toronto. The occasion was a concert sponsored by the Casavant Society, which was named after Casavant Frères, Canada's most distinguished organ builders. A large Casavant organ was part of the opulence of Eaton Auditorium, and until the baroque revival in organ design reached Toronto in the 1960s it was frequently heard in recitals by local and visiting organists.

The Casavant Society was a somewhat loosely knit organization of local organists and people interested in organ music. It gave annual series of organ recitals in Eaton Auditorium, presenting many distinguished visiting and local recitalists. The occasion of Glenn Gould's debut, however, was not a typical Casavant Society program, in that all the performers were in some way connected with Malvern Collegiate Institute, where Gould was a student. Under the heading, "Boy, Aged 12, Shows Genius as Organist," Edward W. Wodson wrote of Gould's portion of the program in *The Evening Telegram*:

Glenn Gould is just a child, really, a loose-jointed, gracious, smiling boy not 13 yet. But he played the organ last evening as many a full-grown concert organist couldn't if he tried. A genius he is, with the modesty that only true genius knows. He played the first and last movements of Mendelssohn's last organ sonata, a movement from a Dupuis concerto, a Bach fugue and for an encore, a Bach prelude. From start to finish and in every detail his playing had the fearless authority and finesse of a master. . . .

He was never at fault. He played Mendelssohn's chorale and lovely variations as only a great artist could. . . .

His feet were as agile as his hands. The Bach G Minor Fugue was

† From 1970 to 1977 Gould made all his recordings for Columbia in Eaton Auditorium.

pedalled as clearly as a song. . . . Not only astonishing technique but interpretive intuition is his in full maturity. He touches the organ with all the reverence it demands. It was a privilege to hear and watch him last evening.[22]

Gould's first public performance as soloist with orchestra was at a Royal Conservatory concert in Massey Hall, Toronto, on May 8, 1946. In one of his most attractive autobiographical essays he gives an account of it:

When I was a tad of thirteen, a misguided pedagogue at my alma mater, the then Toronto (now Royal) Conservatory of Music, suggested that I might prepare for my debut with orchestra . . . and play Beethoven's Fourth Concerto. The suggestion was, of course, enthusiastically adopted but, as I saw it, very little preparation was required: for two years, I had been in possession of an RCA album—acquired with funds painstakingly set aside from my allowance—featuring Artur Schnabel, Frederick Stock, and the Chicago Symphony. . . .

Almost every day during the two years I owned it, prior to the above-mentioned invitation, some or all of the eight 78-rpm sides served as accompaniment for practice-sessions in which I faithfully traced every inflective nuance of the Schnabelian rhetoric, surged dramatically ahead when he thought it wise — that is to say, in most reiteratively inclined and/or motivically awkward situations—and glided to a graceful cadential halt every four minutes and twenty-five seconds or so, while the automatic changer went to work on the turntable.

These changeover points proved an especially important formative influence; without them, the D major second theme, the ambivalent F natural inauguration of the development section, the E minor stretto at bar 235, and, of course, the cadenza—to mention only landmarks pertaining to the first movement — lost emphasis and pertinence and Beethovenian point. Indeed, to this day, I am unable to tolerate any performance of this mellow opus that ignores these obvious points of demarcation, that does not pay at least token homage to that phenomenon of flip-side overlap—which those of us reared in the 78 era came to cherish and anticipate—but strides blithely, uncaringly onward to the finish. . . .

Considering the fact that the subsequent performance was somewhat at variance with rehearsal procedures, the orchestra followed superbly. There was a moment of stress, perhaps, at the D major entry, and the oboes and flutes didn't quite get the point at the E minor stretto, but I left in high spirits, . . . and the press, on the whole, was quite kind. There was, to be sure, one dissenting report from a stringer attached to the morning paper—the Toronto *Globe and Mail*: "Beethoven's elusive Fourth Piano Concerto was left in the hands of a small child last night," he noted. "Who does the kid think he is, Schnabel?"[23]

The "stringer's" actual words were: "Glenn Gould's offering was the opening movement of the Beethoven G Major Piano Concerto. Not too much dynamic range here, phrasing a little choppy and some-times puzzling to one familiar with Schnabel, but with obvious possibilities." He reported that the program also featured Elizabeth Benson Guy, Ronald Stewart, Audrey Farnell and Charles Dobias, and said prophetically: "On the whole, it seems that the Toronto Conservatory is training musicians."[24]

Augustus Bridle reported in the *Toronto Daily Star* that Gould played the allegro moderato of a sonata by Beethoven; it was, of course, a concerto. He included a description of the soloist:

Anglo-Saxon youth, about 14, doing a precarious complex with the assur-ance of a maestro; youth idioms in his manner, none in pianistic art — boyishly counting out every predicament; thrice curtain-called, for a stiff single nod to the crowd.[25]

Edward W. Wodson knew what he was listening to and responded to it sensitively:

The boy's playing showed how beautiful piano music can be — how glorious Beethoven's writing for the piano is — and how awesome are the ways of genius in a child. For Glenn Gould is a genius . . . his butterfly hands made the piano sing as only De Pachmann [sic] used to do. He showed the music lover that scale passages and arpeggios on the humble piano may have spiritual as well as technical beauty and character. His phrasing was elo-quent as poetry chanted by the poet himself.[26]

The following year, on January 14, Gould played the whole of this same concerto (Beethoven's No. 4 in G Major) in Massey Hall, with the Toronto Symphony and a guest conductor from Australia, Ber-nard Heinze. This was a concert for students of the secondary schools in the Toronto area.[27] Pearl McCarthy wrote in *The Globe and Mail*:

The boy played it exquisitely. His is not a heavy tone, but delicacy of phrasing and timing give it clear carrying power. Unfortunately, the young artist showed some incipient mannerisms and limited his self-control to the periods when he himself was playing. As he approaches adult status, he will undoubtedly learn to suppress this disturbing fidgeting while his collabora-tors are at work.[28]

Edward W. Wodson was less interested in the visual spectacle than in the sound of Gould's performance:

The grace and understanding of the boy were never at fault. Phrase after phrase of loveliest pianism would answer orchestral finesse with a solo artistry no less masterly. He sat at the piano a child among professors, and he talked with them as one with authority. It was a joy to hear his beautiful playing and to see him so modest and so utterly self-forgetful.[29]

And Augustus Bridle descended to fantasy:

. . . young Glenn Gould came haphazardly on to play a Beethoven Concerto. Every inch a boy, he sat waiting for his cue to come in — as though he'd have enjoyed a whizzbang at "cops and robbers." But Glenn knew this concerto — one of the trickiest time-scenarios Beethoven ever wrote; so many pages of presto-flutter notes to weave against the ponderous harmonies of the big orchestra; so many manoeuvres with his hankie and a refractory tux-collar . . . as though, between cues, the pianist would have enjoyed biting a big apple. But always the youth was ready to nip in and play up to the big orchestra — with many varieties of presto-digitation, all so boyishly encountered. The lad seemed to enjoy rippling his blithe cadenzas against the more obvious rhythms of the band. The andante was a smooth legato, gliding into the final rondo without a break. All done before the lad was nicely into the swing of it. . . .[30]

At the age of fourteen Gould played his first solo recital. It was a student recital at the Royal Conservatory of Music of Toronto. Recalling this program thirteen years later Gould said that he played "a brace of fugues and some Haydn, some Beethoven, some Mendelssohn, some Liszt (which I haven't played since in public)."[31] He says that he was not nervous:

It was all part of a game, really. . . . In those days, one was blissfully unaware of the responsibility. I just wish I could feel that way again. Now, you accomplish the same thing by sedatives.[32]

His first public recital in the strict sense was in Eaton Auditorium on October 20, 1947. Wodson on that occasion said of Gould's Scarlatti:

Glenn Gould made every note a gem of loveliness. Scales at all sorts of speed were singing things of many-shaded beauty. . . . It was the same with every note of his program. What is called interpretation of Beethoven, Chopin, Liszt and so forth was forgotten. . . . Genius as profound as their own was at the keyboard.[33]

Colin Sabiston wrote in The Globe and Mail:

Here was a player who conceived movements, entire compositions as wholes, and whose every detail was calculated to reveal total structures.[34]

And Augustus Bridle's lurching prose missed the point again:

With infallible accuracy and intense finger-technique he tantalized the mediaeval Italian [Scarlatti!] till he stupefied his audience, especially men. Spiderlike fingers, flexible rubberish wrists, pedals infallible, nose a foot above the keys, he was like an old man on a music-spree. . . .
In a Beethoven Sonata, Op. 37 [there is no Beethoven Sonata Op. 37] he outdid Rachmaninoff for intensively supple art. Vivid re-etching, such as Ludwig never dreamed into a sonata, was the essence of this youth-technique.[35]

This recital was promoted by Walter Homburger, a Toronto-based impresario, who now is also Managing Director of the Toronto Symphony. He was Glenn Gould's manager until 1967.

Gould gave his first network radio recital on Sunday, December 24, 1950, at 10:30 a.m. EST. Here is the announcement published in *The CBC Times*:

Glenn Gould, the eighteen-year-old Toronto Pianist playing the Sonata in B Flat Major (K.281) by Mozart, and Hindemith's Sonata No. 3 (1936).[36]

Gould says that this occasion marks the beginning of his happy relationship with the microphone and the whole apparatus of broadcasting and recording. Since then he has felt completely at home in the studio.

By the time he was twenty, Gould had played four or five concerts with the Toronto Symphony, two with the Royal Conservatory Orchestra, and one each with the orchestras of Hamilton, Ontario and Vancouver, British Columbia. He had toured the western provinces as a recitalist, and had further Canadian tours on his schedule for the near future. And he had played seven or eight network radio performances for the CBC.

For two or three years after ending his formal lessons with Guerrero in 1952, Gould went into almost complete isolation, at Uptergrove for the most part, with his piano, a tape recorder and his dog as companions. His intention was to work as hard as he could at the piano to settle for himself the question whether he had the qualities needed to become a ranking concert pianist. He did, however, accept a few performing engagements in Canada, including broadcasts, and by 1954 was familiar to Canadian audiences.

The year 1954 is of special interest to scholars as the year of the earliest reference to Glenn Gould in *The Music Index*. This reference is to an item in the *Musical Courier* in which Ezra Schabas and Stuart Nall comment on a recital by Gould in Toronto on October 16 of that year. They said, in part:

If his achievements in the music of Bach are matched by comparable insights into works by other masters, the public will soon be confronted with an artist in no way inferior to such artists as Landowska and Serkin.[37]

All this, of course, was leading up to Gould's debut performances in the United States in January, 1955.

We know very little of events preparatory to these performances: arguments with his agent Walter Homburger; discussions with other musicians; general excitement and last-minute practice and changes in the program. We can only be certain that Gould went about it in his own way. Years later he gave accounts of his planning and motives to several interviewers, but it is impossible to separate his after-the-fact impressions from the actual events.

He knew that other young pianists at that time would have gone to New York with a debut program consisting of a Bach transcription, a middle-period Beethoven sonata, some Chopin, and a percussive Russian crowd-pleaser — Khatchaturian, perhaps, or Prokoviev. The important thing was not to be just another bright kid from the boondocks trying to impress "Debutown" (as Gould sometimes calls New York) with his thundering octaves, where they know all about thundering octaves, and would compare Gould not only with other bright kids all doing the same things, but also with the piano immortals. So he decided to go with a program that would claim attention for its unorthodoxy if for nothing else, and which would exhibit his own special capabilities. He also insisted that the program should be one which he would enjoy playing, apart from any other consideration; on this he has insisted throughout his performing career.

In the 1970s it would not seem eccentric to include the G Major Partita of J.S. Bach in a recital program, but in the 1950s the Partitas were not generally accepted fare; they were associated with cultish recitals by harpsichordists or by Myra Hess or Rosalyn Tureck on piano. But this Partita was a long-time favourite of Gould's, so he included it. He also included Beethoven's Sonata in E Major, Opus 109, which everyone knew could only be properly played by a wise musician of mature years and full of the world's wisdom. And everyone knew that the Three-part Inventions (or Sinfonias) of Bach were boring, diddly technical studies for young piano students, but that did not deter him from playing five of them in a group, along with Webern's Variations Opus 27 and the Berg Sonata, neither of which anybody knew. With these pieces, along with some Gibbons and some Sweelinck (whose name nobody could pronounce) Gould had a program he knew would be noticed one way or another.

Gould's United States debut was in the Phillips Gallery in Washington, D.C., on the afternoon of January 2, 1955. Here are some comments by the critic, Paul Hume:

Few pianists play the instrument so beautifully, so lovingly, so musicianly in manner, and with such regard for its real nature and its enormous literature. . . .
Glenn Gould is a pianist with rare gifts for the world. It must not long

delay hearing and according him the honor and audience he deserves. We know of no pianist anything like him of any age.[38]

On the evening of January 11 Gould played his New York debut in Town Hall. This was, of course, the crucial one, and by the standards of the time he had invested heavily in it: $1,300, we are told in a newspaper account, of which $450 was for rental of the hall and the remainder was for advertising and promotion. Gould told an interviewer that he had had a recurrence of his chronic fibrositis shortly before this recital and was rescued by a helpful druggist who provided the appropriate remedy. Apart from this, he says, he was completely relaxed before and during the program.

Here is part of the review John Briggs wrote for *The New York Times*:

The challenging program Mr. Gould prepared was a test the young pianist met successfully, and in so doing left no doubt of his powers as a technician.

The most rewarding aspect of Mr. Gould's playing, however, is that technique as such is in the background. The impression which is uppermost is not one of virtuosity but of expressiveness. One is able to hear the music.[39]

The same critic wrote in the *Musical Courier*:

Gould's complete enthralment with the abstract, abstruse beauties of these contrasting works seems to result in a sense of almost other-worldly dedication. We got the impression that he simply could not perform an inferior or shallow work, or even a happy, thoughtless one; and while most pianists should shun baroque music not intended for the piano, not so Gould, for he grasps its very meaning in such a way that he quite transcends and obviates questions as to whether the keys he touches should actuate wind, plectra, or hammers. Hence the curiously successful matching of the baroque, which so often disregards medium, with atonal music, which fairly denies medium, mode and all. I can only call him great, and warn those who have not heard him that he will plunge them into new and unfamiliar depths of feeling and perception.[40]

The next day Glenn Gould signed a contract with Columbia Records, and a remarkably productive business relationship was launched which continues to the present. But it is noteworthy that he was offered a contract so promptly. Several accounts exist of how this came about, so I asked David Oppenheim, who is now Dean of the School of the Arts in New York University, for the facts of the matter. He was at that time Director of Columbia's Masterworks Division.

On January 10 Oppenheim visited the violinist Alexander Schneider at his house in New York. They listened to a record of

Dinu Lipatti, at the conclusion of which Oppenheim said that he wished there was another such magnificent pianist. Schneider, who had played chamber music with Gould on CBC, said that there was another, and that he would be playing in Town Hall the next night. Oppenheim went to the recital, and knew after a few bars of Gould's playing that this was a great artist, and that Columbia would offer him a contract.

Tired but happy, Gould flew home to Toronto the day after his recital. With him were his contract, his folding chair, his father (who had attended the recital), and Walter Homburger, who told reporters that the contract was the first Columbia Records had ever signed with an unknown artist merely on the basis of his debut.

Gould's first service under this contract was his recording of the *Goldberg Variations* by J.S. Bach, for which the sessions took place in the CBS studios in New York in June 1955. A press release from Columbia Records dated June 25 gives a description of these sessions from which it is easy to make the standard discount for flak, or hype, or whatever was the word at the time.

Columbia Masterworks' recording director and his engineering colleagues are sympathetic veterans who accept as perfectly natural all artists' studio rituals, foibles or fancies. But even these hardy souls were surprised by the arrival of young Canadian pianist Glenn Gould and his "recording equipment" for his first Columbia sessions. Mr. Gould was to spend a week recording one of his chief specialties, Bach's Goldberg Variations.

It was a balmy June day, but Gould arrived in coat, beret, muffler and gloves. "Equipment" consisted of the customary music portfolio, also a batch of towels, two large bottles of spring water, five small bottles of pills (all different colors and prescriptions) and his own special piano chair.

Towels, it developed, were needed in plenty because Glenn soaks his hands and arms up to the elbows in hot water for twenty minutes before sitting down at the keyboard, a procedure which quickly became a convivial group ritual; everyone sat around talking, joking, discussing music, literature and so forth while "soaking" went on.

Bottled spring water was a necessity because Glenn can't abide New York tap water. Pills were for any number of reasons—headache, relieving tension, maintaining good circulation. The air conditioning engineer worked as hard as the man at the recording studio control panel. Glenn is very sensitive to the slightest changes in temperature, so there was constant adjustment of the vast studio air conditioning system.

But the collapsible chair was the Goldberg (Rube) variation of them all. It's a bridge chair, basically, with each leg adjusted individually for height so that Glenn can lean forward, backward, or to either side. The studio skeptics thought this was wackiness of the highest order until recording got under way. Then they saw Glenn adjust the slant of his chair before doing his slightly incredible cross-hand passages in the Variations, leaning in the direction of the "cross." The chair was unanimously accepted as a splendid, logical device.

Gould at the keyboard was another phenomenon — sometimes singing along with his piano, sometimes hovering low over the keys, sometimes playing with eyes closed and head flung back. The control-room audience was entranced, and even the air conditioning engineer began to develop a fondness for Bach. Even at record playbacks Glenn was in perpetual motion, conducted rhapsodically, did a veritable ballet to the music. For sustenance he munched arrowroot biscuits, drank skimmed milk, frowned on the recording crew's Hero sandwiches.

After a week of recording, Glenn said he was satisfied with his recording stint, packed up his towels, pills, and bridge chair. He went 'round to shake hands with everyone — the recording director, the engineers, the studio man, the air conditioning engineer. Everybody agreed they would miss the cheerful "soaking" sessions, the Gould humour and excitement, the pills, the spring water.

"Well," said Glenn as he put on his coat, beret, muffler and gloves to venture out into the June air, "you know I'll be back in January!"

And so he will. The studio air conditioning engineer is getting ready for the workout.[41]

The disc won instant acclaim, became a best seller, and established Glenn Gould as a fully mature artist among the foremost pianists. As Gould later said, it paid the rent for a few years. From the perspective of the 1970s, it is evident that the release early in 1956 of Gould's *Goldberg Variations* recording, and not his New York debut in 1955, is the fulcrum of his career, although the latter was a necessary step toward the former.

In the succeeding months Gould played concerts and broadcasts, and recorded his second release, the last three sonatas of Beethoven (Opus 109, Opus 110, and Opus 111). With these, as with the *Goldbergs*, Gould was recording repertoire which other artists would have attempted not at the beginning but at the end of their careers.

In February 1956 Gould's String Quartet was given its first performance. The players were the Montreal String Quartet, and the occasion was a CBC broadcast. It is in one movement, structurally taut yet introspective and appealing. Gould and others have noticed its debt to Richard Strauss. He said that he gave two or three years of his life to the Quartet, and loves it, but that it did not quite come off, because he was insufficiently acquainted at that time with the technical capabilities of stringed instruments.

In March of the same year Gould played his first concert with orchestra in the United States, the Detroit Symphony, conducted by Paul Paray. They played Beethoven's Concerto No. 4. His first concert with the New York Philharmonic was in January 1957;

Leonard Bernstein conducted and they played Beethoven's Concerto No. 2. The following month he played Bach before a live audience for a CBC telecast from Toronto in which he also conducted Maureen Forrester and an orchestra in the alto solo from Mahler's Second Symphony.

And so it went until May 3, 1957 when, with his manager, Walter Homburger, he set out on his first European tour. It began with two weeks in the Soviet Union. He played four concerts in Moscow and four in Leningrad, beginning in Moscow on May 7 with the following program: J.S. Bach, four fugues from *The Art of the Fugue*, and the Sinfonias (complete); Beethoven, Sonata Opus 109; Berg, Sonata.

Gould was the first pianist from North America, and the first musician from Canada, to perform in the Soviet Union. The newspaper accounts of his visit refer to him as a "cultural ambassador," but it was not diplomatic of him to give lectures (by interpreter) at the conservatories in Moscow and Leningrad on the music of the twentieth century Viennese School, music which was proscribed in the Soviet Union. He says that a few senior musical academicians demonstrated their disapproval by walking out.

It is well known that Gould had wildly enthusiastic receptions from audiences and critics in Russia and in the other countries where he played. His Berlin debut was in May 1957, with the Berlin Philharmonic conducted by Herbert von Karajan, playing Beethoven's Concerto No. 3. H.H. Stuckenschmidt was quoted describing Gould as an absolute genius, the greatest pianist since Busoni.

Early in June Gould played a recital in Vienna before a small but rapturous audience which included Paul Badura-Skoda, Alfred Brendel, and Georg Demus. This was his final appearance of the tour. He had played twelve concerts in one month; in each he had been recalled for many encores. He did not fail to observe that European critics paid little attention to his unique bodily and vocal mannerisms at the keyboard, whereas in Canada and the United States there were some who noticed little else.

He returned home in June, not too exhausted to resume his recording schedule at Columbia Records in New York, and to play several recital and concert engagements in the months following. In May 1958 he played his first concert with the Philadelphia Orchestra. Eugene Ormandy conducted and the work was Beethoven's Concerto No. 4.

In August 1958 Gould played the Bach Concerto in D Minor in

Salzburg with Dimitri Mitropoulos. Three days later, still in Salzburg, he had to cancel a recital because of influenza. In December he played eleven concerts in eighteen days in Israel. This, his second overseas tour, took him also to Germany, Austria, Italy, Belgium and Sweden.

In February 1959 he was awarded the Bach Medal for Pianists by the Committee of the Harriet Cohen Music Awards, London, England. In late May and early June of the same year he played Beethoven concertos at the Royal Festival Hall in London with the London Symphony Orchestra conducted by Josef Krips. (Years later Gould said that Krips was the most under-rated conductor of his generation.) He was scheduled to play all five concertos, but an illness prevented his playing the *Emperor* (Louis Kentner substituted for him). Harold Rutland, writing in *The Musical Times*, described his impressions of Gould:

A good deal of publicity preceded his arrival. He was said to be the first North American pianist to have played in the U.S.S.R., where his success was phenomenal; and in Berlin he was hailed as 'the greatest pianist since Busoni'. One gathered, moreover, that his manner on the concert platform was distinctly unorthodox.

I met him a few days before his concerts began. He was wearing woollen gloves, though the day was warm; and he politely declined to shake hands with me, evidently fearing that my grip might put his hand out of action. Frequently, I understand, he wears two pairs of gloves, and (like Pachmann) he is no lover of fresh air. He was clearly a young man of character and, I would say, intellect. . . .

Although the 'Emperor' is not my favourite concerto, I went to Festival Hall on 25 May to hear Glenn Gould play it, since it would, I thought, show one what his capabilities were. But he was indisposed, with a high temperature, and did not appear. 'That's what comes of coddling yourself in this climate,' said a member of the audience when she heard the news. But I tried again, on 1 June, and heard him play the Concerto in C minor. Yes, his manner was unorthodox; not to say eccentric. He sat on an exceptionally low chair with the piano raised on wooden blocks; he almost lay back and crossed his left leg over his right; now and again he sipped a glass of water; and he beat time with his foot. But he came out to the platform quickly, without any fuss, and as soon as the music started his absorption was complete.

One frequently praises a performance for its clarity. Here, however, there was not only what one might call technical clarity (the part-playing was particularly admirable), but extreme clarity of the mind. Gould knew exactly how he wanted to play the Concerto, and he was playing it just like that. Furthermore, to an unusual degree, he was evidently thinking of the solo part as belonging to the whole texture; he listened keenly to the orchestra, which, under Professor Krips, gave him the maximum of co-operation. To judge by what one knows of Beethoven, I would not say that this was how he played the work; he was probably far more dynamic, even violent. But Gould's performance was finely conceived and finely carried out, with a continually forward impulse, subtle tone gradations, and with never an ugly sound. There were, moreover, no effects superimposed on the music. I felt, on the strength of this performance, that Gould was one of the very few pianists I would be ready to listen to at any time and under any conditions.

However, I cannot help thinking it unfortunate that a teacher or friend, whose judgment he respects, has never taken him in hand and told him home truths about his platform manner. . . . But when all is said, the playing's the thing, and if Glenn Gould should find it impossible to play as well as he does without, let us say, standing on his head, I for one would not object. He would, I am sure, do this if he felt like it, without first asking my or anybody else's permission.[42]

In January 1960 he made his first appearance on television in the United States, with Leonard Bernstein and the New York Philharmonic. He was by then a veteran of Canadian television, where his talk-and-play shows are still a regular feature of the programming. In 1963 and 1964 he gave lectures at the Gardner Museum in Boston and at several academic institutions, including the University of Cincinnati, Hunter College, the University of Wisconsin, Wellesley College and the University of Toronto. The latter granted him an honorary doctorate in June 1964. It is a tradition in that university for a musician, when he receives an honorary degree, to give a brief performance as part of the ceremony. This is what was in the first place expected of Gould, but instead he gave the convocation address. The ratio of talking to playing in his life was by then much in favour of talking. None of Gould's listeners at the convocation could have known that his final public appearance as pianist had taken place three months previously. It had been a recital in Orchestra Hall, Chicago, on March 28, 1964, in which he played fugues from *The Art of the Fugue* by Bach, the same composer's Partita No. 4 in D Major, Beethoven's Sonata Opus 110 and Krenek's Third Sonata.

All his adult life Gould has worked at composing (in several senses of the word), broadcasting, recording and writing. By the early 1960s a conflict was growing between the demands of these activities and the demands of his concert and recital schedule. Numerous cancellations of concert engagements and widely publicized hypochondria attest to this; it was obvious that concerts and recitals would lose the contest. But Gould had been predicting this since his late teen years. It was not his fault if nobody believed him.

Since 1964 Glenn Gould the person has thoroughly merged with the works of Glenn Gould. His life is no longer separate from his works because the major events of his life are embodied in those works. He has continued to live in Toronto a solitary and incredibly productive life, ecstatically committed to the exploration of audio technology and its applications to "music" in his own wide sense of that word, which includes the manipulation of all kinds of sounds, including speech.

CHAPTER 2

Non-Take-Twoness

In 1967, three years after his final recital, Gould said:

Except for a few octagenarians, I'm really the first person who has, short of having a nervous collapse or something, given up the stage.[1]

He gave up the concert stage not because he was getting too few engagements, nor because people were not coming to his concerts. On the contrary, in 1964 he was a superstar who could rely on full houses and more offers of engagements than he could accept. He gave it up not as the result of an impulsive decision, nor of some kind of temperamental renunciation, but so he might be free to realize certain ambitions formulated long before his New York debut in 1955.

These included, in addition to public performing, such activities as composing, writing, and experimenting with applications of technology to music-making. He has since done all these, and is still doing all except public performing. In his mid-twenties it became evident to him that the strenuous life of a touring performer, and the conventional restrictions of concerts and recitals, were preventing the realization of those other ambitions. As someone once put it, Gould gave up the concert stage in order to become less of a performer and more of a musician. People still believe that he will come to his senses or snap out of his sulk and make a come-back to a conventional career as touring soloist. But Gould's withdrawal was no temporary aberration: there is not the slightest possibility that he will return to public performing.

In a broadcast interview recorded in 1959 Gould was asked if he ever went to concerts as a listener. He replied:

No, almost never. I'm extremely uncomfortable at concerts and, for me, the real approach to music is sitting at home . . . listening to recordings.[2]

The American composer Ned Rorem said something similar:

I never go to concerts any more, and I don't know anyone who does. It's hard still to care whether some virtuoso tonight will perform the *Moonlight Sonata* a bit better or a bit worse than another virtuoso performed it last night.

I do often attend what used to be called avant-garde recitals, though seldom with delight, and inevitably I look around and wonder: What am I doing here? What am I learning? Where are the poets and painters and even composers who used to flock to these things? Well, perhaps what I'm doing here is a duty, keeping an ear on my profession so as to justify the joys of resentment, to steal an idea or two, or just to show charity toward some friend on the program. But I learn less and less. Meanwhile the absent artists are home playing records; they are *reacting* again, finally, to something they no longer find at concerts.[3]

Gould says that he becomes claustrophobic in an audience, but not on the stage because there he had room to breathe. He speaks of audiences as "people sitting there with the perspiration of two thousand, nine hundred and ninety-nine others penetrating their nostrils."[4] If for some reason he has an inescapable obligation to attend a concert he will listen standing in the wings rather than sitting in the best seat in the house.† He is convinced that audiences are in the concert hall mainly in the hope of witnessing a spectacular disaster of which the performer will be the victim. Debussy put it this way:

The attraction of the virtuoso for the public is very like that of a circus for the crowd. There is always a hope that something dangerous may happen.[6]

In a circus the acrobat might slip, fall off his wire and be horribly mutilated. In a concert the horn might crack, the pianist might forget his notes and be horribly humiliated. "Blood-lust," Gould calls it. "At live concerts I feel demeaned, like a vaudevillian."[7]

In his concert-giving days Gould overcame his strong negative

---

† In January 1960 Gould went to hear a recital by Arthur Rubinstein in Toronto. Gould did not take a seat in the hall but lurked in the broadcast booth. At the end of the recital he met Rubinstein, who asked: ". . . why didn't you take a seat out front—surely you can't enjoy the sound back here?" Gould replied: "On the contrary, Maestro, I always prefer to listen in the wings."[5]

feelings toward audiences by adopting what he called "an attitude of healthy indifference" to them, pretending to himself that what he was doing up there on the platform he would be doing anyway for his own pleasure, whether or not anyone wanted to hang around and listen.[8]

Gould acknowledges that not all performers share his negative attitude toward audiences. He mentions Menuhin and Rubinstein as artists who need the stimulus of a live audience. Myra Hess would be another example. For her a public performance was an occasion confidently and happily shared with people she regarded as friends. She was nervous, but not because she sensed hostility on the part of her hearers. Rather it was because she feared that she might fail to rise to the greatness of the music she was to play.

Gould had reason to be suspicious of the motives of his audiences and critics. It was sometimes evident that they were more interested in his stage mannerisms than in the music: his visible display was unlike anything seen since de Pachmann. And since our ears can never successfully compete for attention with our eyes, it was frequently overlooked that as music his performing was a new and remarkable phenomenon.

Gould must have known that he was bringing musical performances of extraordinarily high calibre to his audiences. They in turn were no doubt aware of this knowledge on his part, since it is never possible for persons of extraordinary capabilities to conceal entirely their sense of special worth; and it is never quite possible for less gifted people to conceal their resentment of this. I am not speaking of arrogance and our reactions to it; arrogance is used to hide stupidity or cowardice or some other kind of inferiority. I am speaking of the disturbing currents that flicker when someone shows us something we might have seen for ourselves if we had been as perceptive as he. Although we might be grateful for the revelation, we are nevertheless irritated by it, especially when it was our "normal" limitations that prevented our seeing it in the first place. In turn our discomfort is misinterpreted as resentment by the person who brought us the revelation, and his response to this is to adopt a protective attitude of remoteness, which we in our turn misinterpret as arrogance, and we have a vicious circle. We rejoice, secretly, when someone set apart from us in this manner suffers a fall.

Of course this is merely an interpretation and not an explanation of how Gould developed his negative attitude toward audiences. That some artists have a different attitude he does not deny.

He also wishes we could abolish the custom of applauding at concerts. His reasons are that applauding gives the audience a false sense of active participation in the occasion, and that applause misleads performers, luring them into crowd-pleasing tricks of interpretation and personal display. So long as a performer's primary motive is personal display, he cannot give more than secondary attention to the music he is performing. For Gould, all personal display is competitive, and all competition is corrupting. He fears and mistrusts the competitive instinct in humans.

Public musical performances are competitive in several ways: the performer competes against his own recording, or against his previous performances of the pieces; in a concerto the soloist competes against the orchestra; the performer must "conquer" his audience, must have a "triumph" in New York or Moscow.

The motive of personal display tempts the performer to distort the music as he strains after theatrical effects to arouse the gallery. Gould's favourite example of this is his Columbia recording of J.S. Bach's Partita No. 5, recorded in July 1957. He had recently returned from conquering Europe, from "triumphant" appearances in Moscow, Berlin and other cities (to use the language of the press back home). He had played the Fifth Partita or parts of it in almost every program, either as a featured item or as an encore. In order to project the piece into large, crowded concert halls he had acquired stagy habits: expressive dynamics and rubato, and other artful devices. These tricks turned up in the recording, which Gould says is a bad thing because they are not only redundant but distracting. Someone at CBS probably winces every time Gould publicly says that he would like to delete this recording and destroy every copy of it, if this could be done without risk to his royalties.

"Perversions" is Gould's word for such attention-grabbing tricks. He says that they distort the structural framework of the music. For him this is a serious matter because in his way of experiencing music the structure is the essence, the peculiarly *musical* aspect of a piece.

This preoccupation with structure, or "backbone" as he sometimes calls it, belongs to what we roughly classify as the "classical" artistic disposition. By comparison, the "romantic" artist is preoccupied with sensuousness and impulse. Gould prefers coherence of structure to luscious tone, control of detail to emotional impulse. Coherence and control are for the most part lost in the distances and the acoustical underbrush of a concert hall.

Gould dislikes and does not play the kinds of music which seem to thrive best in big auditoriums. Chopin, Liszt and Rachmaninoff come readily to mind; less readily so do Schubert and Schumann (and cousin Edvard Grieg, whose concerto Gould once said he might record, but only as a publicity stunt and to replenish his portfolio if the stock market should sag). He admires what a master such as Arthur Rubinstein can do with this romantic music, but for Gould it has been proven that the repertoire he likes best is better served in the recording studio than in the concert hall. His own Columbia recordings are his proof of this. It has *not* been proven that Chopin, Liszt and the others are better served in the concert hall than in the studio. (These are my words, not his, but they convey the essence of his view.)

Gould has not confined his attack against the concert hall to such descriptions of his personal attitudes towards audiences and repertoire and the career of a performer as we have just examined. He has a set of more objective arguments which have historical and social pretensions.

He claims that there are social and economic forces at work in our culture which have already rendered the concert hall obsolete (except for specialized shrines such as Bayreuth) and which will cause it to disappear from our musical life by the year 2000. The most potent of these is progress in the technology of musical recording, and particularly of the long-play disc, the beginnings of which happened to coincide with his own beginnings as a professional musician. This technological progress has changed not only the mechanics and economics of the music market, but also the nature of musical composing, performing and listening, and the relationships between these.

In the 1960s Gould talked a great deal about the "post-renaissance" specialization which, he said, separates composing from performing, and both of these from listening. He claimed that in the sixteenth and seventeenth centuries nobody performed music who was not a composer as well as a performer; and people who listened to music were all, to a greater or lesser degree, composers and perform-ers. Kings and dukes wrote songs and played the lute.

In the eighteenth century performing became a specialized art in its own right, and audiences no longer consisted almost entirely of people who could write music and sing or play it. The three musical functions became separate, and there began the emergence of the mighty virtuoso performer as the god-like figure so admired since the late nineteenth century. This was a disaster for music, according to

Gould, and the art of music might not have survived had it not been for the advent of recording technology.

Recording has already begun to eliminate the compartmentalization of composing, performing and listening; eventually it will cause the separations to disappear entirely, thereby restoring music to its proper pre-renaissance condition. With recorded music it is now possible for a performer to make artistic decisions which post-renaissance culture allocated exclusively to the composer, and for a listener to make artistic decisions which formerly were made only by composers or performers. These decisions the listener is now able to make by adjusting the controls on his radio or phonograph.[9]

At the centre of the technological debate . . . is a new kind of listener—a listener more participant in the musical experience. The emergence of this mid-twentieth-century phenomenon is the greatest achievement of the record industry. For this listener is no longer passively analytical; he is an associate whose tastes, preferences, and inclinations even now alter peripherally the experiences to which he gives his attention, and upon whose fuller participation the future of the art of music awaits.[10]

Gould's New Listener participates as an artist when he adjusts his phonograph for loudness, balance, clarity and (as has been possible since the early 1960s) tempo. Formerly such adjustments were dictated by the composer caste and carried out (with deviations at peril) by the performer caste. Gould went so far as to propose, quite seriously, what he called the "kit-concept" of the listener's role: the listener would be able to buy a kit consisting of many different recorded performances of a particular work, and with his home editing set he could splice together pieces of tape from these to make a composite interpretation to his liking. The New Listener, as artist, would merge with performer and composer more and more as technology provided the means.

The New Performer, on the other hand, will be freed by technology from his bondage to a small number of pieces with which he has had success in his concerts:

A tremendous conservatism takes over the concert performer—he's afraid to try out the Beethoven Fourth, if the Beethoven Third happens to have been his specialty.[11]

Once liberated from the concert stage the performer can explore the immense repertoire of less well-known music, from the Baroque period for example, for which the recording industry has created a demand. Or instead of specializing in one concerto by Beethoven he can apply himself to them all, one after the other, since having recorded one he can forget it and move on to the next with all his attention. In this manner he can encounter, in the closest possible relationship, a wider range of music than would be possible for him if he were required to maintain a few concert pieces in peak form. The New Performer can be incomparably more adventurous than his predecessor.

The New Composer, in turn, has an advantage totally denied his predecessors: the possibility of recording permanent and authoritative performances of his music, performed by him or by someone else under his guidance. Britten, Copland and Stravinsky are mentioned by Gould, but of course there are others making use of this possibility. Presumably a composer's performance of his own work will settle all questions arising out of the ambiguities of staff notation. If, subsequently, a performer needs to know exactly how the composer wanted a certain passage to be played, he can listen to the composer's own recording.

This possibility might have the effect of restraining performers from trying new and original interpretations. But on the other hand it might have the effect of making composers into better performers, since they will want to be technically capable of playing the music they write; this in turn will further erode the distinction between composing and performing, which can only have the ultimate effect of revivifying the art.

Either way, it would seem, the concert stage loses. If composer-recorded testaments become canonical so that performers must try to make their performances resemble the composers' recorded performances as much as possible, then much of the interest and variety will depart from the concert hall, and a portion of the audience will depart also. Each performance will tend to sound like every other, and we will listen to the composer's recording, the prime source, in greater comfort at home, and more cheaply. On the other hand, as the distinction breaks down between composer and performer, the specialist demon performer, bred and trained to be capable of putting on a show which excites the audience into a frenzy of stamping and cheering, will disappear. The all-purpose musical man is no such freak; his name will never be a draw at the box office. And anyway, Gould says, the "name" or identity of the performer will become insignificant in proportion as the composer-performer-listener distinctions disappear.

Gould says that, apart from other factors, economic pressures will bring about the end of concert halls. Their paying customers are already deserting them for the comfort and privacy of their homes, in which are phonographs, radios and television receivers. For economic reasons few acoustically decent concert halls have been built in recent years, and people who can listen to well-balanced recorded ensembles at home, with the sound adjusted to suit the room, will not want to endure an evening dominated by cello and double bass as the result of an unlucky assignment of seats in a concert hall.

Our expectations of music have been conditioned by the near-perfection that is possible in a recording and impossible in a live performance. The record manufacturer can sell a disc made up of the best parts of several "takes" of a piece, but at a concert "Take 1" is what you pay for and "Take 1" is what you get, whether good or bad. There is no second chance for the concert performer. Gould calls this "non-take-twoness," and it is his chief objection to the concert hall.

Perhaps it is by a bad historical accident that we have come to include the ability to play a piece through with no obvious errors as one of the things we look for in a performing artist. It is bad for several reasons: nobody can be in top form all the time; mishaps occur with delicate musical instruments; stray dogs wander across the stage during the cadenza. It is part of the viciousness of concert hall etiquette that the performer cannot stop and say, "Do you mind if I try that lovely bit again?" Recording has, no doubt, its own viciousness; but a recorded performance avoids this whole problem and the destructive nervous tensions which accompany it.

One of Gould's weakest arguments against the concert hall goes like this:

A great deal of the music that I would play if I, in fact, gave concerts . . . would be music not written for an auditorium seating two or three thousand people; it would be music of Bach or Mozart or Beethoven, written for palaces or churches or homes. And why on earth should I try to play this in an auditorium that seats two or three thousand people?[12]

But from the fact that Bach (to select just one of Gould's examples, and not to contest its literal truth) intended his music to be played in palaces, churches or homes, we cannot conclude that he intended his music *not* to be played anywhere else. Bach did not intend his music to be played on the modern grand piano either, as of course Gould does.

A presupposition underlies Gould's historical-social arguments against the concert hall: that technological innovations not only *can* but *must* be put to use. In his 1966 articles "The Prospects of Recording" he writes about "an endearing, if sometimes frustrating, human characteristic—a reluctance to accept the consequences of a new technology."[13] And where he tells us about the artistic decisions now open to the New Listener, with his phonograph controls, Gould says:

. . . not only *can* the listener become qualified to make such decisions; he *must* become so. This is the future for him.[14]

Comes the Revolution we'll all eat strawberries and cream, whether we like them or not.

There is no evidence that the listener is obeying the imperative thus laid down by Gould, or that there are more composers who are competent as performers than there were fifty years ago. The technological developments predicted by Gould in the mid-1960s have for the most part materialized as he said they would, but the advertisements in the audio press do not suggest that there is a consumer market for them. Nobody is advertising "kits." As for composers who are capable of performing their own works, many of the younger generation work directly on tape with electronic music, rather than writing music to be played on conventional instruments by themselves or by anyone. But in a way Gould could not have expected, the New Listener and the New Composer have merged, and powerfully verified some of his predictions, in the person of Walter Carlos, whose Columbia disc *Switched-on Bach* was released in 1968. Gould was deeply impressed by this disc; it challenged his own preeminence as an innovative interpreter of the keyboard music of J.S. Bach. He wrote:

. . . the "performer" for *Switched-on Bach* . . . is no professional virtuoso taking time out from the winter tour for a visit to the recording studio, but a young American physicist and audio engineer named Walter Carlos, who has no recording contract, whose most esoteric musical endeavor heretofore was the supervision of sound-track material for the Schaefer beer commercial on TV. . . .[15]

The disc was a sensation and a commercial success, and has been followed by similar recordings of conventional repertoire using synthetic sound materials rather than performances in the familiar sense. Walter Carlos is a musical person, but he is not a professional musician, and this for Gould was the most remarkable aspect of the whole affair: the New Listener, freed by technology to become his own composer-and-performer, did not evolve gradually. He burst suddenly upon the scene, five years after Gould began telling us about the historically emergent new role of the listener. Carlos jumped several stages in the process. He did not assemble his music from prerecorded kits; he went straight to sound sources whose environment had previously been the acoustical laboratory, not the concert hall or the conservatory or even the recording studio. And Carlos achieved a degree of technical control and a range of artistic choice which neither Bach nor Gould nor anyone else could have imagined. This he achieved by means of a device called the Moog Synthesizer, which enables its operator to reduce musical problems to their basic constituents—individual tones with their various characteristics of duration, frequency, wave-form and intensity—to record these singly and separately, if need be, or in convenient clusters, and to mix and assemble them by mechanical and electronic means.[16] This device and its successors have to some extent done for music what Gould predicted the kit concept would do: they have enabled the listener to become composer and performer. But the synthesizer has turned out to be too expensive to attract the home listener, or too complicated, or uninteresting. Or perhaps after all it requires a certain amount of musical skill and judgment on the part of the operator, and the New Listener is not ready for this. Ironically, the synthesizer has found its way to the concert stage, at least in pop music, where it is used as a conventional keyboard instrument.

We continue stubbornly to show that endearing, frustrating human characteristic of which Gould wrote—resistance to technological change. Nevertheless technology has had its impact upon music in many of the ways predicted by Gould in the 1960s, even if not always for the reasons he mentioned. Whether their net cumulative effect will be the disappearance of concert halls by the year 2000, who besides Gould would dare predict?

The New Listener has fallen far short of Gould's expectations, and has seldom been mentioned in his writings since 1970. One reason may be that the New Listener has been distracted by technological marvels like the chord organ, by means of which he can mislead himself and his listeners into thinking that he is doing what musicians do.

Another reason may be that, as Gould rightly but astonishingly says in a passage quoted in the next chapter, the listener does not know what he wants: listeners rely on performers the way most drivers of cars rely on mechanics. The ordinary driver does not really know what constitutes mechanical rightness in his car; he leaves this to his mechanic. His confidence in the mechanic is a part of his sense of well-being when he drives his car. Similarly the listener relies upon the performer in a recording, according to Gould. Why, then, would the listener adjust his dials and switches? This is the mechanic's job, not the driver's. If he trusted the performer, the listener would keep his phonograph adjusted to those settings which would enable it to produce sounds most like those originally produced in the studio by the performer, just as a trusting driver would operate his car without altering the brake adjustment or the ignition timing as set up by the mechanic.

Dial twiddling is no more a part of music making than car driving is a part of car making. The dial twiddler may enjoy a feeling of power and ego enhancement similar to that of the driver with his eight cylinder engine, his air conditioning, tape deck, power brakes and steering, many headlights, four-chime horn, and the rest of it. But twiddling dials has nothing significantly in common with organizing and comprehending musical structures. A person can produce an overwhelming mass of sound on his phonograph by turning up the volume, just as he can produce a thrilling burst of speed in his car by stepping on the accelerator. He does not have to be a musician to do the former or a mechanic to do the latter. There is a continuum along which the composer, performer, and *informed* listener have their place, and their places are somewhat interchangeable, as Gould says; but the *man-in-the-street* listener, no matter how complicated and powerful and expensive his phonograph, is not by reason of that phonograph in the continuum.

The informed listener can be compared to a trained and experienced technician who test-drives cars. He is aware in considerable detail how the music is constructed, what options are open at various stages in composing and performing, and how the structure of a given piece is related to the structures of others. The ordinary listener does not even know that a piece of music *is* constructed, let alone *how*. It is not merely that he lacks the skill to play in the same game as composers and performers; his limitation is that he has no idea of the rules of the game or of the criteria of skill in playing it. He is a spectator who knows whether the teams are playing or not, whether the play is fast or slow, exciting or dull, intricate or simple, and who is playing. He knows very little more than that.

At any rate, the new generation of creatively active listeners has failed to emerge. Concert halls are busier than ever, and if they are in difficulties it is not because their audiences have left them and are staying at home twiddling dials.

In April 1966 *High Fidelity Magazine* celebrated its fifteenth anniversary by featuring Glenn Gould's article "The Prospects of Recording." Here he explained how the new technology would bring about an end of the concert hall, and bring in the era of the New Listener.

In April and May 1976 the same magazine celebrated its twenty-fifth anniversary. There was no mention of Gould's "Prospects of Recording," but there was no lack of prophecy. We read that in the year 2001 the home listener will be able to conduct the orchestra as he listens to his records, and the orchestra will respond to his gestures.[17] And we read that in the same year we shall be able to sit at home and push a button that will cause our playback apparatus to simulate the characteristic resonances and other sounds of specific concert halls. The New New Listener, instead of participating actively, will allow himself to be transported in imagination to the Concertgebouw, or the Royal Festival Hall, or to whatever concert hall in which at that moment he would like to hear the music.[18]

The technology for both developments, we were told, already exists. High Fidelity did not say whether we can hope to combine the two, and conduct our own orchestra with our living room responding acoustically like whatever concert hall appeals to us at the moment, or whether we could conduct the allegro movement in Munich and the andante in Milan, if we had the appropriate accessories.

But there are wonders in store. It will be fun to see what Glenn Gould does with them.

CHAPTER 3

A
Higher
Calling

By a charming coincidence the first famous pianist whom Glenn
Gould heard in performance, Josef Hofmann, was perhaps also the
first classical musician to make a recording, which he is reputed to
have done for Charles Edison in 1888.[1] Gould himself made history
as the first major artist to abandon a successful concert career in
order to concentrate upon the recording of music. Hofmann in 1888
was tinkering with a new gadget;[2] Gould in 1964 was risking his
future as a musician.

On the financial side was risk that his records would not sell if he
were not before the public in person. How many people purchase a
record by a particular artist because they, or their friends, have heard
that artist play the piece in a concert hall? How many people buy an
artist's records because they have read about his stage antics? Gould's
concerts and recitals earned him a huge international following.
Journalists adored him for his eccentricities. Would he cease to be
interesting and profitable if he ceased to be on public display?

On the artistic side the prospects must have seemed equally
uncertain. Despite his mistrust of audience motives, and despite his
conviction that applause misguides the performer, was there truth in
the old saying that a performer needs an audience for support, for
excitement, for spiritual nourishment? Would he become dull and
stale without that support? Nobody knew, because it had not been
tried. Admittedly the concert hall has inherent vices and limita-

tions; yet it has inherent advantages as well. There was no doubt that for some people it was possible to have splendid careers as concert artists. Nobody had attempted a career exclusively as a recording artist. Did the recording studio have vices and limitations which had not yet become evident? Scarcely anyone had thought of the recording studio as anything other than a secondary and supplementary place of work for musicians. Would it rise to Gould's expectations?

He did not terminate his concert career abruptly, but tapered off. And when he played his final concert he did not announce publicly that there would be no more. He left open the possibility that he might give concerts on special occasions.

The narrator in a film about Gould's career says:

In 1959 Gould celebrated his twenty-seventh birthday. His ambition is to make enough money by the time he is thirty-five to retire from the concert stage and devote himself to composing.[3]

In 1962 Gould was quoted in these words:

I know that no one believes me, but this will definitely be my final tour. I'll do some special concerts from time to time, but I have no intention of travelling as consistently as I've done in the past.[4]

In Gould's interview with Arthur Rubinstein, published in 1971, Rubinstein twits Gould, saying he has the feeling that Gould will go back to giving concerts. Gould demurs, Rubinstein insists, whereupon Gould says "if this is a bet, you will lose it."[5]

There is only one equally eminent musician before Gould who abandoned an established position in concert life and committed himself to an untried way of being a musician—Leopold Stokowski. Gould said:

In the mid 1930s he relinquished his post as conductor of the Philadelphia Orchestra, in which he single-handedly had transformed the standards of orchestral playing in North America, in order to join Deanna Durbin and Donald Duck on the silver screen in Hollywood. "I go to a higher calling," he was reported to have said to the press conference which was called to announce his departure; and if one can filter out the inevitable quotient of defensiveness which may be assumed to infiltrate a remark of that kind, it was a remarkably revealing comment.

Technology, for Stokowski, *was* a higher calling.

He was, indeed, the first great musician to realize that the future of music would be inextricably bound up with technological progress, and that the communications media were in fact the best friends that music ever had.[6]

Glenn Gould's own view of the relation between music and technology can be summed up in those same words. His transition from the concert hall to the recording studio was a step forward in his career, not a defecting or (as some people called it) a "dropping out." Stokowski did not give up performing in public altogether, as Gould has; he gave up one of the most important conducting jobs in the world, but afterward he played many concerts as guest conductor, and eventually accepted other orchestral appointments; his was not a clean break, as Gould's has been.

But having broken away, Gould did much more than just make recordings. He produced a spate of writings for magazines, radio, television and disc in which he elaborated what he refers to as "a philosophy of recording" which "admits the futility of emulating concert hall sonorities,"[7] and which "runs counter to all the prevailing concepts of that elusive thing called artistic integrity."[8]

In what follows, this "philosophy of recording" will be referred to as "New Philosophy," and it will be contrasted with the correlative "Old Philosophy."† Its main themes and distinctions are illustrated by Gould in many of his anecdotes, of which here are four, selected from the many to be found in Gould's writings. They relate to different periods in his career and tell us of his increasing involvement, as a musician, with technology. It should be kept in mind that he is talking about the technology of recorded sound, and not about the technology of musical instruments.

First is the story of the vacuum cleaner. This has been told by Gould in at least two different versions[9] and with as many different interpretations. He was twelve or thirteen years old at the time of the event he describes, and the music he talks about is the Fugue in C Major, K.394, by Mozart.

It's a wonderful academic study in how to write a fugue and obey the textbook and never quite get it off the ground. But I do like it. I was learning it when I was an early teenager, and suddenly (one day) a vacuum cleaner was started up beside the piano, and I couldn't hear myself play — I was having a feud with the housekeeper at this particular time, and it was done on purpose. I couldn't quite hear myself. But I began to *feel* what I was doing —the tactile presence of that fugue as represented by finger positions, and as represented also by the kind of sound you might get if you stood in the shower and shook your head with water coming out of both ears. And it was the most luminously exciting thing you can imagine — the most glorious sound. It took off—all of the things Mozart couldn't quite manage to do I was doing for him. And I suddenly realized that the particular screen

---

† The word "philosophy" with lower-case initial will be reserved for the conventional sense of the word.

through which I was viewing this, and which I had erected between myself and Mozart and his fugue, was exactly what I needed—exactly why, as I later understood, *a certain mechanical process could indeed come between myself and the work of art that I was involved with.* [10]†

Gould says that this was one of the great moments of his life.

Here we have "music and technology" in the literal, conjunctive sense of "music plus technology." Music is represented by Glenn Gould playing the Mozart C Major Fugue; technology is represented by the housekeeper with the vacuum cleaner. Most musicians would have had to stop playing, but not Gould. The mechanical noise came between him and the work all right, but not as an obstruction. Instead it was taken up by him into a higher aesthetical unity, of which he was then the author, and which consisted of Mozart's music, Gould's piano sounds, and the noise of the machine.

Gould must be aware that this anecdote will seem preposterous; indeed, this may be why he frequently tells it. But he is serious when he says that the incident was "a determining moment in my own reaction to music," [11] so we must take it seriously if cautiously. (Gould's anecdotes seldom lose detail in the retelling.)

For the moment we may accept the anecdote as a suggestion that from an early age Gould was comfortable with the juxtaposition of music and machinery, and was ready to accept the possibility that machinery might be a complement to music rather than an impediment. From this acceptance it is a series of short steps to the home tape recorder and thence to the sound studio, each with its own supplementary or complementary noises.

The second anecdote is of Gould's love affair with the microphone.

In December 1950, I took part for the first time in a CBC network broadcast and made a discovery that influenced, in a most profound way, my development as a musician. I discovered that, in the privacy, the solitude and (if all Freudians will stand clear) the womb-like security of the studio, it was possible to make music in a more direct, more personal manner than any concert hall would ever permit. I fell in love with broadcasting that day, and I have not since then been able to think of the potential of music (or, for that matter, of my own potential as a musician) without some reference to the *limitless possibilities*† of the broadcasting and/or recording medium. For me, the microphone has never been that hostile, clinical, inspiration-sapping analyst some critics, fearing it, complain about. That day in 1950 it became, and has remained, a friend.

---

† Author's italics.

In fact, most of the ideas that have occurred to me as a performer have related in some measure to the microphone. Now I know this sounds like a minute observation capriciously expanded into an imposing theory, but it isn't. The microphone does encourage you to develop attitudes to performance which are entirely out of place in the diffuse acoustic of the concert hall. It permits you to cultivate a degree of textural clarity which simply doesn't pay dividends in the concert hall.[12]

Specifically, this is what happened at the beginning of Gould's "love affair with the microphone," as he himself has called it.[13] He went to the CBC's Toronto studios to play his first network broadcast. His program consisted of two sonatas, one by Mozart and the other by Hindemith. The studio piano had a thick bass sound which gave him a hard time in the Mozart. Later somebody gave him an acetate disc of the broadcast to play at home on his own phonograph. He discovered that by suppressing the bass and boosting the treble he could obtain the sonorities he wanted but could not get on the studio piano. From that moment on Glenn Gould has not been able to accept the doctrine that technology is dehumanizing.

The third of our four anecdotes illustrating the New Philosophy is Gould's story of the recording of the *Goldberg Variations*. Perhaps there are still people around who believe that what they hear on a disc is like what they see in a snapshot: an image of an event in time and place. These people, if we asked them to consider it, would assume that when Gould made his recording of Bach's *Goldberg Variations* the course of events ran like this: Gould took his place at the piano, the producer and technicians sat in their booth, and when everything was ready the tape recorder rolled and Gould played the variations from beginning to end; then Gould got up and stretched, the technicians stopped the tape recorder, and the job was done. Or at least this is how such people might say it *should* have been done if artistic "integrity" was to be preserved. But, of course, this is not how it was done. Gould has described the occasion:

When I recorded Bach's *Goldberg Variations*, I by-passed the theme — the very simple aria upon which the variations are constructed—and left it for recording until all the variations had been satisfactorily put down on tape. I then turned to that ingenuous little sarabande [the aria], and found that it took me twenty takes in order to locate a character for it which would be sufficiently neutral as not to prejudge the depth of involvement that comes later in the work. It was a question of utilizing the first twenty takes to erase all superfluous expression from my reading of it, and there is nothing more difficult to do. The natural instinct of the performer is to add, not to subtract. In any case, the theme, as represented on my recording of the *Goldberg Variations*, is Take 21.[14]

Joseph Roddy in his article on Gould in *The New Yorker* seems to take the naive view when he says, ". . . the young Canadian relates each part of the piece to the whole work in a way that leaves Bach scholars convinced that he knew in the most precise detail how he would play the last variation before he intoned the first one."[15] But what Gould knew "in the most precise detail" was what he already had on tape. Indeed, Gould's memory for the characteristics of each take of a piece is a legend among the musicians, producers and technicians with whom he has worked.

This theme (or aria or sarabande) appears at the end as well as at the beginning of the *Goldberg*. It is interesting to reflect on whether or not Gould and his producer considered using the same take in both places. It happens that the concluding version is *not* Take 21; perhaps they decided that it was excessively neutral for a conclusion. But according to New Philosophy principles there is nothing to prevent the one take being used in the two positions, if this should seem desirable on aesthetical grounds, as it well might. Indeed, this sort of thing was occasionally done in the 78-rpm era, although somewhat apologetically, and saved money for everyone with no genuine loss to the listener. It could be done in certain da capo movements in which the final section is the same as the beginning section of the piece, with no ritenutos or textual problems at the double bar. One side of the disc would contain the first section, the other side the middle section, and there would be an instruction to play the first side again, thus completing the piece at two-thirds the cost. The mere notion of this infuriates some people, but it has happened and it continues to happen; the technology of the New Philosophy era enables the manufacturer to make use of this option without many of us knowing about it.

Our fourth anecdote concerns Gould's recording of the A Minor Fugue from Book I of Bach's *The Well-Tempered Clavier* (on March 17, 1965).

This is a structure even more difficult to realize on the piano than are most of Bach's fugues, because it consists of four intense voices that determinedly occupy a register in the centre octaves of the keyboard—the area of the instrument in which truly independent voice-leading is most difficult to establish. In the process of recording this fugue, we attempted eight takes. Two of these were regarded, according to the producer's notes, as satisfactory. Both of them, No. 6 and No. 8 respectively, were complete takes requiring no inserted splice—by no means a special achievement since the fugue's duration is only a bit over two minutes. Some weeks later, however, when the results of this session were surveyed in an editing cubicle and when Takes 6 and 8 were played several times in rapid alternation, it became apparent that both had a defect of which we had been quite unaware in the studio: both were monotonous.

Each take had used a different style of phrase delineation in dealing with the thirty-one-note subject of this fugue—a license entirely consistent with the improvisatory liberties of Baroque style. Take 6 had treated it in a solemn, legato, rather pompous fashion, while in Take 8 the fugue subject was shaped in a prevailingly staccato manner which led to a general impression of skittishness. Now, the Fugue in A Minor is given to concentrations of *stretti* and other devices for imitation at close quarters, so that the treatment of the subject determines the atmosphere of the entire fugue. Upon most sober reflection, it was agreed that neither the teutonic severity of Take 6 nor the unwarranted jubilation of Take 8 could be permitted to represent our best thoughts on this fugue. At this point someone noted that, despite the vast differences in character between the two takes, they were performed at almost identical tempo (a rather unusual circumstance, to be sure, since the prevailing tempo is almost always the result of phrase delineation) and it was decided to turn this to advantage by creating one performance to consist alternately of Takes 6 and 8.

Once this decision had been made, it was a simple matter to expedite it. It was obvious that the somewhat overbearing posture of Take 6 was entirely suitable for the opening exposition as well as for the concluding statements of the fugue, while the more effervescent character of Take 8 was a welcome relief in the episodic modulations with which the centre portion of the fugue is concerned. And so two rudimentary splices were made, one which jumps from Take 6 to Take 8 in bar 14 and another which at the return to A minor (I forget which measure, but you are invited to look for it) returns as well to Take 6. What had been achieved was a performance of this particular fugue far superior to anything that we could at the time have done in the studio. There is, of course, no reason why such a diversity of bowing styles could not have been applied to this fugue subject as part of a regulated a priori conception. But the necessity of such diversity is unlikely to become apparent during the studio session just as it is unlikely to occur to a performer operating under concert conditions. *By taking advantage of the post-taping afterthought, however, one can very often transcend the limitations that performance imposes upon the imagination.* [16]†

His recording of this fugue is a relatively simple example of what Gould calls "montage." He does not say that every record should be a montage. Many of his own recordings are straight-through performances with no splices, and some of these are from Take 1. For Gould, montage is merely one of the options made available by modern technology; it should be used only in cases where it makes possible a better result than could be obtained from a straight-through recording.

† Author's italics.

These four anecdotes contain the main elements of Glenn Gould's New Philosophy of recording. They demonstrate that he was comfortable from an early age with the combination of music with machinery; that broadcasting and recording have opened up "limitless possibilities" for music and for himself as a musician, and have determined his whole musical outlook; that he makes use of those same possibilities as aids to his own exploration of a piece of music, and by means of them discovers aspects and alternatives which might not otherwise be revealed to him; that he considers the "takes" recorded in the studio to be raw materials for a later creative stage in the making of a recording, namely the editing and splicing stage.

Gould does not say much about the corresponding Old Philosophy of recording, but it is not difficult to make an outline of it. From such an outline, and in contrast, we can take a closer look at the New Philosophy.

The first thing to be said about the Old Philosophy of recording is that it is not really old. It is, I believe, the conservative view held currently by the majority of people who listen to classical records. It is the view that a good recording played on good equipment should bring "concert hall realism" into our homes; this slogan can still be found in audio magazines. "High fidelity" is both aim and criterion: fidelity to the sounds we might expect to hear if we were present at the actual performance. The microphone is a passive extension of our ears; any sounds that might be added by the machinery or the process must be extirpated. The performer is supreme, and the technicians are there to see that his performance, intact and unaltered, is accurately preserved in the final result, the disc. Of their own presence there must be no trace.

If we took a poll among the people in a classical record shop on a busy Saturday we would probably find most of them in agreement with this or a similar account of what recording is all about. If we asked Glenn Gould, he would say that there is nothing wrong with it except that it overlooks the potential of recording as itself an artistic medium. It emphasizes the preservative or archival function of recording, which Gould values. But it ignores the "limitless possibilities" of which he speaks, and it perpetuates the tyranny of a few big-name composers and performers, since it imposes upon the record industry the conservatism that also dominates the concert hall: only those works and those names which can be relied upon to "sell" will be available on records.

The Old Philosophy technology and attitudes belong to the

transitional period from the 78-rpm disc to the long-play disc, roughly 1945-55. The New Philosophy period began in approximately 1960.

As the Old Philosophy is not really old, so the New Philosophy is not really new. In the very early days of recording, what we might call the pre-Old-Philosophy days, things were much the way Gould describes them in his New Philosophy. The Old Philosophy tyranny of composers and performers did not exist. Because the old acoustical recording process was severely limited in range of frequencies and weak in level of sound, and because recording cylinders and discs were of short duration, the composer's design for a piece had to be drastically changed. It had to be reduced to a length which would fit, or broken into sections; the orchestration had to be reduced because there was not much room in front of the recording horn. The first and second violin sections were replaced by four or five Stroh violins, which had horns instead of bellies to amplify the sound, and these had to be aimed at the recording machine. So did the bells of the French horns, which meant that the horn players had to sit with their backs to the conductor, watching him in a mirror. There could be no double basses because their lower frequencies were too low for the machine. A tuba took their place.

If the composer were on hand to see this he might protest, but it would do no good. In those early days it was a matter of recording this way or not recording at all. Not the composers but the engineers told performers what would make an artistically satisfactory impression and what would not. And as in the New Philosophy, the best recordings were those in the making of which the collaboration between engineers and musicians was most harmonious and complete. Rigid distinctions between technical and aesthetical judgments were destructive, as is the case with the New Philosophy.

In the early days of recording, people noticed that one could play intriguing tricks with the phonograph, much as Gould did in his story about the beginning of his love affair with the microphone. Roland Gelatt, writing about the phonograph of the 1880s and 1890s, said:

Someone suggested using the phonograph as a musical composing machine by playing favorite airs backward on it.[17]

Gelatt quotes "a contemporary account" as follows:

It was interesting to observe the total indifference of the phonograph to the pitch of the note it began upon with regard to the pitch of the note with which it was to end. Gravely singing the tune correctly for half a dozen notes, it would suddenly soar into regions too painfully high for the cornet even by any chance to follow it. Then it delivered the variations on *Yankee Doodle* with a celerity no human fingering of the cornet could rival, interspersing new notes, which it seemed probable were neither on the cornet nor any other instrument. . . . [18]

These are homely and frivolous examples of the "limitless possibilities" of the early phonograph. The next example is closer to the New Philosophy.

. . . there are times, I confess, when I enjoy playing romantic or sentimental tricks with it [the phonograph], when I can persuade myself that by playing some orchestral record with the thinnest possible needle I have produced a delicate, distant kind of fairy music, something not at all like the actual orchestra but *with an original quality of its own*.† This can best be done with good but imperfect records, such as the Columbia version of *L'Après midi*, which crackles and is much cut down, yet makes a faint and beautiful concourse of sounds with a very thin needle. [19]

The author of those words, A. Clutton-Brock, has a strong claim to the title of First Gouldian New Listener. In 1924 he was bringing out qualities which were not impressed on the disc, but which originated in the phonograph as a result of his adjustments to it. These adjustments obtained active participation from the machine rather than maximum fidelity to the disc. As Gould has said:

Dial twiddling is in its limited way an interpretative act. Forty years ago the listener had the option of flicking a switch inscribed "on" and "off" and, with an up-to-date machine, perhaps modulating the volume just a bit. Today, the variety of controls made available to him requires analytical judgment. And these controls are but primitive, regulatory devices, compared to those participational possibilities which the listener will enjoy once current laboratory techniques have been appropriated by home playback devices. [20]

In the New Philosophy neither composer nor performer has final control over any stage in the whole recording process; nobody has. Making a recording is a collaborative process which at any stage leaves open further modifications or adjustments at another stage, and there is no final stage because records are listened to repeatedly, and each repetition is subject to the New Listener's judgments and adjustments. The whole process, however, is presided over by a person who comes into prominence for the first time in the New Philosophy — the producer.

---

† Author's italics.

Gould says that the producer is part impresario and part technical engineer. The producer is the company's man-on-the-spot. His responsibilities include seeing that performers are aware of technological possibilities and technicians are aware of musical limitations. The producer is the author of that intermediate product, the disc in the record shop. It is intermediate because in the New Philosophy there is no final product.

In the New Philosophy the producer, the technicians and their apparatus, are not obsequious and unobtrusive as in the Old. They leave the hallmark of their own art upon the disc or tape. The work of a great producer should be as distinctive in the sound of a record as are the works of composer and performer. And to a sensitive listener the producer's work should be aesthetically as significant.†

In the pre-Old-Philosophy period nobody worried about "fidelity"; it was a triumph if the piece was recognizable. Concert hall realism of the Old Philosophy type was an interim goal for technicians and inventors, and it had its day, but the sound engineers surged onward while musicians and record buyers settled down happily at the Old Philosophy stage. What the new technology of the New Philosophy offered was not necessarily better, but it was different, and it held out promises of new possibilities for recorded musical sound to which few musicians have responded: composers still think that performers are performing rightly when they most exactly re-present what is indicated in the score; performers think that technicians are recording rightly when the disc or tape most faithfully reproduces the sounds made by the performers.‡

But consider the motion picture. Early in the history of this art the camera became a commentator on the action, a character in the narrative, an analyst of plot and motive. It is not a mere recipient of images. A finished motion picture does not show scenes and actions in the chronological sequence in which they were actually shot.

Glenn Gould frequently compares the editing of audiotape for a disc to the editing of film for a motion picture, and is impatient with the Old Philosophy attitude that rejects for music, on grounds of "integrity," procedures which have for many years been accepted as basic to film making. Such procedures and many others open up the

---

† Gould has most frequently worked with Andrew Kazdin, his present producer at CBS. Others have been Thomas Frost, John McClure, Paul Myers, Joseph Scianni, and Howard Scott. Keith MacMillan produced the 1953 Hallmark disc. Here is a good place for me to point out that the editor of a book is, like the producer of a disc, an artist in his own right; and that the editor of the present book is Garry Lovatt, whom I thank and admire.
‡ See Appendix — Eighteenth Century Mechanical Instruments.

"limitless possibilities" of which he speaks. Examination of the procedures will be undertaken in later chapters. Here we look at the possibilities in a theoretical way, since they are the grounds of Gould's arguments in favour of the higher calling that is the career of a recording artist.

The two possibilities of the New Philosophy most frequently mentioned by Gould are: greater intimacy between performer and listener, and deeper awareness of the inner workings of the music than are achievable in public performance. There are others, but let us look first at these.

Gould says that in a good recording the listener and performer have a closer relationship than is possible in the concert hall. This claim seems odd to us at first reading. In a recording the two are separated by time and place and also, we might think, by the recording and playback apparatus. Gould will argue that the apparatus does not separate but rather connects, more intimately indeed than does physical proximity. In the concert hall the virtuoso, with his crowd-pleasing mannerisms, is set apart, the great man, the object of worshipful attention rather than the sharer in a profound human experience.

The way in which the performance of music has been changed by its exposure to electronic media is . . . significant. When we listen to the early phonograph recordings by artists reared in the latter half of the nineteenth century, we are struck not by the felicities or the gaucheries of their artistry but by how very different the performing premise seems to have been from that to which we are now accustomed — how very high the level of whimsicality and caprice, how very flirtatious and extravagant the range of dynamics, judging by the levels of distortion in these recordings—in short, to what an incredible extent these artists accommodated their relation to music to the specific situation of the public arena, to what a very large extent they must have depended upon the visual connection, on the supplemental choreography of movement and gesture. Today, the performer conditioned to think in terms of electronic projection automatically comes to think in terms of an immediacy of reception between himself and the individual listener (represented by the microphone or whatever the electronic conveyance happens to be) and, because of this, a fantastically varied and subtle range of interpretive insinuation is possible.[21]

If a performer can disregard the visual aspects of his performance, and if he can subdue his image or identity as a "star," directing his performance not here and now to a crowd, but to one thoughtful listener at the output end of the apparatus, at some other time and place, then it is the presence of the music and its details, not the personal identity of the performer, that will occupy the listener's attention. This is the intimacy of which Gould speaks: an intensely shared attentiveness to the music, between the performer at one end of the technological system and the listener at the other.

The inner workings of the music are revealed to both participants as a consequence of their special attentiveness; the microphone elicits the structural details, or, as Gould puts it, the microphone "dissects and analyzes" the music, equally well with a small and transparent work, say, a Partita by J.S. Bach, and a large, impressive work such as the Second or the Eighth Symphony by Gustav Mahler.

GOULD: . . . I think that's precisely why you will find the Second and Eighth Symphonies virtually leading the *Billboard* charts these days. Because they do so much beg to be dissected, to be analyzed by the microphone —that's precisely what the microphone, in a good production, will do for these works, and why the microphone has managed to rediscover an audience for Mahler. . . .

MCCLURE: Does the average listener want a work dissected, or does he want to be swept away by it?

GOULD: I don't think the average listener perhaps knows quite *what* he wants —and I don't mean that derogatorily in any sense at all. I don't know that there's any reason the average listener *should* know quite what he wants. I don't think that I, as a very average car driver, know whether I'm driving a tight car or a loose car, as a mechanic might define it; I simply know that I'm driving one and it gets me there. Nevertheless, I'm probably vaguely appreciative of the things that a good mechanic can do for that car. In the same way, I think that a listener, whether he knows it or not, is appreciative of what a microphone can do for that work, and I'm quite sure that the Mahler Eighth can create a much more overwhelming effect heard properly at home, intimately and quietly and reflectively, than it can in a concert hall.[22]

What Gould means by "dissection and analysis" is less clear than it might be. It seems that, so far as performance is concerned, they are results of a performer's deliberate effort to emphasize the backbone or structure of a piece, at the expense, if need be, of expressiveness and tone quality. And so far as listening is concerned, it is the result of effort to obtain intense and heightened awareness of the same backbone or structure. Recording technology makes it possible for the performer to bring the listener into closer awareness of the structure than is possible at a concert. Gould has illustrated this on several occasions. For example:

Schoenberg's music, especially his later works, which so decisively influenced the compositional climate of the present day, are suited to the medium of recording, just as surely as are the works of Bach. Like Bach's music, that of Schoenberg is technically complicated, determinedly contra-puntal in design, and more concerned perhaps with the significance of gesture than with the seductive lustre of attractive sound *per se*.[23]

Gould carried dissection and analysis to their extremes in his only recording to date as organist, *The Art of the Fugue, Fugues 1-9* by J.S. Bach. In a broadcast Gould discussed his performance of the third fugue in these words:

What I like about that recording is that, because of the gloriously eccentric registration which that Casavant instrument offered, the central strands of the music are each allowed to have a life of their own — they're not embalmed in reverberation as organ recitals in churches tend to be. We were, of course, very fortunate in being able to record in a church which possessed a remarkably light reverberation. But that recording goes even further: the microphones were placed hard up against the organ chests so that the pipes could speak, as they say, and perhaps even wheeze occasion-ally as well. There was no attempt to glamorize the sound, to surround it with a halo of resonance, or to "mike" it so distantly as to suggest that one was listening to it from far back in the congregation. There was, in fact, no attempt to capitalize on a sense of occasion—on relating our performance of *The Art of the Fugue* to that church, on that winter afternoon and, hence, to create for the listener an artificial sense of participation. Our aim was to ignore the occasion of recording, and to concentrate instead upon the likely circumstances of playback — to think about the living-rooms, studios, automobiles, transistors on a sand dune, in which or through which that recording might conceivably be heard.[24]

The third fugue, which Tovey characterizes as "one of Bach's most beautiful pieces of quiet, chromatic slow music,"[25] is played by Gould in this recording with choppy articulation and in rapid tempo. Apparently his intention was to take advantage of the dry acoustics and close miking to reveal the "backbone." The character-istically New Philosophy aspect of this recording is that the whole process was aimed at the time and place of playback, and away from the time and place of recording.

Here is another passage which illustrates what Gould means by dissection and analysis:

The recordings of Robert Craft . . . tell us a good deal about the way in which performances prepared with the microphone in mind can be influ-enced by technical considerations. For Craft, the stop watch and the tape splice are tools of his trade as well as objects of that inspiration for which an earlier generation of stick-wielders found an outlet in the opera cape and temper tantrums. A comparison between Craft's readings of the large-scale orchestral studies of Schoenberg, especially the early post-romantic essays such as *Verklärte Nacht* or *Pelleas und Melisande*, with the interpretations of more venerable maestros—Winfried Zillig's glowingly romantic *Pelleas* of

1949, for instance — is instructive.

Craft applies a sculptor's chisel to these vast orchestral complexes of the youthful Schoenberg and gives them a determined series of plateaus on which to operate — a very baroque thing to do. He seems to feel that his audience — sitting at home, close up to the speaker — is prepared to allow him to dissect this music and to present it to them from a strongly biassed conceptual viewpoint, which the private and concentrated circumstances of their listening make feasible. Craft's interpretation, then, is all power steering and air brakes. By comparison, in Zillig's of *Pelleas* . . . the leisurely application of rubatos, the sensual haze with which he gilds the performance, as though concerned that clarity could be an enemy of mystery, point clearly to the fact that his interpretation derived from a concert experience where such performance characteristics were intuitive compensations for an acoustic dilemma.[26]

Glenn Gould is not only the principal expositor and apologist of the New Philosophy; he is its most dedicated practitioner. Several people have said that no other musician participates as actively in the technological side of the recording processes—some of his producers regard this as a mixed blessing.[†]

Gould says that he does very little practice at the keyboard in preparation for his recording sessions. Instead he spends time reading scores. He is a very quick study with new repertoire, but he carries an immense amount of music in his head, some of it previously performed by him and some not. His memory includes the parts of other players or singers in ensemble music, and he is renowned for his ability to play their parts as well as his own in rehearsals, not always to their delight. Although from his writings we might never guess it, Gould is tense and anxious at recording sessions — sometimes desperately so, and much more than he was when he played concerts. This may be for the reason that he takes recording seriously, whereas concerts were for him necessary but temporary evils to be got through as best one could. It may also be for the reason that tape is very unforgiving: taped errors are more permanent than errors in a concert, and no amount of editing can make right a thoroughly bad take. In theory at least, a taped performance *can* be perfect in ways no concert performance ever can, and this perfection is a goal seldom absent from the mind of a recording artist. Any recording artist knows what it is like to have played flawlessly and beautifully up to

---

[†] The direct-to-disc recording and manufacturing process is, of course, intractably Old Philosophy and archival, and will no doubt have a vigorous fling despite the high cost of its product. Gould's interest will more likely be attracted by the new digital signal processing methods, which are already at an advanced stage. These methods will open up previously unimagined possibilities for editing and mixing recorded audio materials, and will greatly enrich this art of which Gould is a leader and pioneer.

the last ten or twelve bars, and suddenly to face the horror that the take may be wrecked in the final few measures. At such moments the momentum of the playing ceases to be a joy and becomes a crushing threat. In these conditions private catastrophe is as appalling as is the public variety.

Although he is much less ritualistic than he was in his concert-giving days, Gould still uses the famous folding chair; his arms and hands require massage before a recording session and at intervals during it; he requires a piano technician on stand-by duty in the studio or within easy reach. He prefers to record at night, all night if necessary. Near the end of his concert career he frequently cancelled engagements, pleading illness. But he is scrupulous with his recording, radio and television commitments. Most musicians who have worked with him since the mid-1960s have found him infallibly polite and considerate (and of course enormously stimulating musically), but there are some who speak of difficulties with Gould in earlier days. On mike or on camera he works with an almost unimaginable intensity, indeed almost frightening to people who are not accustomed to it. And he still wants the air conditioning turned off, no matter how hot the lights, although he says he has moderated his stand on this in recent years.

A concert artist keeps a limited number of pieces in top form, ready for engagements in the near future. He works at these pieces daily, in both practice and performance, refining them and making them his own. A commitment to perform a particular piece or program implies months or years of preparation, hard physical and mental work aimed at overcoming technical difficulties and exploring interpretive possibilities, with the intention of being ready on the day.

But not Gould. Take, as examples, his Beethoven sonata recordings of the early 1960s. He said of these works that he had known them since his youth and could play from memory any of them on demand, so the "specialized and very particular look"[27] at them came only about two weeks before the recording date. He compares this apparently suicidal approach with that of an actor in a soap opera who learns his lines the night before the taping session, and then forgets them. "What I forget is not the work, not the notes; but I forget *the particular relationship to the work*."[28]†

The particular relationship is a specific interpretive approach to the piece, or a sense of how it might be treated in performance.

† Author's italics.

Gould arrives at the recording studio sometimes with just one such approach in mind, but sometimes with many different ones. One example he mentions is the recording he made with Leopold Stokowski and the American Symphony Orchestra of Beethoven's *Emperor Concerto*. For this project Gould had two quite different "special relationships" in mind: an extremely fast one, and an extremely slow. Stokowski agreed to try the slow version, to Gould's delight, with the result that can be heard on Columbia MS 6888.

Gould does not say whether they made takes of both relationships. If they had done so, and if a week or more later they had gathered with the producer and technicians in the editing room, to make comparisons and choices, and to combine portions of the various takes, they would have been doing the typical New Philosophy kind of work. This *Emperor* recording is, in fact, a montage and hence a New Philosophy product. But the tempo is consistently slow throughout the concerto so we may conclude that there was no splicing for the purpose of obtaining contrasts in tempo, and that the slow relationship was the only one attempted in the recording studio.

With full orchestra it can be expensive trying out various relationships in the studio. If Bach had written his *Goldberg Variations* for symphony orchestra instead of for keyboard soloist there would not have been twenty-one takes of the aria. Putting it another way, the range of decisions which can be put off to the editing stage is wider in solo music than in concerted music requiring many players. So the New Philosophy probably works better for solo music than it does for ensemble music, despite Gould's cheerful remarks about Mahler's Second and Eighth Symphonies.

Gould expressed all this very persuasively:

GOULD: I've come in with perhaps five or six, as it then seemed to me, equally valid ideas, and perhaps none of them worked, in which case we would come back in a week and try a seventh. If two or three did work, we then repaired to an editing cubicle, within a week or so, and listened to them. And, really, the week, at least, is necessary for some kind of perspective. The judgments you make a week later are never those you think you are going to make on the spot, on the spur of the moment—it never turns out that way. The things that seemed best, and most inspired, and most spontaneous, at the time, are very seldom that. They're usually contrived, they're usually affected; and they're usually filled with all kinds of musical gadgetry that one doesn't want in a recording.

MCCLURE: You mean part of your creative process is going on in the editing room?

GOULD: Absolutely. . . . We don't treat [the taped recording] as the finished product in the studio.[29]

His anecdote about the Fugue in A Minor is Gould's favourite illustration of the manner in which taped raw material from the recording studio is worked upon in the editing booth as a further stage in the process. It will be recalled that two quite different versions (relationships) were cut up and spliced together at several points to produce the disc version. Paul Myers was the producer for this recording, so his description of Gould at work is of special interest, particularly for its account of what we have been referring to as dissection and analysis.

He is never concerned with traditional views of interpretation, nor with the already-recorded versions of a work which are regarded as the yardsticks of performance. Instead, he prefers to perform a piece almost as though it were newly composed, awaiting its first interpretation. When he is in the studio, he likes to play as many as ten or fifteen interpretations of the same piece—each of them quite different, many of them valid—as though examining the music from every angle before deciding upon a final performance. This, in itself, is a rarity, for there are few pianists who have the technique equal to the task. His provocative musical ideas, backed by complete integrity of purpose and thorough academic understanding of the technical workings of a piece, make him either a musical devil's advocate or *enfant terrible*, depending on your point of view. One thing is certain: a Glenn Gould performance is unmistakably original and the result of extensive study and consideration, both at and away from the piano.

All this might suggest a misrepresentation of the music he performs, but it has always been my experience, with these facts in mind, that Glenn Gould's approach to music and the opportunity he gives the listener to reconsider his attitude towards a particular work—to "rethink" the entire piece, if necessary—achieve a deeper and more complete understanding of it. This is especially true of the solo repertoire, where the demands of the orchestra do not impinge upon the freedom of his interpretation. I have also found the greatest enjoyment from listening to a Gould performance of a work I believe I already "know" for, as he pulls it apart and reconstructs it in this unique manner, he reveals new facets of the music which I, for one, may never have considered.[30]

Glenn Gould, age 13, at the organ in the Concert Hall (since demolished) of the Royal Conservatory of Music of Toronto. Page Toles

ABOVE *Gould (age 23) in the Concert Hall of the Royal Conservatory of Music of Toronto, 1956. Taken during a photo session for an article in Maclean's Magazine.* Paul Rockett

BELOW *Conductor Leonard Bernstein and Gould during a recording session at Columbia's 30th Street Studio, New York City, in 1957.* CBS

ABOVE *Six distinguished Canadians brought together for a newspaper feature celebrating Canada's Centennial in 1967. Left to right: Morley Callaghan, Sir Ernest MacMillan, Kate Reid, A.Y. Jackson, Glenn Gould and Marshall McLuhan.* The Toronto Sun

BELOW *Studying the score and sipping Poland water during a union break in a public rehearsal at Massey Hall, Toronto, December 1960. Walter Susskind conducted the Toronto Symphony.* David Wulkan

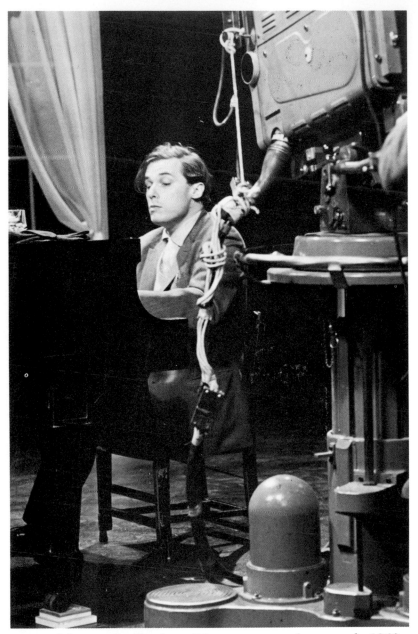

ABOVE *Music and technology. Filming a* CBC *telecast, early 1960s.*
CBC Photo Department – Herb Nott

RIGHT *Legs crossed, chair patched with adhesive tape, fallboard of the piano removed. Taken in the late 1950s, this photograph shows the flat, stroking action Gould used at that time for playing music by J. S. Bach.* CBS

ABOVE *Elbows extended in Gould's characteristic* con amore *attitude, 1960.* CBC Photo Department – Robert C. Ragsdale

BELOW *Leonard Bernstein, Glenn Gould and Igor Stravinsky were photographed during a break in the filming of the 1960* CBS *television program "Leonard Bernstein and the New York Philharmonic." This was Gould's first appearance on television in the United States.* CBS

Left hand conducting the right. Late 1960s. CBS

ABOVE *Taken after a performance of a Bach concerto at the Stratford (Ontario) Festival. Gould was Music Director at the Festival in the early 1960s.* James R. Murray

BELOW *Gould addressing Convocation, University of Toronto, June 1, 1964, on the occasion of being granted an honorary degree.* University of Toronto Department of Information Services – Jack Marshall

Creative cheating on a hot June day, 1970, in the Toronto freight yards. Gould was posing for a photograph to promote the film version of his documentary The Idea of North. CBC Photo Department – Harold Whyte

In 1973 Gould and CBC producer Mario Prizek discuss a score for the program "Music in Our Time: The Age of Ecstasy." The piano is Gould's CD 318; his famous chair is in the foreground. CBC Photo Department — Harold Whyte

ABOVE *During the preparation of "Stokowski: A Portrait for Radio," December 1969, Gould and Stokowski were photographed in the maestro's apartment overlooking Central Park, New York City.* CBC Photo Department

BELOW *Violinist Yehudi Menuhin and Gould were photographed in October 1965 in rehearsal for a CBC telecast. Menuhin in his autobiography affectionately wrote of Gould as ". . . that most exotic of my colleagues. . . . Perhaps no one in the world knows . . . more about the recording and broadcasting of music."* CBC Photo Department

In the Green Room, Eaton Auditorium, Toronto 1971, Gould and technician Lorne Tulk listen to the playback of a recording made for the European Broadcasting Union. Walter Curtin

A photographing session in Studio "G," CBC Toronto, 1974, hastily improvised for Rolling Stone Magazine: not his piano, not his chair, and certainly not his posture at the instrument. Walter Curtin

ABOVE *Gould at the end of a long mixing session in a* CBC *studio, Toronto, 1974.* CBC Photo Department — Robert C. Ragsdale

BELOW *''Conducting'' the technician in a* CBC *studio, mid-1970s.* CBC Photo Department — Robert C. Ragsdale

Portrait, 1974. CBS

Gould posing as one of his fictional characters, Sir Nigel Twitt-Thornwaite, "Dean of British Conductors," in a television cameo promoting a CBC radio series, 1974. CBC Department – Robert C. Ragsdale

CHAPTER 4

Action
At A
Distance

Neighbours at Uptergrove, where the Goulds had their cottage, remember Glenn as "a rather solitary little boy with strong opinions and a hatred of cruelty, who was happiest in the hours when he was free to practise the piano."[1] Gould's hatred of cruelty and his need of solitude are interwoven themes which touch upon nearly every aspect of his musical thought.

In the schoolyard at Williamson Road Public School those strong opinions provoked the rough treatment bright children receive from dull ones. In his *New Yorker* article on Gould, Joseph Roddy quoted him:

I suppose it was only natural that the fact that I was unable to come to terms with my associates forced me to take refuge ever more intently within the shelter of my own imagination.[2]

But music, which can in this manner provide a refuge from cruelty, is cruel in its own way, which is the way of the arena: audiences lusting after the spectacle of bloodshed; performers competing against other performers for the public's favour. Glenn Gould's writings and recordings are evidences of his intention to separate music from cruelty, to show that competition is not a law of civilized life. Nature may be red in tooth and claw, and competition in the struggle for survival may be a law of nature, but technology (Gould says) intervenes in human culture between man and nature, between man and the beastliness that is in men (at least in the hearts of men such as sit in audiences at concerts and bullfights).

Anthony Storr's fascinating book *The Dynamics of Creation* is a study of the creative personality. In the following passage he describes the schizoid type of creative artist and the considerations which determine his vocational choices:

. . . since most creative activity is solitary, choosing such an occupation means that the schizoid person can avoid the problems of direct relationships with others. If he writes, paints or composes, he is, of course, communicating. But it is a communication entirely on his own terms. The whole situation is within his own control. He cannot be betrayed into confidences which he might later regret. He can express whatever he does want to reveal with such exactitude that there is less chance of being misunderstood than might obtain with more casual and spontaneous exchanges. He can choose (or so he often believes) how much of himself to reveal and how much to keep secret. Above all, he runs little risk of putting himself in the power of another person. As we have seen, the tragedy of the schizoid person is that he fears love almost as much as he fears hate; for any close involvement carries with it the risk of being overborne or "swallowed" by the other party. Some form of interaction with other people is felt to be necessary, as it is to all of us, but this interaction is better undertaken at a safe remove. To show oneself only through the medium of a book, a picture, or a string quartet, is to protect oneself whilst at the same time enjoying the gratification of self-revelation.[3]

Joachim Kaiser, an influential German critic, says:

In what other branch of musical reproduction does everything still depend so much on the individual, on his ability to perceive, shape and dispose, as in piano playing? Even the solo violin, even the prima donna, generally needs an accompanist or an accompanying orchestra. . . . Only the pianist . . . is completely on his own, and offers in the age of teamwork, of division of labour and the security of numbers, the image of the great, self-reliant subject.[4]

Thus, according to Storr the schizoid type of creative artist has by his choice of occupation chosen isolation; according to Kaiser the pianist is the most isolated of musicians. And Gould is surely the most isolated of pianists: "the recording experience is the most womb-like experience that one can have in music," he says. "It's a very cloistered way of life, and indeed I've given up all that was non-cloistered in my musical life."[5]

The uncloistered musician is constantly exposed to outside influences. In youth his teacher is an outside influence. In maturity he may himself become a teacher, in which event his pupils' responses to him and to the music they study will influence him. He goes to concerts and is influenced by the ideas and attitudes of the performers he hears, and by other people's responses to those performers. He gives concerts and is influenced by the approval and disapproval of audiences and critics. The smallest mishaps to his health, his disposition, his instrument, or in the weather, can raise him up or smash him down, and he is all but helpless in the face of them. But the cloistered musician is protected from these exigencies, or (what is the same thing) he thinks he is.

Gould considers himself to be largely self taught, claiming that he did not really begin to study music until after he discontinued lessons with Alberto Guerrero.[6] The greater part of his musical learning has been done in isolation, with recordings and radio, scores, books, and his unique way of thinking at the keyboard and about it. He thus protected himself against pressures to conform to other people's notions of piano playing and repertoire.

Among the things he admires about certain composers is their refusal to conform to prevailing trends, to join the mainstream: Hindemith, Ives, Schoenberg and Richard Strauss are examples, and above all so is J.S. Bach. Gould has said:

When creative people . . . need sympathetic understanding, I feel it's a shame; the line of productivity and creation is more direct than this. . . . Also, I'm fascinated with what happens to the creative output when you isolate yourself from the approval and disapproval of the people around you.[7]

Of teaching Gould says:

It is something that I have never done and do not imagine that I shall ever have the courage to do. It strikes me as involving a most awesome responsibility which I should prefer to avoid.[8]

I'm afraid of teaching. I find it extremely stimulating when I'm in the mood to sit down and talk with people and analyze music, but I'm subject to periods of noncommunication, so it would be very draining to have to do it at prerequisite hours. Also, I need spinal resilience when I'm confronted with opinions not my own.[9]

The person who successfully resists outside influences is entitled to claim that his abilities and his achievements are his own and nobody else's. This possessiveness is not peculiar to the successful creative genius, but is common to the type, and is part of his security in a situation which in ordinary experience is insecure: the situation of a person who knows that he has no friends within hundreds of miles, but who cannot be sure that there is no enemy behind the nearest tree. This possessiveness sometimes turns out to be false security, a brave facade. Gould has written an article in which he refers to himself as a hermit,[10] but we may doubt that he would be comfortable entirely alone in a true wilderness, with none of the material or social amenities of civilization.

For the liner to his disc *The Idea of North* Gould wrote:

The north has fascinated me since childhood. In my school days, I used to pore over whichever maps of that region I could get my hands on, though I found it exceedingly difficult to remember whether Great Bear or Great Slave was farther north — and in case you've had the same problem, it's Great Bear. The idea of the country intrigued me, but my notion of what it looked like was pretty much restricted to the romanticized, art-nouveau-tinged, Group of Seven paintings which, in my day, adorned virtually every second schoolroom, and which probably served as a pictorial introduction to the north for a great many people of my generation.

A bit later on, I began to examine aerial photographs and to look through geological surveys, and came to realize that the north was possessed of qualities more elusive than even a magician like A.Y. Jackson could define with oils. At about this time, I made a few tentative forays into the north and began to make use of it, metaphorically, in my writing. There was a curious kind of literary fall-out there, as a matter of fact. When I went to the north, I had no intention of writing about it, or of referring to it, even parenthetically, in anything that I wrote. And yet, almost despite myself, I began to draw all sorts of metaphorical allusions based on what was really a very limited knowledge of the country and a very casual exposure to it. I found myself writing musical critiques, for instance, in which the north— the idea of the north—began to serve as a foil for other ideas and values that seemed to me depressingly urban-oriented and spiritually limited thereby.

Now, of course, such metaphorical manipulation of the north is a bit suspect, not to say romantic, because there are very few places today which are out of reach by, and out of touch with, the style and pace-setting attitudes and techniques of Madison Avenue. *Time, Newsweek, Life, Look* and the *Saturday Review* can be airlifted into Frobisher Bay or Inuvik, just about as easily as a local contractor can deliver them to the neighborhood newsstand, and there are probably people living in the heart of Manhattan who can manage every bit as independent and hermit-like an existence as a prospector tramping the sort of lichen-covered tundra that A.Y. Jackson was so fond of painting north of Great Bear Lake.

Admittedly, it's a question of attitude, and I'm not at all sure that my own quasi-allegorical attitude toward the north is the proper way to make use of it, or even an accurate way in which to define it. Nevertheless, I'm by no means alone in this reaction to the North; there are very few people who make contact with it and emerge entirely unscathed. Something really does happen to most people who go into the north—they become at least aware of the creative opportunity which the physical fact of the country represents and, quite often I think, come to measure their own work and life against that rather staggering creative possibility—they become, in effect, philosophers. [11]

Torontonians use the expression "up north" in a special way that needs explaining. When a Torontonian says that he is going "up north" for the weekend, he has in mind a destination considerably short of the Arctic Circle; indeed it is probably south of the latitude of, say, Venice or Astrakhan, Portland Oregon or Portland Maine. In fact he probably has in mind a trip of about a hundred miles. This at any rate was approximately the distance from home in Toronto to the cottage at Uptergrove; yet for the young Glenn Gould that hundred miles "up north" meant more than just going to the cottage. It meant getting away from schoolyard toughs and schoolroom bores. From the despair and depression of a winter weekday in Toronto, "up north" must have seemed the image of a rustic paradise, away from all that. Some years later, when Gould was touring the concert circuit, Uptergrove was his home base where he rested and spiritually replenished himself between concerts.

But there is not much real solitude there. The Gould cottage sat companionably among other cottages, with a road along the back. In front the lake teemed with snarling motor boats on a summer day. However, the cottage was equipped for all seasons, so "up north" for Glenn may more typically have meant going there on winter weekends when there were few people about. We have already noticed that his childhood image of Beethoven was associated with snow and frozen lakes and the drive home to Toronto on Sunday afternoons, listening to the New York Philharmonic. Gould has made a few trips much farther north in Canada than Uptergrove, and has been deeply moved by the independence of people living in isolated northern places. His musical equivalent of this experience is the Fifth Symphony of Sibelius. (The reader is urged to sit alone on a stormy winter day and listen to this music to feel the "Ibsenesque gloom" to which Gould is strongly attracted, and which he associates with wild terrain and dull, low skies.)

Gould's musical preferences are strongly influenced by northerliness. He is ill at ease with the passionate, sunny Mediterranean temperament in all its manifestations, but particularly the Spanish bullfight and the Italian opera. He thinks these depend equally upon herd responses to violent spectacle, and upon flashy personal display.[12]

By contrast, he associates northerliness with moral rectitude, adherence to law (including the laws of God and of counterpoint, and hence J.S. Bach), and blue-nosed Protestantism. In an article published in 1974 Gould hints that he equates "separation from the world" with latitude: the higher the latitude the greater the degree of separation or isolation.[13] It is not possible to quote all his many remarks on these connections between North, solitude, the music he prefers, and the moral conduct he esteems. They reiterate his individualistic stand in moral and aesthetical matters; he seldom deviates when pursuing these connections. For him "the line of productivity and creation" runs directly from individual to individual, and it can be assisted by technological means that *separate* us in space and time as beings capable of hating and hurting each other, capable of passion and enthusiasm and other impulses. But these same technological means *connect* us as beings capable of comprehending one another at a high, pure, abstract level of enlightenment. They enable us to act at a distance.

The telephone is Gould's paradigm of action at a distance. In his private life he avoids person-to-person contact as much as possible, and keeps in touch with his friends by telephone. His long-distance telephone bills must be awesome. For him to *see* the person he talks to is to be distracted; he can have a more satisfactory relationship when the visual element is filtered out by distance while the telephone bridges the auditory gap between himself and his interlocutor.[14]

The hardiest of all Glenn Gould apocrypha has to do with the telephone, and with action of an undesirable kind at a distance. In this story Van Cliburn or Alfred Brendel, or almost anyone, is passing through Toronto and during a stopover at the airport telephones Glenn Gould for a friendly chat. After an initial exchange of pleasantries the caller mentions that he has a cold, then sneezes. Gould in hypochondriac panic hangs up. (The Gould apocrypha never rise above this level of humour.)

An interviewer asked Gould if he eats much. Gould replied that he eats very little, and feels guilty about it when he does. Then the interviewer asked him if he needed people. Gould replied:

People are about as important to me as food. As I grow older I find more and more that I can do without them; I separate myself from conflicting and contrasting notions. Monastic seclusion works for me.[15]

He once said in a telecast:

Solitude is the prerequisite for ecstatic experience, especially the experience most valued by the post-Wagnerian artist—the condition of heroism. One can't feel oneself heroic without having first been cast off by the world, or perhaps by having done the casting-off oneself. . . . To such men [Arnold Schoenberg, for example] isolation fashioned a heroic life and heroism was the patron of creativity.[16]

Immanuel Kant said:

To be sufficient for oneself, and consequently to have no need of society, without at the same time being unsociable, i.e. without flying from it, is something bordering on the sublime, as is any dispensing with wants.[17]

That genius flourishes in solitude is a notion foreign to the Canadian musical scene, where budding musicians are required to compete like gladiators and to be graded like eggs, to strive against each other for prizes and high scores. Glenn Gould was caught up in this situation as a boy, and has vigorously opposed it in his writings. He epitomized it when he said of Canadians:

We're not a nation of doers, we're a nation of evaluators.[18]

This is nowhere more evident than in the non-professional musical life of Canadians, at least in English-speaking Canada. Gould had in mind two musical institutions which have burgeoned in Canada as nowhere else: the graded musical examination system and the competitive musical festival.

Graded examinations in music are administered by several conservatories and university music departments in Canada; the Royal Conservatory of Music of Toronto has probably the most widespread examination system. The Royal Conservatory publishes a syllabus of studies in piano, violin, voice, theory, and other musical subjects, with the materials and requirements arranged in ascending order through Grades 1 to 10 (a few subjects have fewer grades in the sequence). At the top of the scale is a diploma, "Associate of the Royal Conservatory of Music of Toronto". (Gould was awarded the equivalent of this diploma at the age of twelve, with the highest grades in all of Canada.) Candidates are examined at local examination centres across Canada and at a few places in the United States. In 1971[19] there were 54,000 candidates for examinations in all grades and all musical subjects; there were 250 local examination centres. These are figures for the Royal Conservatory only, but it is evident from them that the grading and evaluating of music students is not a small enterprise in Canada. Most children who take private music lessons are required, by parents and teachers, to take these examinations. Such expressions as "Grade 5 piano," or "Grade 3 theory," or "Honours in Grade 2 violin" are supposed to stand for exact and meaningful positions along an objective scale of talent, merit and achievement. This supposition has never been seriously challenged, so ingrained is the national characteristic of which Gould speaks. The fact that nothing quite like these musical examination systems exists in any other country seems not to have occurred to anyone, or if it has, its significance has been missed.

Any evaluation by numerical or letter grade is, in Gould's terms, a kind of competition. The most extensive and ferocious competing in Canadian non-professional music takes place in music festivals and there is scarcely a community of any size in English-speaking Canada which does not have one.[20] (In Chapter 1 Toronto's Kiwanis Music Festival was mentioned.)

These music festivals are tournaments with many different classes of competition: solo and ensemble classes for various instruments, voice, choir, and so forth, at several levels of achievement. They are an even bigger operation than the graded examination systems. In 1971 there were more than 160 festivals in Canada; approximately 500,000 persons competed in them; cash prizes exceeding $165,000 were awarded to winners; there were more than 600 adjudicators; the total income of music festivals in that year exceeded $800,000, of which less than $100,000 came from public sources. Approximately thirty percent of the income was from admissions, sales of programs and advertising.[21] Considering that admission charges are usually modest, and that each competitor (including each child in a school choir) has numerous proud relatives, the number of people who paid to attend must have been enormous.

Of these music festivals Gould wrote:

There is . . . a minor-league festival tradition in English Canada — one which is concerned not with the do or die fortunes of budding professionals but with an annual series of regional adjudications for students, presided over by superannuated British academicians. At these events—such is their aura of charity and good fellowship—a mark of 80 is automatically accorded a contestant merely for showing up (79 is considered a stain upon the family honour and reserved for platform indiscretions of a most grievous order, such as sticking out one's tongue at a fellow competitor or playing one's test-piece caution-to-the-winds, and with a most un-British brio).
    The adjudicators, moreover, being compelled to deliver their remarks before the assembled parents, neighbors, and schoolmates of the respective contestants, develop an altogether endearing strain of report-card euphemism: "I say, that's jolly good, Number 67—smashing spirit and all that. Have to dock you just a point for getting tangled at the double bars, though. Four times through the old exposition is a bit much of a good thing, what?"[22]

Gould wrote this in 1966. In 1971 only thirty-two of the 600 adjudicators were from the United Kingdom (the statistics are mute on how many of these were "superannuated"). But otherwise, and allowing a notch or two for literary license, the competitive music festivals in Canada today are much as Gould described them.

He wrote this article as a report on a different kind of competitive festival, the kind at which not students but young professional musicians compete for cash and fame. It was the First International Violin Competition in Montreal, held in 1966. He says of this and similar musical competitions:

[Adjudicators tend to be] capable and respected . . . musicians whose own careers have attracted heretofore something less than universal renown. And it is . . . characteristic of musicians thwarted in their aspirations for international acclaim to decry the unaccountable mysteries of personality, to downgrade those virtues of temperamental independence which signal the genuine recreative fire. . . .

Prodigality may, indeed, be courted in the competitive quest, but originality must at all costs be discouraged. It is, surely, one of the considerable ironies of the contemporary musical scene that these gatherings of the best young talent from each continent ignore the ethnographic revelations implicit in their regional distinctiveness in the interest of preserving a consensus of mediocrity—a mean line of temperamental indifference. . . .

It is sometimes argued that without the competitive frenzy consensus engenders, the aspirants would fail in the perception of their own potential. But I suspect that what happens, rather, is that, because of consensus, the observant contestant—and no other kind turns up a winner—becomes uncomfortably aware of the potential of his fellows, becomes conscious of all the misguided traditions which constitute "style" in musical performance —his initiative blunted by the supreme fallacy that performance is essentially a repetitive act—and this precisely at that time in his life when a muted response to the world outside and the sharpest attention to the vibrations of the inner ear could most propitiously shape and characterize his art. Competitions, then, rarely benefit the supreme artist whose career would come to pass regardless. . . .

It would be foolish to discriminate against a level of competence without which our musical life would be the poorer. But while it is entirely proper to speak of competent electricians and plumbers, and hazardous — if not, indeed, in contravention of civic maintenance bylaws — to bargain for ecstatic ones, the notion of ecstasy as the only proper quest for the artist assumes competence as an inclusive component. The menace of the competitive idea is that, through its emphasis upon consensus, it extracts the mean, indisputable, readily certifiable core of competence and leaves its eager, ill-advised suppliants forever stunted, victims of a spiritual lobotomy.[23]

In a 1962 interview Gould said:

Throughout my teens, I rather resisted the idea of a career as a concert pianist. . . . I imagined that only a career that was musicologically motivated was worthy, and that everything else was a little bit frivolous. I saw myself as a sort of musical Renaissance Man, capable of doing many things. I obviously wanted to be a composer. I still do. Performing in the arena had no attraction for me. This was, at least in part, defensive. Even from what little I then knew of the politics of the business, it was apparent that a career as a solo pianist involved a competition which I felt much too grand ever to consider facing. I couldn't conceive of myself ruthlessly competing against other seventeen-year-olds who quite probably played the piano much better.[24]

The spectator in the arena, who regards musical performance as some kind of athletic event, is happily removed from the risk. He takes some kind of glee in what goes on there, but this is entirely separate from what is really going on: an effort by the performer to form a powerful identification with the music. A performance is not a contest but a love affair.[25]

Gould's most elaborate argument against competitiveness was developed in a 1972 broadcast.[26] It is a reminder that Gould is never more serious than when at his most waggish. He comments on international chess and hockey, and assumes character roles as an Italian pugilist, a silly-ass Englishman and a Viennese psychiatrist. At the same time, however, he makes a number of important points against human aggression.

Gould in this broadcast argues against "the whole phenomenon of the competitive fact." Sports, games, commerce, fighting—all are equally forms of aggression. He quotes chess champion Bobby Fischer: "I like to see them [i.e., his opponents] squirm. I want to crush their egos." This is a murderous urge. Murder is not only of the body; there is psychic murder as well. Bodily murder is observable, psychic murder is insidious. The distinction between body and spirit is a peculiarly occidental development which conceals and even sanctions the psychological damage caused by our competitiveness.[27]

In any kind of competition we assume that only the loser loses (the prize, a job, position in the hierarchy of champions, or a contract). But how do we know that the victor has not also suffered damage, although of an unobservable kind? Or that the loser has not lost something more fundamental than prize, job, reputation, etc.? Can we ever count the full cost of either victory or defeat?

The impulse underlying all competitive activities is domination. This is true not just of trials of skill or of strength, but of all forms of competition. "The competition in sport," he says, "is a metaphor for other types of competition as well." Some people insist that competition is a law of life derived from our jungle ancestry. Human society is competitive, and that's just the way it is, they say. To this Gould replies with a question: "Are you satisfied with society as you know it?" He says that we now have the power to opt out creatively: ". . . there's a younger generation . . . to whom the competitive fact is not an inevitable component of life, and who do program their lives without making allowances for it."[28]

Gould suggests one way of opting out creatively from our competitive society: accept the alternatives offered to us by technology. Technology introduces a protective shield around humanity which removes the necessity for humans to measure themselves against one another, on either a bodily or a psychical scale. We are no longer frontiersmen, competing in the rough wilderness like animals for food and shelter.

At this point in his argument Gould quotes a radio interview with Jean Le Moyne, who has been a profound influence upon his ethical thought. Le Moyne, in his slow, quiet way said:

The much-maligned mills of the Victorian era were of course terrible, because the kind of machine they were using there provoked a kind of super-concentration of humanity and work. The conditions were really terrible. But those very dreary and bleak mills have clothed more humanity than all the charity of all the kings, and all the lords, and all the saints, of humanity. Our most terrible technologies, the ones that frighten us—for example, the oil technology, when you see refineries at night with flames and all that— the heat that is distributed through them is much more than all the wood that was chopped. And I think in that way technology exercises a sort of charity upon which we have not reflected yet.

There is real charity in the machine. It is there to help man. Of course it can be perverted. In that way we are not very free among our own creations. But in themselves they are good. . . .

The network of machines and techniques that encompasses the earth is the ensemble of all the networks: the radio network, the television network, the oil network, the hydraulic network, the railroad network, telephone, telegraph, and all that. So that today it is almost impossible to consider a machine isolated from the rest. It is part of all the rest. So that there is only one machine in fact encompassing the earth. And this has a meaning: that machine, stemming from the activity of man, is between man and nature like a second nature, offering to us its mediation. We cannot go to nature now without going through the network.[29]

There is a competitive streak in everyone, including Glenn Gould himself. Friends of his family remember croquet games on the lawn in front of the cottage in which it was desperately important to young Glenn that he should win; in later years he drove powerful cars at high speeds. And sometimes his piano playing on television seems competitive, or at least a *tour de force*. An example of this would be his transcription of Ravel's *La Valse*, which he played on CBC television in 1975. This work, in its original form (or, more accurately, forms), is already a giddy parody of the sentimental Viennese waltz. Gould's transcription is a parody of those nineteenth-century piano transcriptions of orchestral and operatic masterpieces, and works by Bach for organ, to which he objected in his youth. In his playing of this transcription he seemed bent upon surpassing those virtuosi who dust off the more spectacular transcriptions of Liszt to perform them in concerts or on records, and to dazzle us with the sheer physical improbability of their display. Gould outdid them all in dazzle.

There is a romantic streak in Gould too, of course, which he keeps under control by arguing in support of classical, regulated musical structures, and by recording fugues, canonic variations, and other technically elaborate and emotionally disciplined kinds of music. He strives to keep within bounds both the competitive and the romantic sides of his nature. In himself and in other people it is the things we do for their own sakes and not for glory or power or thrills that he most esteems, along with a responsible and disciplined style of thinking and doing.

But even when we are not seeking glory or power we are not free from an odd kind of competitiveness: competitiveness against self. Arthur Rubinstein relates that he once found himself up against the astonishing virtuosity of Vladimir Horowitz:

Horowitz was seducing Paris—literally snatching her from me. I saw in him a new Liszt, able to vanquish a whole generation. . . . I doubled my fists, but as a pianist cannot in the nature of his profession keep them doubled for long I opened them again and set myself to work very hard. I had vengeance to wreak, not on Horowitz but on myself. . . .[30]

Ernst Bacon put it this way:

A concert is like a tennis match, except that the opponent is not across the net, but you.[31]

There is no escaping it: competitiveness is an important factor in our development both as individuals and as a species. It lends poignancy to our play, and provides motivation in our growth, our education, and our work. Without it there would be no innovation or change, technological and otherwise. In every human activity there occurs measurement of individuals by standards of more and less, better and worse.[32] There could be no orchestras or opera or dance companies without auditions in which some candidates are accepted and others refused on the basis of competitive evaluation.

Some people are more competitive by nature than others; and fortunately it is possible, as Gould says, for the less competitive to opt out and let the pack go thundering past. In the jungle an uncompetitive human would perish of starvation or exposure; in primitive society he would be enslaved. But the charity of the machine protects uncompetitive persons from the worst that heedless nature or schoolyard bullies or grasping tyrants can inflict upon them, according to Gould and Le Moyne.

I intend to challenge Le Moyne's fantasy of the charity of the machine, but for the moment will accept that technology makes it possible for the uncompetitive person to opt out without peril. Presumably he could opt out *un*creatively as well as creatively, although Gould does not mention this possibility. But the creative opter-out must *create* something, or the word "creative" is wrongly used. What does he create? What is there in his manner of opting out that is lacking in *un*creative opting out?

Two difficult but crucial notions are, taken together, Gould's answer to this question. Both are mentioned in the preceding quotations about competitiveness, but he does not elaborate upon them. They are *ecstasy* and *the non-repetitiveness of musical performance*.

The creative opter-out, then, creates two things. He creates a state of affairs in his own mind, and in the minds of other people, for which Gould's word is "ecstasy." And he creates a state of affairs in the perceivable world — a unique, one-time performance of a particular musical work significantly different from any other performance of that same work. He creates the first by creating the second, and technology gives permanence to both by making possible a permanent image or record of the second. There may be other states of affairs an opter-out could create, but we cannot deduce these from Gould's writings, as we have done with the two mentioned here. Let us examine both more closely, beginning with *ecstasy*.

Ecstasy is by strict definition a solitary condition, an individual person's standing-outside-himself. It is not euphoria and not exaltation. A crowd might be exalted by a spectacle; that is to say, it might be collectively moved to an extreme state of fear, pleasure or grief. But it would be odd to say of a crowd that it stands outside itself. Of course it is also odd to speak of an individual standing outside himself, since this locution implies two selves, or a pseudo-self and a true self, one doing the standing outside and the other being stood outside of. Odd as it is, we are familiar with this manner of speaking. An individual may be exalted, of course, no less than a crowd. To be exalted is to be lifted up; figuratively a crowd or a person can be lifted up without excessive contradiction or oddity.

That may be bad etymology but it is good Gould. He uses the word "ecstasy" with the strict meaning I have mentioned: a condition in which an individual has some sense of standing outside himself. Gould uses it with heavy emphasis upon the solitary aspect. It is not a condition attainable collectively by a crowd, as, for example, an audience at a concert.

The word is closely related in Gould's usage to another word, "narcissism." As he uses them the two words shed light on each other, but he has dropped "narcissism" in his more recent writings. In 1962 he wrote:

. . . I believe that the justification of art is the internal combustion it ignites in the hearts of men and not its shallow, externalized, public manifestations. The purpose of art is not the release of a momentary ejection of adrenalin but is, rather, the gradual, lifelong construction of a state of wonder and serenity. Through the ministrations of radio and the phonograph, we are rapidly and quite properly learning to appreciate the elements of aesthetic narcissism—and I use that word in its best sense—and are awakening to the challenge that each man contemplatively create his own divinity.[33]

It is not obvious what Gould meant by "aesthetic narcissism" and by narcissism "in its best sense." We have to dig.

There is a familiar sense in which making works of art is a self-expressive activity: artists make works of art in order to clarify something within themselves of which they are uneasily and obscurely aware, some drive or want or mystery. Gould is not talking about this.

He is talking about what art shares with prophecy: the capacity to serve as a mirror to those who contemplate it. If one contemplates a work of art with intense concentration, penetrating from its pleasing surface to its disturbing depths, what does one find? Perhaps one finds the inner, vulnerable secrets of the artist who made the work. Or perhaps one beholds a revelation of the cosmos or Divine Truth or of the human condition.

Perhaps what one discovers is none of these, but is nothing less than one's own real self, revealed in its weaknesses and strengths, its simplicity and complexity. I should not try to explain a poetically obscure statement of Gould's by substituting for it an equally poetic and obscure statement of my own; but what I think his statement about "narcissism" means, and would like my own to mean, is this:

that while a work of art might please its beholder, it also presents him with an occasion for introspection of a special and potentially salubrious kind; and that to indulge in such introspection is an active, proper response to a work of art and a condition without which nobody can produce a work of art. To respond passively, or to respond merely by adding one's voice to the voice of a howling mob at a spectacle, is to shirk a responsibility to oneself, to miss an opportunity to come to terms with oneself. As Karlheinz Stockhausen said about his *Stimmung*, a work for six vocalists:

Stimmung is indeed meditative music. Time is suspended. One listens to the inner self of the sound, the inner self of the harmonic spectrum, the inner self of a vowel, *the inner self.*[34]

Gould quoted this in his telecast "The Age of Ecstasy." I think we shall come no closer to a statement of what he means by the words "ecstasy" and "narcissism."

He uses "ecstasy" indiscriminately for a quality of the music, a quality of the performance, an attitude of the performer, and an attitude of the listener. But this lack of discrimination is intentional, and is the essence of Gould's meaning: that "ecstasy" is a delicate thread binding together music, performance, performer and listener in a web of shared awareness of *innerness*.

On rare occasions at a concert performance there is a moment of powerful magic in which performer and audience seem to merge in oneness, in total sympathy. This can be felt, but it cannot be explained. Gould has experienced it, as have many performers and listeners. He values it highly,† but is uneasy with it because he cannot control it. I think this is not ecstasy but exaltation. For ecstasy there must be not just a merging of self with other selves, but of self with the innerness of the music. A performer alone with his piano (or other instrument, although as Joachim Kaiser says, the pianist is more alone with his instrument than is any other musician) has moments, many moments, of transcendental luminescence, of ecstasy indeed, in which this merging of self with music occurs.

Gould is in an ecstatic condition during the whole of the time he plays. "Alone" is the key word: alone with his piano at home, in the recording studio, or on the concert stage while indulging in the deliberate self-deception that the audience is not really there. A truly intent listener at the output end of the system, at his loud-

---

† "Occasionally something quite lovely will happen at a concert, of course, and then I'll wish the audience were twenty thousand instead of two thousand."[35]

speaker, may share the ecstasy. The system separates Gould physically from the listener and assures Gould of his solitude; but it also connects him with his listener at the purely intellectual and auditory level at which Gould works to achieve this condition for both himself and his listener.

This, or something close to it, is what Gould means by "aesthetic narcissism." In the noisy herd at a concert it is absent. When it is present in an individual's experience, it is the result not of one single great moment, but of a cumulative tendency to lower one's guard, to remove layers of social protectiveness and private delusion. In the herd we bellow because everyone else is bellowing. In solitude we find reconciliation.

An antonym of "ecstasy" is "apathy," which is a good word for the individual's state of mind in a crowd. He may intone the ritual responses ("bravo!" or "Kill the umpire!"), but this is not active participation. The performance is happening to him and around him. The ecstatic, on the other hand, is an agent, not a patient; a doer, not an "undergoer." He is the cause, or at least a contributing cause, of his own mental condition; and he is to this extent designer and executant, composer and performer, of the structured event that is his awareness at that moment or in that interval of time.

From Gould's article on competitive music festivals two main and very important points emerge: first, there is no genuine musical experience without ecstasy; second, ecstasy cannot be measured or compared, because it is unique to each self on each occasion, wholly private to the self or between two selves intimately connected by experience deeply felt and shared.† With the second I cannot disagree, because (unless I have misunderstood Gould's remarks on this difficult subject) it merely adumbrates his own meaning of the word "ecstasy." I question the first, however, because most people seldom experience anything with the degree of intensity suggested by the word "ecstasy." Gould *seems* to experience everything at a very high level of awareness; the rest of us experience things mostly at lower levels than are normal for Gould. We are not introspectively challenged by our experiences the way he is, although our responses may give us as much pleasure as his give him.‡

The two most important questions about ecstasy, for our purposes, are these: can it be recorded? can it be spliced?

I said earlier that for Gould a piece of music is not merely a

---

† *See* Appendix — Ecstasy and Authenticity.
‡ *See* Appendix — Ecstasy on Demand: Richard Strauss.

collection of acoustical events; and that for him music is more a form of cognition than of sensation. There is no question that acoustical events (that is, events capable of being heard) can be both recorded and spliced. In this sense music is nothing more than a matter of getting the correct notes into the correct sequence. But most people would insist that music is more than that. "Ecstasy" might be that something. It is not an acoustical event or a collection of acoustical events.

On the question of whether it can be recorded or spliced we shall explore Gould's answers in Chapter 8. We must for the present leave Gould's notion of *ecstasy* and move on to his notion of *the non-repetitiveness of musical performance*.

By this he means that each separate performance of a piece should be unique in the history of that piece, and in the personal history of the performer. He means something more than that a performer should keep his performance "fresh" and "vital," to use words familiar to readers of popular musical criticism. It will help to clarify this if we consider the opposite view.

In its extreme form the opposite view is that for any particular piece of music there must be one correct way of performing it, an abstract paradigm performance of it. This cannot exist in fact, but a good performer strives towards it, a good performance is good insofar as it resembles it, and a bad performance is bad insofar as it does not. It is unattainable, but thinkable as the goal toward which all practice and all performances are aimed. In a less-than-extreme form this view is that a performer works diligently to bring "his" performance of the piece to a peak, to a condition in which it reflects his characteristic manner of performing, and at which he will thereafter try to maintain it. In both forms of the view, performance is regarded as a repetitive act. "Get the piece right and then keep playing it that way" would be the slogan, as if performing a piece of music were a routine operation like cleaning the sink or paying the bills.

Competitive evaluation presupposes the extreme form of this view: that there is a perfect, though unattainable, performance of the piece in the adjudicator's imagination, against which he measures all actual performances; or, as is more likely, that there is in his imagination an amalgam of several performances, combining (according to his taste and background) the best features of each, against which he makes his comparisons. And if, instead of being the only adjudicator, he is one of a panel or jury, he will take care to avoid revealing that his own tastes and background are "different," lest he himself be tacitly adjudicated by his colleagues on the panel. This is what Gould had in mind when he spoke about the deadening effects of consensus.

Adherents to the view that performance is essentially a repetitive act will expect a recording of a piece to be a crystallization of what the performer would always do with the piece if he could always perform at his best. This recorded performance would be quintessentially "his." Listeners would then compare one performer's recorded version of the piece with another's, to see which comes closest to the paradigm.

Glenn Gould has nothing like this in mind when he goes to the recording studio, and he would reject any suggestion that he should be working toward a paradigm version for the microphone. One reason for his rejection would be that this kind of thinking draws attention away from the music and directs it toward the identity of the performer: "Rubinstein's Chopin" as compared with "Ashkenazy's Chopin."[36]

Another reason relates to ecstasy. Ecstasy not only separates the individual from the crowd, it separates his experiences one from another. There is not an all-purpose ecstasy that belongs to each experience of a particular piece of music, or a Brahms ecstasy or a Bach ecstasy. We lack a form of the word which would enable us to speak of "an ecstasy" without awkwardness. We need it because ecstasy is a condition of here-and-now, belonging to *this* occasion of playing or of hearing the piece. The ecstasy of the moment, and not some paradigm image of the piece, is what defines and distinguishes that moment and that playing or hearing of the piece. A near-paradigm performance would be repeatable; an ecstasy is not.

It is possible to perform a piece of music many times with the notes in correct sequence, with suitable alterations in tempo, phrasing, dynamics and the rest, but with no trace of ecstasy. Ecstasy throws the playing into peril because it urges the player to abandon inhibitions and conventions. It might make a kind of sense to compare non-ecstatics to other non-ecstatics and assign grades to them in a competitive festival or in a musical examination. But ecstasy cannot be assigned a grade. It inhabits our solitudes and our isolated moments of deepest reflection.

In his arguments against competitiveness as a law of life and of human culture Gould frequently invokes the views of Jean Le Moyne, particularly those contained in the radio interview quoted above.

In 1968 Le Moyne and Gould were jointly awarded the Molson Prize of the Canada Council. Walter Carlos' *Switched-on Bach* was released that same year, and so also was Gould's article about it.[37] Gould admired the Carlos disc, but was shaken by it. It appears that Le Moyne's published writings provided a conceptual framework within which Gould could come to terms with this new thing, this almost totally technologized Bach. In addition to the article mentioned above, Gould produced a radio documentary on *Switched-on Bach* for the CBC; it included an extended interview with Jean Le Moyne.

Jean Le Moyne was born in Montreal in 1914. He has had mainly a literary career, as journalist, translator, literary critic, essayist, film writer and producer. His only book is *Convergences*,[38] which was published in French in 1961. It contains essays written in the years 1940-1960 on many topics: religion, literature, women, French-Canadian culture and politics, cinema, music and others. He may have endeared himself to Gould for his love of Bach and his "unswerving resistance" to Mozart.[39]

Like Gould, Le Moyne is a man of abounding intellectual curiosity. Each in his way is a master craftsman: Le Moyne as essayist and Gould as keyboard player (among other things). Here is a description of Le Moyne's prose: ". . . chatoyant, fortement imagée, manque peut-être de sobriété et confine même à une certaine préciosité, à une sorte de baroquisme."[40] Gould's prose is like that too.

Gould has quoted the Le Moyne interview on several occasions in support of his own theories of music and technology. If we subtract the informality and the *baroquisme*, what remains is something like this: first, that technological advances have potential for human good; second, that between ourselves and the natural world we have placed an interlocking hierarchy of technological systems which is itself a single, all-embracing system, whose power for human good we either take for granted or overlook in our concern over its potential for evil. Thus stated the theory is unobjectionable, provided no argument of consequence is built upon it. But Gould builds such an argument, so it needs a certain amount of critical examination.

Le Moyne makes quantitative judgments and comparisons: benefits to mankind in the form of clothing and warmth, he says, outweigh some of the sufferings of mankind. The atrocious working conditions in nineteenth century mills are the ones he mentions, but we could add suffering due to industrial pollution for another example. There are evils included in the cost of the benefits; Le Moyne merely says that the good outweighs the bad. Presumably if there were no mills and no oil more people would be naked and cold. But is it better that a few people should suffer acutely for the benefit of many, than that everyone should suffer but not so acutely? No final answer is possible, but philosophers of the tradition known as "utilitarianism" have been working on this problem for more than a century, and have greatly clarified the question.

Since the seventeenth century there have been scientists and philosophers who displayed this same sweet optimism: technological and scientific progress cannot do otherwise than improve our lot, cannot fail to save us from natural disasters and our own savagery. To understate it: things have not turned out that way. We are threatened by our machines not only when they work properly, but when we become dependent on them and they fail. They do sometimes fail, of course; and they do not always improve our lot when they work. Lewis Mumford gave a topical illustration:

Compare our present situation with that which accompanied the relatively technically primitive era of the seventeenth century. In that time a good London burgher, like Samuel Pepys, a practical man, a hard-working administrator, would select the servants in his household partly on the basis of their having a good voice, so that they might sit down with the family in the evening to take part in domestic singing. Such people not merely listened passively to music, but could produce it, or at least reproduce it, in their own right. Today, in contrast, we often see people wandering around with a portable radio set on Riverside Drive, listening to a radio musical program, with no thought that they might sing a song freely in the open air without invoking any mechanical aid.[41]

Do the skills of the New Listener, no matter how highly developed, and no matter how elaborate his machinery, compare with the skills required to sing a melody or to carry a part in a part-song? Indeed, are his skills in any way to be compared to singing or playing or composing, at no matter how elementary a level? Has technology silenced the song that is within most of us?

We may suppose that Glenn Gould means no more by his acceptance of Jean Le Moyne's notion of the charity of the machine than this: that an entirely negative attitude toward "the technological" as opposed to "the human" is untenable. With this it is possible to agree while rejecting, as I think we must, the metaphysical notion of an objective and inherent good in the technological network. Gould is trying to make us understand that it is possible for people to show their better natures to one another without being in physical proximity, and that technology helps make this possible. With this also we can agree.

I believe this is what Gould is explaining in some remarks he once made concerning the early days of radio:

It's always seemed to me that when those first people sat glued or wired to their crystal sets, what they really were recognizing was the phenomenon of another human voice. It wasn't the facts of the news reportage; it wasn't the vital weather information; it was the sheer mystery and challenge of another human voice — five blocks away and yet heard. It didn't matter whether what was being said was being said accurately or inaccurately, or was senseless or serious; none of that counted. What really counted was that there was a way of communicating *something*, no matter what, one person to another, while not being in the same room, in the same acoustical area.[42]

Gould used his hauntingly beautiful essay "The Search for Petula Clark" to make the same point, among others. In it he says that in the isolation of Northern Ontario radio is "the surest evidence that the 'outside' . . . is with us still."[43]

There are human voices out there.

Glenn Gould most clearly reveals his anti-competitive attitude in his dislike of bravura concertos for instrumental soloist and orchestra. Of composers, he mentions Liszt, Grieg, MacDowell and Gottschalk as among those who are guilty of writing them,[44] but he also dislikes the concertos of Mozart and Beethoven, if we credit his liner-note remarks on several of these. His reasons will be no surprise: the concerto overemphasizes the "identity" of the soloist; the soloist is cast in a competing role against the orchestra; the whole thing is intended to be a spectacle.

He put these words into the mouth of a fictitious psychiatric patient on the couch:

Doctor, I have this incredible fixation. I want desperately to be up on a stage, at a piano, in front of an orchestra, subduing that orchestra with my playing, having them copy my phrases, embroidering the phrases more delicately than they can and, in the end, to be applauded for my efforts while my colleagues in the orchestra sit there subdued.

He says of this:

I don't think it's at all rare to have that particular kind of exhibitionistic tendency turned loose against—as opposed to on behalf of—an audience. And I think there is a kind of underlying neurosis when one feels that compulsion to aggressiveness.[45]

Gould spoke those words to a real-life psychiatrist in a radio interview, which accounts for the exaggerations. But the passage gives a clear idea of Gould's resistance to the whole conception and tradition of the virtuoso solo concerto, a conception which contains the essence of Gould's reasons for leaving the concert stage. The concerto is intrinsically competitive and aggressive, he says, and the public's expectations of it are demeaning to the performer. He says:

We exaggerate the protagonist's role in concertos. We exaggerate a sense of dualism as between orchestra and soloist, as between individual and mass, as between masculine and feminine statements, as Tovey put it. This is a great mistake.[46]

On two famous occasions Gould tried to mitigate this dualism. The first was a performance of the Brahms D Minor Concerto in 1962 with Leonard Bernstein and the New York Philharmonic. Just before the performance Bernstein read a statement to the audience in which he disassociated himself and the orchestra from the interpretation proposed by Gould, who intended to experiment with the work, to see what would happen if it were treated in an understated manner with the solo exhibition reduced to a minimum by means of restrained dynamics and consistent tempos.

. . . I wanted to play both the outer movements . . . [so that] the main themes and second themes were played in exact tempo unless otherwise indicated by Brahms. Unfortunately, a whole virtuoso tradition has been built up otherwise.[47]

The other occasion was the recording session for his recording with Leopold Stokowski and the American Symphony Orchestra of Beethoven's *Emperor Concerto*. This was in 1966. Gould and Stokowski agreed upon an interpretation in which the work was treated not as a display piece for soloist with orchestral accompaniment, but as a symphony with an orchestral part for piano.
    Gould says:

The great evil of the concerto is that attention is being directed away from the person who is listening. It would seem to me that one ought to make the listener aware of an inward-looking, rather than an outward-looking, process. Surely everything that is mixed up in virtuosity and exhibitionism on the platform is outward-looking, or causes outward-lookingness; and I think that's sinful, to use an old-fashioned word.[48]

Old-fashioned it may be, like pride, lust, anger, and emulation; but in the marketplace and the arena, as in the jungle, there is no escaping these and other forms of sinfulness and their manifestations in human cruelty. There is escape in solitude, however; in turning from the crowd and realizing one's better nature by means of creative introspection or (as Gould calls it) ecstasy.

CHAPTER 5

The Musical Mind
&
The Music Itself

Given solitude, given ecstasy, given that music is more mental than physical, what kind of mind must a person have who thinks this way about music? What goes on in that mind? What kinds of objects does it contemplate?

People who know Glenn Gould only by his reputation for clowning, or from his more eccentric interpretations on disc, dismiss him as completely mad. Reviewers have done this in print, to Gould's amusement. But "crazy" people do not figure out what they want to do with their lives and then arrange things so they can do exactly that. No crazy person could stand the pace at which Gould works. He is *different*, of course, but that does not mean he is crazy. Before I began serious study of his writings I thought he was inconsistent and unpredictable in his published utterances, but in fact he is remarkably consistent in his main lines of argument. He earns a handsome living, but his personal style is austere and private. No reputable psychiatrist would diagnose a person as crazy who was merely different, who seemed inconsistent in his public utterances (but in fact was not), and who did not squander his earnings like a drunken sailor.

Gould is fascinated by psychoanalysis and psychiatry, and mentions them in at least a dozen places in his writings. His interest is that of a person who is alert to the intellectual currents of his time, rather than one who is preoccupied with his own psychological health or disposition.

Two psychiatrists have been interviewed by Gould in radio broadcasts, Peter F. Ostwald and Joseph Stephens. Dr. Ostwald lives in San Francisco. As a young man he studied composition with Arnold Schoenberg, and Gould interviewed him on the subject of Schoenberg as teacher. Ostwald is the author of two books: *Soundmaking* and *The Semiotics of Human Sound*. In the latter book Ostwald says that there is a connection between humming and "a more general withdrawal from the realities of the outside world."[1] This could be applied to Gould's vocal noises when he plays the piano. If "the realities of the outside world" include the external and audible aspects of his own playing, then Gould's humming while he plays can be interpreted as an unconscious attempt by him to cut himself off from those realities, which inevitably fall short of his mental images of the music he plays.

Dr. Stephens lives in Baltimore. He was introduced in his broadcast as "psychiatrist and harpsichordist." Gould interviewed him on the subject of the psychological make-up of musicians who yield to the urge to play concertos in public. Dr. Stephens refused to be bullied by Gould in this interview, and did not budge from a thoroughly conventional position regarding concertos and concerto players.

Two fictional psychiatrists have been born of Gould's typewriter, S.F. Lemming and Wolfgang von Krankmeister. S.F. Lemming, M.D. makes his appearance on the liner of Gould's recording of Liszt's transcription of Beethoven's Symphony No. 5 in C Minor. He is presented as the author of a so-called "research report" in *Insight*, identified as the "digest of the North Dakota Psychiatrists' Association." The research report concerns the recording session for this disc.

As recording ensued, however, it became evident that career-disorientation was a major factor. The work selected by the artist was, in fact, intended for symphony orchestra and the artist's choice clearly reflected a desire to assume the authoritarian role of conductor. The ego gratification of this role being denied by a lack of orchestral personnel, the artist delegated [sic] the record's producer and engineers as surrogates and, in the course of the session, attempted to demonstrate approval or disapproval of various musical niceties by gesticulating vigorously and in a conductor-like manner.

These words have the earmarks of a complicated in-joke between Gould and the producer and technicians with whom he worked at that time at Columbia Records. Gould's conducting of himself with a free hand if he had one, and his nose if he did not, has been the subject of many jokes since 1955.

Wolfgang von Krankmeister appeared in a broadcast which we examined previously in connection with competitiveness. Among the skits in this production, all played by Gould himself, is one involving von Krankmeister, who is a noisy paranoiac with what is intended to be a Viennese accent.

Joseph Roddy in *The New Yorker* quoted Gould as saying that he has never undergone psychoanalysis.† Later in a broadcast Gould said that he has not discussed the psychological significance of his doodling with his friendly neighbourhood psychoanalyst. He cheerfully talks about his physical disorders, his hypochondria, and his dependence upon tranquilizers and sedatives; perhaps he will let us know about it in the same uninhibited way if ever he should have psychiatric treatment.

Gould's mental health is, of course, a private matter, none of our concern in this book. But the same cannot be said of his artistic personality. As we saw earlier, Anthony Storr in *The Dynamics of Creation* gives an interesting description of the relation between creative genius and the need for solitude in the case of the schizoid creative personality. We noticed that Storr's description fits Glenn Gould neatly. And so does Dr. Storr's description of the obsessional artistic personality.

Perhaps the most striking feature of the obsessional temperament is the compulsive need to control both the self and the environment. Disorder and spontaneity must be avoided so far as possible, since both appear threatening and unpredictable.[3]

"Take-two-ness" is the opposite of "disorder and spontaneity;" the unplanned and unpredictable elements of a musical performance can be edited out or a take can be rejected. Gould does not work without this sort of control over his productions. He does not like so-called "chance" music, and has made a radio documentary (its title is a very Gouldian pun, "Anti Alea")[4] reflecting this bias. Another broadcast contains his objections to improvisations in music.[5] Returning to Storr:

The tight control which has become habitual often makes it difficult for obsessionals to dive, to turn head over heels, or to vault a gymnasium horse;

† Gould's actual words are: "It seems that I perform in the eighteenth and twentieth centuries and compose in the nineteenth. That must be just jammed with psychoanalytic significance, but I have never paid to find out what it means." Taken literally this does not preclude that Gould has consulted one or more psychoanalysts.[2]

all activities which necessitate letting go at a critical moment.[6]

Glenn Gould displays reluctance to "let go" in at least two facets of his creative work, composing and humour.

As composer he has difficulty letting go in the sense that he cannot complete the projects he starts. Apparently he cannot take the attitude, "It's done, such as it is, so forget about it, let it go." In 1959 he said in an interview that he had many compositions lying around at home, most of them "of about one page duration, planned for sixty-four, and suddenly abandoned at the end of one."[7] A few years later he said the opposite in another interview: "I specialize in unfinished works. I don't write to the end of the first page and quit, as many people do. I write to the next to the last page and then quit. . . . somehow I allow that last page to elude me."[8]

As humorist he has difficulty letting go or terminating a joke, particularly when he is doing a skit in dialect. He once said that a virtue the great fugue writers had in common was that they always knew when to stop.[9] Gould possesses this virtue in only a limited degree, both as humorist and as fugue writer. But evidently he is aware of this fault, for in his one published fugal composition he has the words, "Never be clever for the sake of being clever," sung in a devastatingly clever and allusive setting, with many repetitions. The point is deliberately hammered flat.[10] As Anthony Storr says:

. . . creative activity may represent an attempt on the part of an obsessional character to transcend the limitations and restrictions of his own personality, or even to escape altogether from the body.[11]

This passage brings to mind Gould's notion of "ecstasy." And it relates to Gould's theoretical position in musical aesthetics: that musical reality is primarily thinkable and only secondarily playable and hearable; music is more mental than bodily in its essence. Once again Storr has a relevant observation:

. . . a ritual may actually serve a valuable purpose by putting a person in touch with his own inner life, or by inducing in him a state of mind conducive to health and progress.[12]

Gould had a repertoire of rituals and ritual objects in his concert-giving days; some of them survive. They include pre-performance soaking and massaging of the arms, a long drooping silence before playing, and a refusal to listen to any other music before playing Beethoven. (Joseph Roddy in The New Yorker quotes Gould as saying: "Before Bach I can listen to Strauss, Franck, Sibelius, juke boxes—anything. But nothing before Beethoven. I have to wind myself into a kind of cocoon before playing him. I go in like a horse with blinders."[13]) The ritual objects included a small carpet under his feet, a bottle of Poland water at his side, numerous medications, and his battered, squeaky chair. This chair can be heard in most Gould recordings, and is as much a secondary trademark of his performance as his vocal noise.

Creative genius works in solitude, seeks to control the self and the environment and in seeking tries to impose inward order upon outward disorder. It tries to transcend the limitations of the outward and physical, and to maintain active contact with the inner life. Artur Schnabel, from his own vast experience as a performing musician, wrote at considerable length about the inner life, the mental and spiritual condition of the musician. He has had a profound effect upon Glenn Gould, who has said of Schnabel:

His characteristic is that he would be almost wholly unconscious of the pianistic resource and would make no attempt to exploit it at all, but, rightly or wrongly, he would use the piano to convey his own peculiar analysis of what he was playing.[14]

It seems odd to speak of a pianist who was unconscious of the piano, who did not exploit the piano. But Schnabel's own remarks confirm what Gould says of him. Of his teacher, Theodor Leschetizky, Schnabel said:

He said to me repeatedly throughout the years, and in the presence of many other people: "You will never be a pianist. You are a musician." Of course I did not make much of that statement, and did not reflect much about it; even today I cannot quite grasp it. However, he made the distinction.[15]

Schnabel grasped the distinction clearly enough to give an illustration of it:

My rival at Leschetizky's was a youth three or four years older than I. To him Leschetizky could have said: "You will never be a musician; you are a pianist." His name was Mark Hambourg. He really had elemental qualities. His thunderous octaves, incomparable ones, had real fire, were not mechanical. He made a big career, was a very popular virtuoso.[16]

Schnabel clearly understood what Leschetizky's words meant, and was content with being in that sense a "musician" rather than a "pianist," because to be a musician was for him a higher estate. By "pianist" Schnabel meant "virtuoso" in an unflattering sense of the word: a noisy extrovert, a demon performer who craves adulation from the crowd. By "musician" he meant a person of more introspective and solitary disposition. Two remarks of Schnabel's about Leschetizky (whom Schnabel considered a "virtuoso") confirm this:

He saw music as a, so to say, public function. For him it was not music itself which gave to the musician, who took. For him the musician, as a person, was the giver, and he who listened took. . . . When Leschetizky . . . denied that I should ever be a pianist but said that I was, from the beginning apparently, a musician, he meant perhaps to indicate that my type "takes" from music.[17]

For "pianist" read "virtuoso performer." Mark Hambourg was one of these; he did the giving and the audience did the taking of the music. When we go to a concert we take what the virtuoso gives: "his" Beethoven, for example.

But Schnabel sees music as a private function, not a public one. The giving is done not by the performer but by what Schnabel calls "the music itself." The receiving is done by the person who plays the music, whether or not he plays it before an audience.

Leschetizky's limitations showed in his comparative indifference to, or even dislike of, the kind of music in which the "personal" becomes just an ingredient of the universal. He had, for instance, not much use, or love, or curiosity, for the second half of Beethoven's production. The more glory the music itself emanates, the less it leaves for the performer. It was such transcending music which he seemed to evade, by instinct. . . .[18]

Schnabel says, and Gould would agree, that the virtuoso avoids the kind of music that itself emanates glory, because this glory of the music itself diminishes the glory of the virtuoso as giver. Beethoven's last three sonatas are famous examples of music that emanates its own glory; it is interesting that Glenn Gould's earliest Beethoven recordings were of these three sonatas, recorded when he was not yet twenty-four years old.

The following words of Schnabel could have been written by Gould in explanation of his notions of ecstasy and the non-repetitiveness of musical performance:

Art is not convenience, is not just *one* feature of some structure; it is an independent organism and each single representation of it is independent as well. It is its intrinsic nature to be released by the noblest aspiration of man and addressed to the noblest aspiration of man, to be released by man's profoundest demands on himself, by his conscious desire for contact with invisible reality and unequivocal truth.[19]

Schnabel says that "in writing and performing music, musical ideas and intentions must precede the appearance of the music itself."[20] The music does not come into existence as a result of someone's playing it ("giving" it); its existence is prior to its performance. "Only when the musical idea precedes the musical performance can the maximum of concentration, always required, be secured."[21] "First hear, then play!"[22]

According to Schnabel, music has its being and its roots in the imagination. A piece of music exists in its entirety apart from and prior to its materializations in notation and in sounds produced on musical instruments. The virtuoso ". . . in his endeavor to satisfy the technical demands of his instrument . . . can easily neglect the creative task, to the extent of obliterating the imaginative side of the music, for which even the quintessence of dexterity and an infallible apparatus cannot serve as substitutes."[23] He says:

. . . I do not believe that great composers are ever inspired by the specific qualities of instruments. . . . I believe that the conception of musical ideas in the composer's mind is followed by a gradual inner indication as to which of the available instruments might best be suited to convey those ideas.[24]

When the composer chooses (for example) the piano as the available instrument best suited to convey his musical ideas, it becomes a part of the external world upon which, as Anthony Storr says, the creative genius seeks to impose order—an order whose source is his inwardness. With this notion of genius as a source of order, we can sharpen the distinction between "musician" and "pianist." The "pianist" competes for public favour, which is external, unpredictable and disorderly. The "musician" shuns outward disorder when he cannot impose order upon it; he focusses his inwardness upon the music itself, which he can control, and which he does not *give* to the hundreds or thousands of people in the audience, but *takes* in his inner solitude, whether or not there are listeners present. As composer, the "musician" tries to transcend the physical limitations of musical instruments; he thinks primarily in pure musical ideas or conceptions which exist only inwardly. Schnabel says:

The process of artistic creation is always the same—from inwardness to lucidity.[25]

Glenn Gould never heard Schnabel in person, and did not read Schnabel's books until his maturity. He says that he formed his impression of Schnabel's musical personality and philosophy from his recordings alone. That his own musical philosophy has so much in common with Schnabel's can only be accounted for as one of several respects in which these two extraordinary men are similar, including their ambivalent attitude toward the piano.

From an unexpected source comes another description of someone who is a musician, not a pianist:

Liszt, speaking of one of his pupils, said: "What I like about So-and-so is that he is not a mere 'finger virtuoso': he does not worship the keyboard of the pianoforte; it is not his patron saint, but simply the altar before which he pays homage to the idea of the tone-composer."[26]

It will be evident by now that Gould, like Schnabel, holds the view that music is primarily mental, and secondarily physical. The philosophical name for such a view is *idealism*. *Empiricism* is the name for the opposite view. In empiricist theory, as it applies to music, our musical ideas or mental images are not the roots and the essence of music. They are secondary and derived from our sense-experiences of audible, tactile and visual stimuli, including the sounds and the feel of musical instruments as we play them, the sounds as we hear them, and the whole visual experience of reading musical notation and watching other people and ourselves playing and singing, whistling, tapping, humming, skipping and so forth.

Gould is an idealist when he admires Schnabel for his indifference to the piano, when he prefers certain composers because they write music in disregard of musical instruments, when he talks about "backbone," and when he says of himself as a composer that he writes not for specific instruments but for undefined open score. On the other hand, he is an empiricist when he talks about what he calls the "tactilia" of piano-playing—the relation of hand to action to sound (the topic of the next chapter).

Similarities in their early musical development may have had similar effects upon the musical philosophies of Gould and Schnabel. Both were born musicians, so precocious as to give the impression that they did not have to learn music because music was already in them. Technique came to both with much less than the amount of physical drill and effort we ordinarily associate with the training of celebrated performers. Schnabel said:

There is no rivalry between perseverence (the capacity to sit, if it is a question of the piano) and genius (which is located elsewhere). A genius could scarcely be expected to spend hours and hours every day just in order to train his fingers and muscles. Also, that would be quite futile and superfluous, except for the satisfaction of athletic ambitions.[27]

The musical growth of such a genius will, at least in its early stages, be askew: as thinker of musical thoughts he will get ahead of himself as pusher of piano keys. He will learn to *think* a piece, and having thought it, go to the piano and play it without having to assemble and integrate sets of isolated skills with scales, arpeggios, trills and other physical devices upon which most pianists must labour.

As an infant Gould could read from score and hear in his imagination intervals which he could not span on the keyboard. Where other (and not necessarily lesser) musicians develop their mental images in consequence of their physical contact with instruments, Schnabel and Gould developed their mental images to a considerable extent by pure thought alone, away from their instruments. And having developed them, they were able to materialize them at the piano without repetitive physical effort.

The three-year-old Glenn Gould, with his then small hands and his big musical ideas, was perhaps compelled, while experimenting at the piano keyboard, to sing or hum notes which he could not reach, or which he could not combine, because of his undeveloped hands. This is one possible explanation of the famous humming and singing he does to this day while playing the piano. Dr. Peter F. Ostwald's explanation of this phenomenon is mentioned earlier in this chapter. Gould has given two different explanations of his own. One is that his singing might have been an unconscious attempt to compensate for the mechanical deficiencies of the piano he was playing, an attempt to produce the kind of mechanical articulation he hears in his imagination and wants to hear from the piano, but which the piano cannot produce.[28] The other explanation is equally dependent upon his mental images:

> I think there's a wishful thinking aspect. . . . THAT is the way I would like my phrases to be made, and I'm never able to do that at the keyboard.[29]

In the first of his own explanations he blames the piano; in the second he blames himself.

Each of these four explanations describes a musician trying to produce, in the external or physical world, events which are correlative to antecedent mental events which are his mental images of the music itself. A very young but rapidly developing musician will find his mental reach exceeding his physical grasp; and unless he puts complete confidence in the mental while waiting for the physical to catch up, he will be discouraged and fall by the wayside. Accepting the mental, and placing such confidence in it, at so early an age, is all that is required to make a musical idealist of a person: an idealist in the sense of one for whom musical ideas are more real than their physical embodiments.

Nothing shows more clearly the idealism in Glenn Gould's

musical philosophy than his likes and dislikes among composers. He once said that Stravinsky and Bartok are the two most overrated composers of the twentieth century. And he has always had an uneasy, largely negative attitude toward Chopin.† The reason for his attitude in each case is the same: that these composers were more empirical than idealistic, to put Gould's views into the language of this present discussion. They wrote music which was inspired by the specific qualities of instruments. In his late twenties Gould was interviewed on this subject by Vincent Tovell for the CBC.

TOVELL: You don't find yourself wanting to play Chopin, for instance?

GOULD: No, I don't. It's something that just doesn't go on me. I play it in a weak moment, maybe once or twice a year for myself, but it doesn't convince me. . . . When I hear it superbly played by the right person, I can be convinced by it, if only briefly. Chopin was obviously a tremendously gifted man. I don't think, however, that he was a great composer. In large-scale structures, he failed almost altogether. I think that, as a miniaturist, he was superb; as a setter of moods, unparalleled; as someone who understood the piano, certainly unprecedented. But, still and all, he is not a composer that I rest easy with.

TOVELL: It's not enough for you, then, that the composer be a pianist's composer in the sense of knowing exactly what you can get from the piano.

GOULD: No. As a matter of fact, most of the composers that I play are in my repertoire for other reasons altogether. . . .

TOVELL: What composer would you say has written most perfectly for the piano?

GOULD: Well, I think I would be like everybody else and probably say Chopin: *if* the piano means to you what it meant to Chopin—let's put it that way. It doesn't mean that to me. Because, if the piano is to be used to its fullest, it means an indulgence in many things for which I have a very strong aversion. One of them is the pedal.[31]

Three of the composers whose works Gould most likes to play are Orlando Gibbons, J.S. Bach and Arnold Schoenberg. He says that all three are strong in organizational matters, and indifferent to the particular sonorities of musical instruments. They worked primarily with mental images whose materializations in score and in performance were for them secondary. Thus as composers they are idealists.

Of Gibbons Gould has said:

. . . despite the requisite quota of scales and shakes in such half-hearted

---

† There are no works by Chopin in the Gould Discography. As a youth Gould performed a few Chopin pieces in recitals; he played Chopin's Sonata No. 3 in B Minor, Op. 58, in a CBC broadcast.[30]

virtuoso vehicles as the *Salisbury Galliard*, one is never quite able to counter the impression of a music of supreme beauty that somehow lacks its ideal† means of reproduction. Like Beethoven in his last quartets, or Webern at almost any time, Gibbons is an artist of such intractable commitment that, in the keyboard field, at least, his works work better in one's memory, or on paper, than they ever can through the intercession of a sounding-board.[32]

Gould means the same thing when he talks about the "sublime instrumental indifference" of J.S. Bach, as he has done on many occasions and more or less in those words. He has said of *The Art of the Fugue*:

Despite its monumental proportions, an aura of withdrawal pervades the entire work. Bach was, in fact, withdrawing from the pragmatic concerns of music-making into an idealized world of uncompromised invention.[33]

"Pragmatic concerns of music-making" refers to the writing of music for performance on specific instruments; we would say "empirical" rather than "pragmatic" if we wanted to be strictly consistent with the usage of the present chapter. "Uncompromised invention" means composing without requiring to take into account such factors as tone-quality, range, dynamics, and articulation. Without here entering the debate over whether Bach wrote*The Art of the Fugue* for keyboard instruments or not, we can say that this is less obviously keyboard music than is a suite or a toccata by Bach, and this is the distinction Gould is talking about.

He approaches this question in another way, still speaking of Bach's music. If a piece of music is not written for any instrument in particular, then it is equally suited (or equally unsuited) to several different instruments.

Like *The Art of the Fugue*, *The Well-Tempered Clavier*, or excerpts therefrom, has been performed on the harpsichord and piano, by wind and string ensembles, by jazz combos, and by at least one scat-scanning vocal group as well as upon the instrument whose name it bears. And this magnificent indifference to specific sonority is not least among those attractions which emphasize the universality of Bach.[34]

In a telecast Gould once performed certain fugues from *The Well-Tempered Clavier* on piano, harpsichord and electric organ, a few measures on one instrument spliced to a few measures on another, and so on. This was intended to demonstrate the indifference of Bach's music to specific sonorities.

Concerning Arnold Schoenberg Gould has said:

---

† Gould uses the word "ideal" in its vernacular sense of "the best imaginable," and not in the technical sense of the present chapter.

To some extent . . . it is possible to trace the development of Schoenberg's stylistic ideas through his writing for piano; and in doing so, one comes to the conclusion that, with the appearance of each successive work, the piano *per se* meant less and less to him. Mind you, it would be unfair to imply that Schoenberg was unsympathetic to the mechanics of the instrument. There is not one phrase in all of his music for the piano which is badly conceived in terms of execution on a keyboard.

Schoenberg does not write *against* the piano, but neither can he be accused of writing *for* it. There is not one phrase in his keyboard output which reveals the least indebtedness to the percussive sonorities exploited in an overwhelming percentage of contemporary keyboard music.[35]

I do not recall any reference by Gould to the possibility that a composer might combine the idealistic *and* the empirical, to produce music having both strong organization on the ideal level and a distinctive instrumental sonority on the empirical. He appears to be saying that the two are mutually exclusive. But, as he and Yehudi Menuhin agreed in a televised discussion, Bach's C Minor Sonata for violin is not "conditioned by the nature of the instrument"; yet "Bach was such a good instrumentalist that whatever he did write for the violin is eminently playable."

Transcription of a musical work is a test of whether it was composed idealistically or empirically. To transcribe a work is to materialize it on instrumental resources other than those for which it was originally composed. Thus there are, for example, orchestral transcriptions of piano pieces, piano transcriptions of orchestral pieces, woodwind transcriptions of string pieces, and so forth.

Pieces which can be transcribed without significant alteration reveal the idealistic approach to composition of such composers as Gibbons, Bach and Schoenberg. Pieces which cannot be transcribed without significant alteration reveal the empirical approach of a composer such as Chopin, whose musical ideas are controlled by his unique sense of piano sonorities (though not to as great an extent as Gould says they are). Berlioz and Tchaikovsky are also empirical composers; like Chopin they were particularly responsive to the sonorities of different musical instruments, and this responsiveness controlled their musical thinking. Gould might say that they thought in sonorities rather than in structures. Music by all three of these empiricists has been transcribed. It can be done, sometimes with good results. But the organizational backbone is less evident and less solid in the music of empirical composers than in the music of idealists. To this extent empirically composed music depends more upon specific sonority than does idealistically composed music, hence empirical music is more susceptible to loss or damage in transcription than is idealistic music.

This might be easier to grasp in the more familiar terms of visual art. An engraving could be made for the purpose of printing it on paper in one colour, say green pigment on white paper. But it could be printed in different pigments on different colours of paper, with no loss of detail and no damage to the whole, provided there is appropriate contrast between figure and ground. (It would not do, for example, to print pale green on pale green.) Given adequate contrast, the delineation should remain intact and the work should survive undamaged, because it *is* primarily a delineation. It is only secondarily an arrangement of colour. We might not like the new colour, or we might resent it because we were accustomed to the original, but the delineation would be unchanged and indifferent to specific colourations. Idealistic music survives transcription to different sonorities in this same way.

But some works of visual art are primarily colour and relationships among colours; they are only secondarily delineations. To change the colouration is to alter their primary characteristics, and this cannot be done without loss or damage. We might try, of course, to produce equivalent (literally equi-valent) relationships among the new colours; this is a theoretical possibility. But it would call for a degree of artistic competence equal to the original artist's own.

Something like this latter is what Glenn Gould has attempted in his transcriptions for piano of three orchestral pieces by Richard Wagner: the Prelude to *Die Meistersinger*, the "Dawn" and "Siegfried's Rhine Journey" music from *Die Götterdämmerung*, and the *Siegfried Idyll*.

Gould is a tireless extemporizer of transcriptions at the piano, particularly of works by composers whose music he likes but who have not written much for piano. Richard Strauss, Sibelius and Wagner are notable instances.

I have the most hair-raising piano transcriptions of Strauss tone poems that you'll ever hear. I play them privately. I've done my own transcription of the overture and last scene of *Capriccio*, Strauss's last opera.[36]

Gould's recording of Liszt's transcription of Beethoven's Fifth Symphony has been much admired by some critics.[37] In Chapter 1 we saw that Gould did not play piano transcriptions of Bach's organ works at a time when they were in vogue as piano recital pieces. His reason was not that he objected to transcriptions on principle, although many musicians do, but that people were ignoring the suites and fugues of Bach, ecstatic music, and being carried away by the flashy transcriptions.

Columbia Records released with Gould's Wagner transcriptions a leaflet in which Gould discusses his procedure as transcriber. We can learn a few things from this about Gould's notion of what Schnabel called "the music itself," and how the music itself is related to its materializations in specific sonorities.

He says that Wagner's early works are not inherently pianistic, mentioning in particular the Overture to *Tannhäuser*, the Act Three Prelude of *Lohengrin*, and the Overture to *Rienzi*. These works are not inherently pianistic because "relatively speaking they're harmonically static."

. . . they're fitted out with glorious themes which, as themes, can be made to work very well indeed on the piano, but the accompanimental figures sound like the proverbial oom-cha-chas at a church social. Now this is fine in an orchestral texture. It's all part of the post-Weber heroic opera style. You can repeat the same chord *ad infinitum* and, as long as you emphasize the beat with some assistance from the percussion battery or by constantly modifying the orchestral color involved, all's well. But it doesn't work on the piano precisely because you emphasize percussive elements on that instrument at your peril.

The *Siegfried Idyll*, on the other hand, is a "natural" for piano transcription: ". . . it makes all its dramatic points through counterpoint, never through percussive effect." Gould says that his task as transcriber was "to rebuild the piece for piano." Rebuilding is what Liszt did *not* do in his Wagner transcriptions:

Liszt . . . was too faithful to the score for his own good. You know, in an orchestral work, you can put in all sorts of octave doublings, for example, and, according to the diverse impulses of the instruments involved, you will have a rich and glamorous texture. Do the same thing on the piano, even with the options available to ten fingers and, although you may get marks for authenticity, what you end up with is mud, glorious mud. Liszt, of course, is much more puritanical than I am in a funny sort of way. He tends to solve these problems by left hand tremolandos—or even worse, right hand tremolandos—which, to me, always sound like the worst excesses of Aunt Sadie at the parlor upright. . . .

I simply decided that—well, for instance, that you can't hold a chord indefinitely on the piano without allowing for diminishing returns—pun intended—and you certainly can't expect that chord to build dynamically as, in the string choir, it can be made to do. So what I did, on occasions like that, was to activate inner voices, make them imitative, wherever possible, of Wagner's motivic conceits, stagger incoming motives, and so on — anything to preserve a realistic sense of time and movement. For instance, there's one ten-bar sequence which occurs about one and a half minutes into the *Idyll*, and in which the orchestral textures are singularly uneventful . . . which makes for problems because, as I've said, a string choir can sustain one chord for four bars, say, but a piano simply cannot — at least, not without making it sound like a transcription.

That is a crucial point: a transcription should not sound like a transcription. The transcriber should not merely rework the original score for different instruments; rather he should reach back mentally beyond the original score and aim to materialize the music in its new sonorities, working from "the music itself." This, in effect, is what Gould says he did.

I decided to pretend that Wagner had an acute pianistic sense — which, insofar as we can judge from the accompaniments to the *Wesendonck* songs, the only relatively "mature" piano-writing he got involved with, he didn't. But I decided to pretend that he had keyboard flair to match his orchestral flair though, of necessity, representing a difference in kind, and I deliberately dispensed with all textural scruples and tried to imagine what might have been if someone with both orchestral and pianistic flair — Scriabin, let's say — had had a hand in it.

For the purpose of rebuilding the piece for piano, Gould reached back beyond Wagner's original score to an imaginary one, an instrumentally indifferent score which could be as readily materialized in one kind of instrumental texture as in another. This imaginary score was "the music itself." Imaginary scores such as this are the musical objects which musical idealists contemplate. Whether listening to a performance, or performing, or reading a score or recollecting it, they do not listen *to* the instrumental sounds, real or imagined, but listen *through* them and by means of them. This is the answer to the third of the three questions with which this chapter began: What kinds of objects does the idealistic musical mind contemplate?

But as in all things Gould has to make it wildly difficult for himself, as is evident in another version of his anecdote of the vacuum cleaner. In it he tells of his discovery, while practising a fugue by Mozart, that the noise of a vacuum cleaner did not block out the sound of the music. On the contrary, the sound of the music was enhanced by the uproar.

. . . in the softer passages I couldn't hear any sound that I was making at all. I could feel, of course — I could sense the tactile relation with the keyboard which is replete with its own kind of acoustical associations — and *I could imagine what I was doing, but I couldn't actually hear it.* But the strange thing was that all of it suddenly sounded better than it had without the vacuum cleaner, and those parts which I couldn't actually hear sounded best of all. . . . what I managed to learn through the accidental coming together of

Mozart and the vacuum cleaner was that *the inner ear of the imagination is very much more powerful a stimulant than is any amount of outward observation*.[38]†

This is perplexing, of course. Not even Gould's most faithful readers could be expected to agree that music sounds better when it cannot be heard, which seems at first glance to be what he is saying. But Gould is here playing upon two senses of the word "sound": the external or physical, and the internal or mental. He describes a trick by means of which a pianist can force himself to disattend to the physical sounds of his playing in order to attend more acutely to their corresponding imagined sounds. These imagined sounds are "the music itself," and for Gould they are more compelling, more interesting, and more "real" than physical sounds could ever be.

---

† Author's italics.

CHAPTER 6

The Musical Hand
&
The Keyboard

> *The Centipede was happy, quite*
> *Until the Toad in fun*
> *Said, "Pray which leg goes after which?"*
> *And worked her mind to such a pitch,*
> *She lay distracted in the ditch*
> *Considering how to run.* [1]

An interviewer asked Glenn Gould about his singing while he plays the piano: what function does it serve? Gould replied:

That's very difficult, and it's one of those centipedal questions—you know, Schoenberg once said that he would not willingly be asked by any of his composition students exactly why such-and-such a process served him well, because the question made him feel like that centipede who was asked in which order it moved its hundred legs, and afterwards he could move no legs at all—there's something impotent-making about that question. I'm rather afraid of it. [2]

There are good reasons for this fear, as Arthur Koestler explains:

When we exercise a well-practised skill the parts must function smoothly and automatically—they must never occupy the focus of attention. This is true whether the skill in question is riding a bicycle, playing the violin, enunciating the letter "M," or forming sentences according to the rules of grammar and syntax. . . .

   The paradox of the centipede is a consequence of the hierarchic organization of the nervous system which demands that the highest centres should be occupied with the task in hand conceived as a whole, and leave the execution of the component sub-tasks and sub-sub-tasks to the sub-centres, etc., on lower levels of the nervous system. A brigadier does not give orders to, and concentrate his attention on, individual soldiers during action; if he does the action goes haywire.[3]

Gould tells of a classical centipedal experience in which a lower-level problem arose and blocked his playing of a piece of music:

Years ago I was playing for the first time Beethoven's Sonata no. 30, Opus 109. I was about nineteen at the time and I used to try out pieces that I hadn't played before in relatively small Canadian towns, and this one fell into a program that I was giving about 120 miles from Toronto—a university town called Kingston. I never bothered to practice very much — I now practice almost not at all—but even in those days I was far from being a slave of the instrument. I tended to learn the score away from the piano. I would learn it completely by memory first, and then go to the piano with it afterwards—and that, of course, was another stage in the divorce of tactilia from expressive manifestations of one kind or another. No, that's not quite accurate, because, obviously, certain expressive manifestations were built into the analytical concept, but the tactile assumptions were not.

Now, Opus 109 isn't a particularly difficult or strenuous piece, but there is in it one moment which is a positive horror, as you perhaps know, and that is in the fifth variation in the last movement — a moment which is an upward-bound diatonic run in sixths. It's an awkward moment, not only in terms of black-versus-white note fingerings but also in terms of that break in the keyboard around two octaves above middle C where problems of repetition most often show up. For at that point you have to change from a pattern in sixths to a pattern in thirds, and you've got to do that in a split second. I had always heard this piece played by people who, when that moment arrived, looked like horses being led from burning barns—a look of horror would come upon them, and I always wondered what was so intimidating about it.

Anyway, about two or three weeks before I was to play the thing for the first time, I started to study the score, and about a week ahead of time I started to practice it (which sounds suicidal, but that's the way I always operate). And the first thing I did, foolishly—very bad psychology—was to think in terms of: Well, let's try the variation, just to make sure there's no problem—it had never *seemed* to be one when I sat down and read the thing through when I was a kid . . . but better try it, better work out a little fingering system just in case, you know. And as I began to work out my system, one thing after another began to go wrong. Before many minutes had elapsed I found that I'd developed a total block about this thing. And three days before the concert, the block, which I'd tried to get rid of by all kinds of devious means — not playing the piece at all, for instance — had developed apace, so that I couldn't get to that point without literally shying and stopping. I just froze at that particular moment.

I thought, something's got to be done about this—I've got to change the program or delete the variation or pretend that I know something about the autograph that they don't. So I decided to try the Last Resort method. That was to place beside the piano a couple of radios, or possibly one radio and one television, turn them up full blast . . . turn them up so loudly that, while I could feel what I was doing, I was primarily hearing what was coming off the radio speaker or the television speaker or, better still, both.

Here again are the familiar ingredients of Gould's anecdote of the vacuum cleaner. In the first version of this anecdote (Chapter 1) the extraneous noise demonstrated to Gould that music and machinery are compatible. In the second version (Chapter 5) he learned from it that the inner hearing is a more powerful stimulus than the outer. Now, in this story of the Last Resort, the noise becomes a means to overcome a tactile problem in piano playing.

The classically centipedal element in this story is Gould's becoming stuck when forced to turn his top-level attention to a sub-sub-problem: which finger to put down where. He continues:

I was separating, at this point, my areas of concentration, and to such an extent that I realized that *that* in itself would not break the chain of reaction. (It had already begun to make its mark, the problem had begun to disappear. The fact that you couldn't hear yourself, that there wasn't audible evidence of your failure, was already a step in the right direction.) But I realized that I had to do something more than that.

Now, in this variation, the left hand has at that moment a rather uninspired sequence of four notes, the third of which is tied over the bar line. There's not too much you can do with those four notes, but I thought —all right, there are, we'll say, in terms of accent and so on, maybe half a dozen permutations that would be possible [sings several of the permutations], and I played them as unmusically as possible. In fact the more unmusical the better, because it took more concentration to produce unmusical sounds, and I must say I was extremely successful in that endeavor. In any event, *during* this time my concentration was exclusively on the left hand—I'd virtually forgotten about the right—and I did this at varying tempi and kept the radios going, and then came . . . the *moment*. I switched off the radios and thought: I don't think I'm ready for this . . . need a cup of coffee, made a few other excuses, and then finally sat down. The block was gone. And now, every once in a while, just for the hell of it, I sit down and do that passage to see if the block's still gone. It still is, and it became one of my favorite concert pieces.[4]

This is a kind of squinting to bring the peripheral vision into action, or an averting of the gaze while dealing with a distasteful situation, or a stepping back in order the better to leap. But the centipedal interpretation covers it best. The pianist while actually playing the piano no more thinks in terms of fingers following other fingers than does the centipede of his feet while walking. But once the question was raised, and no answer was forthcoming, Gould's attention shifted down the hierarchy, from the ideal level to the tactile, and his playing went haywire.

Otherwise put: a matter which ordinarily would be looked after with no upper-level attention had come to the notice of the upper level and was hindering its functioning. The problem was to restore this matter to its proper level. The solution was first to make it impossible to hear what those fingers were doing, and second to deflect upper-level attention from that problem to some other lower-level detail. By these means Gould succeeded in breaking the problem's hold upon the upper-level attention.

We might wonder why Gould found it necessary to go to such elaborate lengths, and why he needed the extraneous uproar. If it was a mere finger problem, it should have been possible to solve it on, say, a dummy keyboard; this would seem to have been a much more simple and pleasant way to play without hearing oneself playing.

But Gould needed the uproar as a stimulus to his musical imagination. Besides, it would have taken more than two loudspeakers going full blast to make a grand piano completely inaudible to the player. That there should have been some music there to hear, though with great difficulty, is an essential component of the Last Resort method; with a dummy keyboard there would have been no music to hear, nothing except inane clicking. Gould needed the stimulus of the extra effort his auditory imagination had to make to reach through the uproar to the music. The uproar was the source of an extra boost of energy to his already energetic musical imagination, rather like administering an electric shock to a fibrillating heart to restore it to an orderly mode of working.

Gould's own explanation of the Last Resort is likewise clinical. He compares the Last Resort with a method of dental anaesthesia in which the patient wears headphones through which he hears faint scraps of seemingly-familiar music obstructed by a barrier of random noise. The mental effort required to pull the music out of the noise diverts the patient's attention from the pain of the drill.[5] In both the Last Resort and the anaesthesia there is a barrage of chaotic noise with which the imagination struggles. In the Last Resort the imagination strives to project its images upon the elusive screen of random noise; in the anaesthesia the imagination strives to pull out or even to construct images from the noise. Each case calls forth an extra organizational effort on the part of the musical imagination — an emergency spurt of energy to help the imagination impose inward order upon outward disorder.

Gould has told two other centipedal anecdotes. I call them "The Chickering in the Desert" and "The Half Hour." The first is a story with Biblical locale and atmosphere. He has told it in three different versions.[6] On tour in Israel (1958) he was having piano trouble. In Tel Aviv the only available piano had an uneven action which he described as "power steering." It "had a nice sound but an extremely difficult action," he says. It tended to play the pianist, rather than the other way around.

Full of anguish he went forth alone, driving a Hertz rental car, into the desert to think. There on a sand dune he sat for an hour rehearsing in his head the concerto he was to play that night (Beethoven's Second), not upon the mental image he had of the Tel Aviv piano, but upon his mental image of the familiar old Chickering back home at the cottage in Uptergrove, Ontario. Every note was rehearsed mentally as if upon the Chickering, with its characteristic feel, sound and surroundings. Desperately clinging to this image he went on stage that night and tackled the piano as if it were the Chickering. He found at first that he could barely move the keys, that he was playing in a very restricted dynamic scale. But rhythmically the piece settled down as he had not been able to get it to do in rehearsal on this piano. After a few moments of panic he began to enjoy the sensation, which was one of distance, of physical removal from the Tel Aviv instrument. When the performance was over he left the stage in a state of exaltation and wonder. Of what happened next there are two versions in print and one on disc.

In one print version a lady came backstage and said enthusiastically that she had heard him play the same concerto a few nights before, but this time he had seemed in an elevated frame of mind, as if at a greater emotional distance from everything. Gould took this as evidence of the communication "of total spirit" that is possible between performer and listener, even in a live performance, and he says that he has never forgotten it.

In the other print version, and in the disc version, the same lady has quite a different speech. She says, in a middle-European accent, that the performance was "absolutely zee most extraordinary Mozart I have ever heard in my life!"

The final centipedal anecdote is Gould's story of "The Half Hour."

I was recently talking to a group of educators about the problems concerning the teaching of pianists in institutionalized technical "factories." You see, I think there's a fallacy that's been concocted by the music teachers' profession, to wit: that there's a certain sequence of events necessary in order to have the revealed truth about the way one produces a given effect on a given instrument. And I said: Given half an hour of your time and your spirit and a quiet room, I could teach any of you how to play the piano—everything there is to know about playing the piano can be taught in half an hour, I'm convinced of it. I've never done it and I never intend to do it, because it's *centipedal* in the Schoenbergian sense—that is to say, in the sense in which Schoenberg was afraid to be asked why he used a certain row in a certain way, saying he felt like the centipede, which doesn't want to think about the movement of its hundred legs because it would become impotent; it couldn't walk at all if it did think about it. And I said: Therefore I'm not going to give this half-hour lesson, but if I chose to, the physical element is so very minimal that I could teach it to you if you paid attention and were very quiet and absorbed what I said and possibly you could take it down on a cassette so that you could replay it later on, and you wouldn't need another lesson. You would then have to proceed along certain rather disciplined lines whereby you observed the correlation of *that* bit of information with certain other kinds of physical activity—you would discover there are certain things you can't do, certain kinds of surfaces you can't sit on, certain kinds of car seats that you can't ride in.

And by this time I was getting a great laugh—they regarded this whole thing as a routine, which it was *not*. I was trying to make quite a serious point, which was: that if this were *done*, you would be free of the entire tactile kinetic commitment. No, *correction* — you would not be free, you would be eternally bound to it, but so tightly bound to it that it would be a matter of *tertiary* interest only. It would be something that could be "disarranged" only by a *set* of circumstances that would confuse it.[7]

This story illuminates The Last Resort better than it does The Chickering in the Desert, suggesting as it does that there are different levels of "interest" or attention, that the tactile is at the tertiary level, and that a shifting of levels produces a disarrangement in one's playing. The Tel Aviv piano was "a set of circumstances" which could produce such a shifting of levels. Gould overcame it by a deliberate self-deception: that he was back in Uptergrove playing his Chickering. Like the Last Resort method, this was a means of deliberately and effectively ignoring the tactilia in order to obtain access to the music itself and to materialize this in spite of material obstacles: in the Last Resort case, his finger technique; in the Tel Aviv case, an uncongenial piano. On this piano the centipede could find no secure footing, so it convinced its feet that they were walking on the familiar keyboard of the Chickering, which they did, though gingerly.

The tactile level of interest, Gould says, is tertiary; presumably the secondary level is auditory and the primary level is purely mental or "ideal"—the pianist's awareness of the music itself. If something goes wrong at the secondary or the tertiary level, and that level is not able to restore the situation to normal, then the next higher level is brought to bear on the problem. But this can be awkward because the higher level must for the moment relinquish its more general supervision in order to take care of details to which it is not usually called upon to attend. At any rate, something like this is what Gould has in mind in his three centipedal anecdotes. Each tells of his attempt to grasp and reveal the music itself, and of his own sublime instrumental indifference. This indifference is evident in some remarks by Gould quoted in an interview:

I don't happen to like the piano as an instrument. I prefer the harpsichord. Of course I'm fascinated by what you can do with the piano, and I can sit for hours and play it, but I love to force it out of its inhibitions. My sense of tactilia is that of the harpsichordist, so I'm at home as a Baroque musician. Also, I trained as an organist and that gives me a sense of horizontal line rather than vertical line.

The interviewer wrote: "Here reason tottered."[8] Yet despite Gould's professed instrumental indifference we learn a good deal about his musical thinking from what he tells us about his encounters with various musical instruments.

The organ, on which he had his introduction to the music of Bach, determined his whole perceptual set as a performer, composer and thinker of music, as was also the case with certain other keyboard masters. Mozart said that the organ is the king of instruments; Beethoven's piano touch, like Gould's, was shaped by organ playing in his youth; Robert Schumann recommended organ practice as a way to achieve greater clarity in composing and piano playing.[9] Gould said something very similar in 1962: ". . . every pianist should play the organ. It demands *real* phrasing."[10]

Gould's piano playing has the organist's control of both attack and release, unaided by damper pedal, and the organist's accentuation by spacing rather than by weight of touch. Arnold Schultz noticed this:

The artists who are as consistently sensitive to the endings of their tones as to their beginnings, who in passage work are as intent upon the evenness of the fall of the dampers as they are on the evenness of the hammer attack form for me a somewhat limited aristocracy of pianism. Horowitz, Schnabel, Kapell, Hess, Gieseking and Glenn Gould are some of the names that come to mind.[11]

The organ has influenced Gould's composing as well as his piano playing. He says that it accounts for his thinking musically in terms of a separate bass line not playable on the piano by two hands but demanding a third hand or a pedal keyboard.[12]

Debussy's "M. Croche" detects this same characteristic in Beethoven's compositions for piano:

Beethoven's sonatas are very badly written for the piano; they are, particularly those that came later, more accurately described as orchestral transcriptions. There seems often to be lacking a third hand which I am sure Beethoven heard; at least I hope so.[13]

We have already seen that church choirs and organs figured in Gould's family background. He made himself familiar with the organs in churches near home and the cottage; he heard various organists in recitals and in church services. He says that the Sunday morning radio organ recitals of E. Power Biggs were a formative influence in his childhood.

In 1944, while still a pupil in organ of Frederick C. Silvester, Gould took the Grade 8 examination in organ at the Royal Conservatory of Music. He took Grade 9 the following year. The examiner in both grades was Healey Willan, who was one of the most famous church musicians in Canada, and was known affectionately as the Dean of Canadian composers. At around this same time young Gould's exceptional talents as organist were pressed into service, with the result described in this strange story by Richard Kostelanetz:

At eleven, during the war, he was organist at a local Anglican . . . church; but since he would often lose his place whenever the congregation sang, his forgetfulness led to an embarrassing mistake which brought his rapid dismissal.[14]

The church was St. Simon's in Toronto. Gould was not an appointed and salaried organist there, but was unofficially assisting the organist, Eric Lewis. My guess is that Gould had difficulty with the Anglican chant, as does every organist not raised in that tradition; he also had trouble with a foot slipping and sounding a loud pedal note at an awkward moment in the spoken part of the service.

His debut on the organ at Eaton Auditorium on December 12, 1945 has already been described. Apart from a few minor pre-service recitals in Toronto churches, this was Gould's only public appearance as organist. In High Fidelity Magazine of March 1962 he is quoted by Roland Gelatt as saying that he had not played an organ recital in fifteen years, but was anxious to make an organ recording for Columbia Records. The publicity release for the disc The Art of the Fugue, Fugues 1-9 quotes Gould saying that he had not touched the organ since he was a boy, but this is not true. *Maclean's Magazine* of April 28, 1956 has a wonderful photograph by Paul Rockett of Glenn Gould at the organ in the Concert Hall of the Royal Conservatory of Music of Toronto, cap, muffler, fingerless gloves, overcoat and all, playing and conducting in full cry.[15]

Gould's boyhood encounters with the organ were summarized by him in a 1959 radio interview:

The organ was a great influence, not only on my later taste in repertoire, but I think also on the physical manner in which I tried to play the piano. It was an invaluable training. It's something I think a lot of people could profit by. I was playing the organ when I was around nine or ten, and playing mostly Bach and Handel. It was really through the organ that my interest in these composers began. It was simply transferred to the piano. . . .

I was playing the piano at the same time, and trying to combine this with going to school, which got very difficult; eventually, something had to give and it was the organ that gave. But, by that time, certain aspects of organ playing — the physical aspects — had made a great impression on me. I learned that when you played Bach, the only way to establish a phrase, a subject, a motive of any kind, was *not* to do as one would with Chopin—you know, try to make a crescendo in the middle of the thing—but to establish it by rhythmic gasps and breaths. One had to have an entirely different approach, something that was based, really, on the tips of the fingers being responsible for the whole action, something that could almost produce the wonderful whistling gasp of the old organs. So that expression, consequently, was accomplished with practically none of the slurrings and over-fadings, not to speak of pedallings, with which Bach is so often played on the piano. And I really feel that this is entirely due to the fact that, at an early age, I was playing the organ.[16]

Elsewhere in this same interview Gould mentions that the pedal voice in organ music gave him a sense of spread that cannot be obtained in any way other than by playing the organ. In an article about Richard Strauss published in 1962 Gould says: "One would almost suspect that Strauss conceived of the cellos and basses with his feet (as an organist might do . . .)."[17]

This expression, "conceived with his feet," is of great interest to us, because it suggests an empirical rather than an idealistic attitude. Many of Gould's remarks about musical instruments, and particularly about the organ, are strongly empirical in their presuppositions: the organ gave him a sense of spread, a special awareness of the bass line, and a tendency to let the tips of the fingers do the work, he says. In this manner of thinking musically, the tactilia control the mental images, and not the mental images the tactilia, as in idealism. The instrument is the source of the ideas—ideas which Gould absorbed in his piano playing and in his composing.

Probably all musicians, when confronted with the necessities and limits of music making on actual instruments, are empiricists. The idealist is at his best at the level of abstract musical theory, or when working in undefined open score.

As a mature artist Gould has had only one major encounter with the organ: the recording of his disc *The Art of the Fugue*, *Fugues 1-9* by J.S. Bach. Most of this disc was recorded on an organ of what was then considered very advanced design, installed by Casavant Frères at All Saints' Kingsway Anglican Church in Toronto during the year 1960. It was a magnificent work in the North American Baroque Revival style, with many high-pitched stops and a huge pedal division. There were doubts, of course, among members of the congregation, about this expensive and strange-sounding instrument. Organists in Toronto had strong opinions about it, not all of them favourable. Organists are not renowned for keeping their opinions to themselves, so word of the new organ reached Glenn Gould. He visited the instrument and decided to make recordings on it.

In January 1962 Columbia Records sent a crew and the necessary equipment to Toronto to record the first nine fugues of *The Art of the Fugue* by J.S. Bach with Glenn Gould playing this organ; the disc was released three months later. On the liner it is described as "Volume I" of *The Art of the Fugue*, which suggests that "Volume II" was intended to appear in due course. The liner notes also state that the nine fugues were recorded at All Saints' Kingsway, but this is not quite true. Gould and the recording crew ran out of time in Toronto with the job incomplete, so at least one of the nine was recorded in a theological college chapel in New York City. Gould likes to challenge people to tell which fugues were recorded in which church. Fugues Five, Six and Nine display a prominently out-of-tune tenor B-flat on a flute stop, but I have found no other reliable clues to go by in this game. Both organs were large and varied in tonal resource; audio engineers can add or subtract differences in sound. The game is a silly one anyway, and it merely reinforces Gould's New Philosophy doctrine that the time and place of recording need be of no significance in the final result.

The disc was not acclaimed by reviewers. Indeed, not even his more eccentric Mozart interpretations have received as bad a press as this disc. The main objections were that Gould's playing was too loud, too fast, too choppy, and, of all things, that the contrapuntal interplay of voices was in some fugues muddy.[18] And now, more than a decade later, there is no sign of Volume II, although Gould has performed some of the fugues following the ninth, on CBC radio, beautifully played on the piano. Glenn Gould, who in 1962 said that he would like to record the organ sonatas of Mendelssohn, and that he intended to make at least one organ recording each year,[19] has done nothing of the kind. This is much to be regretted.

What happened? We may take it that Gould did no systematic work at the organ in the years between his Eaton Auditorium performance and the recording sessions at All Saints' Kingsway. He says that he did no practising on the organ for these sessions, and that his registrations were casually put together as he went along. He agrees with an interviewer who said that he treated the organ as if it were a piano, working ". . . against the grain of the predominant temperamental characteristics of each instrument."[20]

In the language of organists "registration" means the selection of stops or registers to be brought into play by the several keyboards of an organ. Tone-quality and loudness are varied, not by weight of touch, as on the piano, but by adding or subtracting stops and by the use of other mechanical devices, of which one is of special interest here, the octave coupler. It is of interest because it accounts for the muddiness of which some reviewers complained. Obscurity of counterpoint is the last thing we expect to find in a Glenn Gould recording of Bach, but in this case the complaint is justified.

It is the more astonishing because that organ was unique in its time and place for clarity and brightness of tone; these were among the qualities which attracted Gould to All Saints' Kingsway in the first place. No expense had been spared to secure what was thought to be the Baroque conception of an organ suitable for contrapuntal music.

Brightness in organ sound can be obtained by adding stops which speak at octaves and other harmonic intervals above the fundamental pitches of the notes being played; this has the effect of enhancing contrapuntal clarity. Brightness of a kind can also be obtained by adding a super-octave coupler, but at great cost in clarity, since the middle voices will much of the time be lost among octave duplications mechanically imposed by the coupler.

It is evident that Gould ignored the remarkable capacity of this instrument for both brightness and clarity of counterpoint, and that he gave little thought to the manner in which organists of the Baroque built up their organ sounds, to the merits of clean and simple combinations based on an eight foot flute and a four foot principal (of which two types alone this instrument could have provided more than a dozen permutations). Let me risk a guess at how this could have happened.

For this we go back to the precocious ten-year-old listening on a Sunday morning to E. Power Biggs on the radio, playing Bach on that modest pioneer of the Baroque Revival in North America, the Aeolian-Skinner organ in what was then called the Germanic Museum[21] at Harvard University. The next day he goes to practise on one of the small organs at the Royal Conservatory, on which he could by no means have reproduced the contrapuntal clarity of the organ on which Biggs played. But by using super-octave couplers he could have produced something like the brightness.

Every organist had to do this sort of thing on the organs which were available then. Frederick Silvester may have introduced Gould to this way of getting a "baroque" sound from a non-baroque instrument. My guess is that such dependence upon super-octave couplers remained with Gould, and misled him when nineteen years later he played an organ in which he could have found, if he had bothered to seek, degrees of clarity combined with brightness which even for Biggs in 1942 could have been no more than a dream. Things in the organ world had changed greatly during those years.

That he had not kept up his organ playing shows particularly in his use of the pedal keyboard. He used no pedal in Fugues One, Four and Five; I think also in Fugue Three, but I am not sure. In Fugue Eight he has no pedal except for some discreet reinforcement of the bass line at the end.

There can be no objection to his decisions against using pedals in these fugues, which together account for more than half the playing time of the disc. But in the remaining fugues we listen in vain for a sign of any strategy or plan for the pedals. In no instance does he use pedal for each "real bass" entry in a fugue;[22] this weakens the structure, which we do not look for in the work of an artist who is preoccupied with backbone in music as Gould claims to be, and as his piano records attest.

It might be asked: what decisions are to be made here? Did Bach not indicate which parts were to be played on manuals and which on pedals in his organ music? The answer is affirmative. He usually indicated this, and where he did not there are conventions which leave little doubt in the matter. But this music, *The Art of the Fugue*, is *not* organ music. It does not belong to the canon of Bach's works written for performance on the organ. This canon includes his chorale preludes, his many toccatas, fantasies, preludes, variations, and fugues designated by him as organ pieces—an enormous repertoire for the organ. But *The Art of the Fugue* belongs among what are called Bach's "didactic" works. In them, Bach, the great teacher of all musicians, shows what can be achieved by a stupendous contrapuntal intelligence working with minimal constraint from the physical demands and limitations of musical instruments; with, perhaps, no concern that they should be playable at all.[23]

If the people at Columbia Records had intended to display Gould as a master organist in the way that his piano records display him as a master pianist, he could have recorded Bach's Toccata and Fugue in D Minor, or the G Minor Fantasia and Fugue, the F Major Toccata, or the "Little" G Minor Fugue, which he had performed at Eaton Auditorium in 1945. These are organ pieces, and there are many others by Bach to choose from.

But Gould's album, *The Art of the Fugue, Fugues 1-9*, is not a showpiece; it is a set of essays—one essay about each of the first nine fugues, each in the form of an extremely original and revealing interpretation. Like every Gould recording it is a mine of fresh insights and novel perspectives. And it exceeds almost every other Gould recording in its exuberance. With joyous excitement he analyzes and dissects these fugues for his own and our better understanding of them, using to the hilt the resources of the New Philosophy.

Gould has not written or talked much about his encounters with harpsichords. His only harpsichord recording is *Handel: Suites for Harpsichord, Nos. 1-4*. It was recorded in March, April and May 1972 and released in October of the same year. Apart from this and a few brief spots for radio and television he has done little harpsichord playing. He has not lived intimately with the harpsichord as he has all his life with the piano, and as he did with the organ between the ages of nine and thirteen. He says:

I love the sound of the harpsichord and the effects that are possible with it, but it upsets my piano playing. It's just too disturbing to make the transition from one instrument to the other.[24]

The basic tactile difference is between snapping a hammer into free flight toward the strings, as in a piano, and plucking a string, as in a harpsichord. Gould's Handel record and his harpsichord broadcasts confirm that he does not accommodate to this: he slams the keys into their beds. A harpsichordist begins his withdrawal at the point in the descent of the key where the string is plucked. This point is normally a significant distance from the key-bed, and in fast passage-work a harpsichordist touches the bed lightly if at all. He seldom depresses the key to its full extent.

Another tactile problem is width of keyboard. This has always been a critical matter for Gould, and unfortunately most harpsichords are built with keyboards narrower than standard for grand pianos.[25] Gould says:

I don't own a harpsichord and never have, and there's only one harpsichord in the world that I can play, and that's one that many pro-harpsichordists turn up their noses at — the Wittmayer — simply because its tactilia, and particularly the width of its keyboard, are as close to the piano as one can get. I love it, however, and the particular Wittmayer that I used was owned by a choirmaster here in Toronto who just has it for his own amusement. It's the equivalent of a baby grand, a five- or six-foot instrument, and it lacks certain amenities such as a lute on the four-foot, which I would dearly like to have and which any self-respecting harpsichord offers.[26]

Only one harpsichordist is mentioned by Gould as having had some influence on him in his youth, Wanda Landowska. Her influence was largely negative:

. . . I knew many of the Landowska recordings when I was a kid, but I don't believe I've heard any of them since I was about fifteen, and Edwin Fischer I never knew at all. Rather than the playing of people like that, I was much more familiar when I was growing up with the recordings of Rosalyn Tureck, for instance, than I ever was with Landowska. In fact, really I didn't like Landowska's playing very much, and I did like Tureck's enormously — Tureck influenced me.[27]

An interviewer said to Gould:

I've noticed, in these recordings [Gould's organ and harpsichord discs], that you seem to work against the grain of the predominant temperamental characteristics of each instrument. For instance, on the harpsichord, where you can't easily duplicate the arched line and sustained legato of the piano, you seem to aim for just those two qualities. In your piano recordings you aim for the immediacy of attack provided more easily on the harpsichord. And on the organ, you produce a sense of spriteliness more characteristic of both the piano and harpsichord.

Gould replied:

Yes, I think you're absolutely right, there's a kind of cross-fertilization involved here. I'll let you in on a secret, however, in regard to both the organ and the harpsichord records: both of them were done literally without practicing on those instruments at all; my preparation for both was on the piano exclusively. . . . Anyway, the registrations for that record were worked out movement by movement as the sessions progressed. I did exactly the same thing with the organ record. Of course, I was somewhat more experienced as an organist because I had played the organ as a kid, but I hadn't played it *since* I was a kid, and again I set up registrations only at the last minute.

Particularly noteworthy is Gould's "secret": all his practising for both the organ and the harpsichord records was done on the piano. He did not seek out "the predominant temperamental characteristics of each instrument," but imposed the characteristics of the piano upon each.

Gould continues:

It's part and parcel of the anticipatory syndrome that I've often talked about in relation to conducting. With the harpsichord, of course, one deals with a particular set of tactile problems and a more or less immediate response to their solution, whereas when one conducts, the tactile problems are, in a sense, imaginary, and the response to their solution is delayed—but there are certain parallels nonetheless. On the harpsichord, for example, it's very easy to achieve the sort of secco, pointillistic, détaché line that I've always tried to produce on the piano with varying degrees of success. On the other hand, having achieved it, you can't influence it dynamically and you're left, so to speak, beholden to the generosity of the ear which is sometimes prepared to read dynamic implications into rhythmic alterations. But this introduces another set of problems, because, on the harpsichord, you have a choice between rhythmic inexorability and its converse, which is infinite rubato, a kind of sound-world which really never comes to rest on any bar line. I was determined to try and find a way around that problem. And I thought, well, the best solution would be to pretend that I'm not playing the harpsichord at all. . . .[28]

This is our third instance of self-deception as an artistic device: first, that the audience is not really there; second, that the Tel Aviv piano is really the Chickering; third, that the Wittmayer harpsichord is Gould's own Steinway piano.

Such self-deception is not unique to Gould. Every performer relies on something like it. In its mildest form it is the self-deception that says, "I am good enough to be up here doing this in front of all those people," or "I am about to give the best performance of this piece that has ever been given." At some level, carefully but not always successfully suppressed, the performer knows that it is not really so, that he is a fake. But without self-deception he would not last more than a few seconds as a performer. Role playing, including the role of a person good enough to be onstage playing a role, is not the exclusive preserve of actors.

There should be no objection to Gould's pretense that the harpsichord is not really a harpsichord but a piano; this is an artistic decision and he is the artist. It would have been objectionable, however, if he (as distinct from the CBS promotional writers) had pretended to be a harpsichordist in the Handel recording or an organist in the Bach organ recording. Gould makes neither pretense. In each case a supreme keyboard artist is taking a merry spin, an outing, a holiday from the piano, but with the piano unmistakably his home base. On the piano he is able to produce almost any articulation he wants, including articulations imitative of the harpsichord or the organ. On harpsichord or organ he looks, listens, feels and thinks beyond the present tactilia to the imagined tactilia of his own piano, as he did in Tel Aviv.

In 1961-62 Gould had a strange encounter with an instrument called by him and its manufacturers the "harpsi-piano." It deserves no more than passing mention since it appears to have had no lasting affect upon Gould's notion of tactilia. Roland Gelatt described it as ". . . an instrument concocted by the Steinway people to convey the timbre of the harpsichord with the volume of the piano."[29]

John Beckwith called it "that offensive bastard the Gould tack-piano" and gave a more specific description of it than Gelatt's:

This is a small Steinway grand with steel T-pins in the hammers, in imitation of the least interesting attribute, the click, of its magnificent cousin the harpsichord. . . . The tack-piano is simply not a particularly interesting compromise.[30]

Gelatt says that Gould "toyed with the notion" of recording J.S. Bach's *The Well-Tempered Clavier* on the harpsi-piano. Fortunately this infatuation was short-lived, and the harpsi-piano is nothing more than a dimly remembered episode in Gould's search for an instrument which produces the sounds he hears in his imagination, and whose tactilia are wholly assimilatable. ("Assimilatable" is Gould's own word; we return to it shortly.)

We come now to pianos and Glenn Gould's encounters with them. He would have us believe that his attitude toward pianos is one of indifference, but this is difficult to accept, since whether he likes it or not it is as a pianist that he presents himself to the great majority of people.

He has written at length about several pianos, and about two in particular, the 1895 Chickering and Steinway CD 318, both of which he owns. The Chickering is in storage in his apartment in

Toronto; CD 318 was until recently at Eaton Auditorium, where it was used exclusively for Gould's recording sessions, and whence it went on occasion to the CBC's studios for videotaping sessions. Other pianos have come and gone, but these are the ones about which he has written in most detail. Of the Chickering he wrote:

I found . . . that there were certain instruments that became prerequisite [sic] for me, certain instruments against which I tended to gauge all others. . . . I had, in those days [mid-1950s], an extraordinary instrument which was built in 1895, in the city of Boston, by the company of Chickering. It had precisely those qualities—a tactile grab and immediacy — that I had always believed pianos could have, but it was a turn-of-the-century instrument with all the sound liabilities thereunto pertaining. And, when I was in search of a more contemporary, more viable instrument for concert use, I decided that I was going to try and design it with something like that characteristic. In the days when I trod the boards and toured the concert circuits . . . there was hell to pay, really, if I had to encounter a piano that was too different. And one did, sometimes; because certain action characteristics were just so unassimilatable in relation to the piano that was my standard and the basis of my judgment.[31]

Gould says that in its external design the Chickering was one of the last classic pianos built in America:

. . . classic by virtue of the fact that it had a lyre that looked as if it were off the cover of the old B. F. Wood edition—short, stubby legs and slightly square sides. This piano was the prototype of the piano that I now use for my recordings [CD 318] and the other one that I have in my apartment as well, in that I discovered a relationship of depth of touch to aftertouch, which admittedly had to undergo a considerable amount of modification for a Steinway. It couldn't just be transferred across the board (no pun intended), and both of the pianos that I own were modified along the lines of this turn-of-the-century Chickering.[32]

He speaks of this instrument almost reverently:

It is quite unlike almost any other in the world, an extremely solicitous piano with a tactile immediacy almost like a harpsichord's. It gives me a sensation of being so close to the strings and so much in control of everything, whereas modern pianos seem to have power steering—they drive you, instead of the other way around.[33]

The Chickering may be Gould's dream of perfection, but it is the nightmare of every piano technician who has worked on a Steinway for him, trying to adjust the action to what Gould at that moment remembers as the feel of the Chickering's. (The Chickering may be seen and heard, with Gould playing, in the National Film Board's "Glenn Gould: Off the Record.")

About Steinway CD 318 Gould published (1964) an essay on the liner of his recording of the *Two- and Three-Part Inventions* by J.S. Bach:

The instrument represented on this disc is a pre-World War II Steinway which answers to CD 318, and to which I feel a greater devotion than to any other piano that I have encountered. For the past few years, it has been reserved exclusively for our sessions at Columbia Records—not as great a sacrifice on the part of the makers as you might imagine, since no one else has ever expressed the slightest interest in it. This has enabled me to carry out some rather radical experiments in regard to the action of this piano—in effect, to try to design an instrument for baroque repertoire which can add to the undeniable resource of the modern piano something of the clarity and tactile felicity of the harpsichord.

For those sessions in which more recent or more conventionally pianistic repertoire has been our concern, we have not made any special demands upon this instrument, but prior to each of the Bach sessions of the past few years, CD 318 has undergone major surgery. The alignment of such essential mechanical matters as the distance of the hammer from the strings, the "after-touch" mechanism, etc. has been earnestly reconsidered in accordance with my sober conviction that no piano need feel duty-bound to always sound like a piano. Old 318, if released from its natural tendency in that direction, could probably be prevailed upon to give us a sound of such immediacy and clarity that those qualities of non-legato so essential to Bach would be gleefully realized.

In my opinion, the present disc brings us within reach of this objective. The operation, performed just before the sessions which produced the "Inventions," was so successful that we plunged joyfully into the recording without allowing old 318 its usual post-operative recuperation. Consequently, our enthusiasm for the rather extraordinary sound it now possessed allowed us to minimize the one minor after-effect which it had sustained—a slight nervous tic in the middle register which in slower passages can be heard emitting a sort of hiccup—and to carry on with the sessions without stopping to remedy this defect. I must confess that, having grown somewhat accustomed to it, I now find this charming idiosyncrasy entirely worthy of the remarkable instrument which produced it. I might even rationalize the matter by comparing it with the clavichord's propensity for an intra-tone vibrato. However, in our best of all worlds, we would hope to preserve the present sound while reducing the hiccup effect; so, as the television card says on those occasions when sound and video portions go their separate ways—"STAY TUNED IN: WE'RE FIXING IT."

Gould made a first attempt at recording the *Two- and Three-Part Inventions* during the last three months of 1963. He did not complete the project, and dropped it for about ten weeks. Then in March 1964 he came back to it, started all over again, and recorded the whole set in two days; these versions are on the Columbia disc.

Perhaps he abandoned the first attempt because he was unhappy with the tactilia of the piano, could not come to terms with it, and then fussed with it for ten weeks to get it the way he wanted. One can imagine the tension at Steinway & Sons, since Gould's ideas of "immediacy and clarity" are unconventional, to say the least. When the instrument seemed to be as close to what he wanted as it was likely to get, ten weeks later, he returned with it to the studio for what must have been a hectic two days. The people at Steinway & Sons and at Columbia Records were perhaps unhappy with the very features of the piano which pleased Gould most, hence his strange apology in the liner notes.

The adjustments of which he speaks left the instrument with a tendency to chatter or bounce back, on some notes more than others; the sound is uneven from one note to the next. These aberrant qualities bring to mind what Gould called "the wonderful whistling gasp of the tracker action of the old organs." It is almost as if Gould proposed to rise above the physical limitations of pianos by modifying his instrument to sound as unlike a piano as possible. In his recording of the *Inventions* he succeeded in producing not the sound of a non-piano, but the sound of a mangled piano. The greater then is the wonder that his performances on this disc are so lucid and appealing. It is as if Gould deliberately went about making things as difficult for himself as it was possible to do, so he could overcome the mechanical and tactile obstacles he had created for himself.

The origins of CD 318 can be roughly traced. This piano arrived in Toronto from Steinway & Sons in New York in September 1945, and Gould first encountered it then. It was on consignment to the T. Eaton Company's piano department. For several years the piano travelled around the country as required by concert pianists who had arrangements with Steinway for the use of their instruments. This is hard service for a piano.

Around 1960 Gould became seriously interested in CD 318. He had its action adjusted to the shallow draft he favours for Baroque music, and it went with him on some of his travels during the concluding three or four years of his career as recitalist and concert artist. There were problems with Canadian Customs each time it came back to Toronto from an engagement in the United States. Since it was legally the property of Steinway & Sons, Customs wanted to collect duty on it. Gould bought it just to put an end to this nonsense. In 1968 an interviewer asked Gould about CD 318, having noticed that it looked "a little bit shabby and down-at-the-heels." Gould replied:

Well, it's followed me about for rather a long time. . . . It's not quite "Government-Issue." It's a vintage Steinway—I think 1938 or '39—with substantial improvements, as I would like to think of them, that began around 1960. We've put about seven years into refining certain qualities that it seemed to have natively, and to perfecting them along lines that seemed to me important if one's going to use the piano to peruse the Baroque repertoire, especially. It was essentially designed for Bach. At one time, I found it important to have a different sort of piano for every kind of music that one played. I no longer do. I use it for everything now: it's my Richard Strauss piano, it's my Bach piano, it's my piano for playing William Byrd, the English Tudor composer, and that I've lately been doing with great delight.

It's a chest of whistles, it's a set of virginals, it's just about anything that you want to make of it. It's an extraordinary piano. I think also it can be made to sound a bit orchestral; we've tried to do that in the Beethoven Fifth Symphony as arranged by Liszt. We've played it very orchestrally and it has a lot of fat and fluffy sounds in that recording because we wanted it to sound that way.[34]

That last sentence reveals that Gould's "wants," his mental images of musical sounds, have broadened considerably since the Uptergrove days of the Chickering.

CHAPTER 7

Burnished Singing Tone

Glenn Gould does not tell us what he is seeking from his endless, agitated tinkering with his piano. Possibly he does not know or, more likely, he does not want to look into the matter for fear of centipedal consequences.

It may come as a surprise that Gould is not seeking beautiful tone. This, after all, is what most musicians look for when they go shopping for an instrument. They play a note and listen to it and pronounce it beautiful or not. But Gould says that he is not interested in beautiful tone in this sense: "As long as the piano has a good action, the sound isn't too important."[1] He says that a "burnished singing tone" is not his goal.[2] But this should not be surprising because it is clear that he is more interested in structure than in sensation, and that for him music is more an activity of intellect than an agreeable stimulation of bodily senses.

So I offer this as a safe preliminary conjecture: that Gould is seeking to reduce to a minimum the extent to which the instrument comes between what he thinks and what he hears, between "the music itself" as an object of pure thought and the instrumental sounds as objects of sensation. In aid of this he seeks three things: "tactile grab and immediacy,"[3] direct control as opposed to "power steering,"[4] and "assimilatability."[5] All three have been mentioned previously; let us now examine them more systematically.

The guitar, the harp and strings *pizzicati* have in highest measure

what I understand Gould to mean by "tactile grab and immediacy."
Among keyboard instruments the harpsichord ranks highest in this
respect because of its direct plucking action.[6] The organ ranks
lowest.

On organs there is a pronounced time lag between the moment of
pressing down a key and the moment of hearing the onset of sound
from the pipe or pipes. Undoubtedly Gould first noticed this as a
child while playing his grandmother's parlour harmonium; reed
organs are notoriously slow and mushy. Later he adjusted to the time
lag on the organs in the Concert Hall at the Royal Conservatory and
in Eaton Auditorium. Both were very slow, by reason of action and of
distance between pipes and consoles. It is not an easy adjustment; on
many organs there can be a time lag of as much as a tenth of a second.
While playing fast passage-work the organist must touch the keys
well in advance of hearing the notes. Indeed, he must touch each
note prior to hearing the onset of the preceding one. Organists have
an old joke about playing a fugue and then sitting back to listen to it.
In addition, of course, an echoing auditorium causes the notes to
continue long after the organist has released the keys.

Considered merely as mechanical devices, all keyboard instruments have bearings, levers and linkages, which present problems of
inertia, slackness of connection, flexibility and elasticity of materials. And all moving parts require time to complete their mechanical
cycles. Time lag can never be eliminated, but it can be reduced by
reducing any of these factors as much as is practicable, thus increasing "immediacy." For example, bearings and linkages can be adjusted
to be as tight as is consistent with freedom of motion; "draft" or depth
of key-travel can be reduced. Gould makes such adjustments, and
finds that they reduce the amount of attention he must give to the
tactile characteristics of his instruments.

As for direct control, professional car drivers dislike power steering because it prevents their "feeling" the interaction between
wheels and road. They want the steering mechanism to be a means of
feeling the road, and not something which comes between the driver
and the road. It is an extension of his own sensory apparatus. A
skilled driver's control of his car depends in part upon his sensitivity
to pressures transmitted through the steering wheel, from the road to
his hands; and anything that diminishes those pressures, diminishes
his sensitivity and hence his control. He needs also to have a steering
wheel in which a small turn produces a small response in the car, a
large turn a large response, a quick turn a quick response, a slow turn

a slow response. Control is again diminished if responses are dispro-
portionate or inconsistent, and the car gives the impression of
controlling itself. It was in something like this manner that the Tel
Aviv piano seemed to Gould to have "power steering." Its action was
uneven and unpredictable.

A philosopher, the late Michael Polanyi, gives the best account I
know of the sort of thing Gould seems to mean by "assimilatability":

When we use a hammer to drive in a nail, we attend to both nail and
hammer, *but in a different way*. We *watch* the effect of our strokes on the nail
and try to wield the hammer so as to hit the nail most effectively. When we
bring down the hammer we do not feel that its handle has struck our palm
but that its head has struck the nail. Yet in a sense we are certainly alert to
the feelings in our palm and the fingers that hold the hammer. They guide us
in handling it effectively, and the degree of attention that we give to the nail
is given to the same extent but in a different way to those feelings. The
difference may be stated by saying that the latter are not, like the nail,
objects of our attention, but instruments of it. They are not watched in
themselves; we watch something else while keeping intensely aware of
them. I have a *subsidiary awareness* of the feeling in the palm of my hand
which is merged into my *focal awareness* of my driving in the nail. . . .

Subsidiary awareness and focal awareness are mutually exclusive. If a
pianist shifts his attention from the piece he is playing to the observation of
what he is doing with his fingers while playing it, he gets confused and may
have to stop. This happens generally if we switch our focal attention to
particulars of which we had previously been aware only in their subsidiary
role.[7]

Learning any skill involves transferring our focal attention *from* the
detailed manipulation of instruments *to* the result of exercising that
skill with those instruments. In the case of the skill of hammering
nails, the result is a nail in process of being driven home truly. In the
case of the skill of playing the piano, the result is an auditory
phenomenon whose coherence or structure is what Polanyi speaks of
as "the piece" and what I take to be "the music itself." Focal
awareness is on a higher level than subsidiary awareness, according
to Polanyi, and in this he agrees with Arthur Koestler's account,[8]
and with Gould's designation of the tactilia as "tertiary." Polanyi
tells *how* the hierarchy works, how the lower and higher terms interrelate: we attend to the focal by attending from the subsidiary. In
Gould's language, the subsidiary would be the tactilia.

Polanyi says:

Our subsidiary awareness of tools and probes can be regarded now as the act
of making them form a part of our own body. The way we use a hammer or a
blind man uses his stick, shows in fact that in both cases we shift outwards

the points at which we make contact with the things that we observe as objects outside ourselves. While we rely on a tool or a probe, these are not handled as external objects. We may test the tool for its effectiveness or the probe for its suitability, e.g. in discovering the hidden details of a cavity, but the tool and the probe can never lie in the field of these operations; they remain necessarily on our side of it, forming part of ourselves, the operating persons. We pour ourselves out into them and assimilate them as parts of our own existence. We accept them existentially by dwelling in them.[9]

We may say, then, that for Gould a piano action is "assimilatable" if it does not require of him that he bring his focal attention to bear on it; or, as Michael Polanyi would say, if the pianist is able to pour himself out into the action and assimilate it. Polanyi's word for this is "indwelling."

One might object that assimilatability and indwelling are nothing more than the result of habit: Gould assimilates by becoming familiar with or accustomed to the feel of the action of a particular piano. But this would be a weak objection, because there is active habituation as well as passive. In passive habituation we accept the way things are and operate within their limits; in active habituation we assimilate those limits and reach beyond them by means of them. We indwell them, and integrate them at higher levels of coherent activity. All skills and all creative and inventive activities depend upon our doing this, according to Michael Polanyi.

It seems from his recordings and from his own accounts of them that Gould failed to assimilate the actions of harpsichords and organs, to come to terms with their tactilia. So he compelled himself to pretend that he was playing on his piano instead.

So far as tactilia are concerned there is almost nothing in common among the actions of organs, pianos and harpsichords. Weight of touch produces no effect upon loudness on the organ, and very little if any on the harpsichord; hence, so far as "control" is concerned these instruments are at least as different from the piano as they are in respect of "tactile grab and immediacy." Thus, for any pianist a drastic redirection of focal attention from the music itself to the tactilia is demanded when he goes from piano to harpsichord or organ. This would be particularly the case if the pianist had not remained in regular contact with those two instruments, as Gould has not.

In his case the effects of this drastic redirection of focal attention can be observed in his harpsichord and organ discs. In the former, as I have mentioned, he slams the key into its bed; it is like a centipede jabbing to find its footing on unfamiliar ground. In the organ disc we cannot hear the action noises, as we can on the harpsichord disc, but Gould plays in an extremely staccato manner as if he were consciously or unconsciously keeping spaces between notes to make splicing easier in the event that his discomfort with the instrument resulted in slips for which splicing would be the remedy. Both the harpsichord slam and the organ staccato entail a great deal of fussiness with the hands, we can imagine, almost as if the performer were trying to push away the tactilia and the sounds of the instrument to enhance his self-imposed delusion that he is really playing the piano. This is mere conjecture, of course. But if it has merit, then a new question demands consideration: what aspect in particular of piano sound was Gould trying to hear in place of the actual sounds of harpsichord or organ? My answer is a further conjecture: Gould was trying to hear the characteristic sound of his own piano's action, something like "chink."

This sound is most evident in Gould's recording of the Bach *Inventions* and in his recording of pieces by William Byrd and Orlando Gibbons; but it is present in every recording he has made on Steinway CD 318. It is the sound this piano would make if it had no strings—a compound of the impact and other noises produced by the touch and by the mechanism. A sloppy, deep action absorbs more of these noises than does a tight, shallow one, but it is audible in some degree in every note on every piano.

I am suggesting here that Gould's quest has been for a pronounced "chink" (as I call it), and that his many adjustments to the action of his piano are made with the intention of enhancing it.

This may seem farfetched. But it has been known for fifty years that the distinctive sounds by which we recognize different types of musical instruments owe less to the sustained sounds of those instruments than to the transient cluster of noises required to get each note started. The "chink" of a piano is one of several components in that cluster.

A few simple experiments with audiotape will produce startling proof of this. Here are two. Record on tape the sound of a high note, say G at the top of the treble staff, on flute, then clarinet (actual pitch), then violin, sustaining each note for at least five seconds. Then cut away from the tape the beginning of each, so that only the steady tone remains. Splice the tape together again, and play it for your musical friends. They will not find it easy to identify the different instruments. The other experiment is to record on tape a note or a chord played on the piano, and treat it in the same way, cutting out the "chink." It will sound in playback like a diminuendo on a harmonium or an accordion. You will not recognize the sound as that of a piano, and you will find the effect a bit unnerving. But you will have established for yourself that chink is an essential and distinctive ingredient in the sound of any piano.[10]

The chink, in normal circumstances, is absorbed within the so-called "sound envelope" of each separate note or group of simultaneously sounded notes in the music to which we are listening. It contributes to the unique, audible appearance of each.

When we hear a piano technician repeating a note over and over, we begin to notice the chink because it irritates us; but it is physically no less present as a sound when a pianist in performance plays the same note. But because in this case the notes are perceived not individually but within constellations of notes, or because, as Polanyi would say, each note is integrated within a coherence or a higher unity to which we attend focally, we cannot give focal attention to the chink; yet we are implicitly aware of it at the subsidiary level. Similarly we might hear the unpleasant whistling of a person practising sibilants at a speech therapy session, or in a tongue twister which repeats "s"; but when the same person speaks normally we hear what he is saying and we do not hear whistling noise, although it is "there" and although we are aware of it subsidiarily. We could not comprehend the meaning of the speech if we were not. However, if we listen to this same person speaking normally while we are feeling out-of-sorts or ill-disposed towards him, the whistling noise will assert itself; our attention will shift to this subsidiary detail of speech. It is much the same with chink in pianos.

Chink is not just an incidental noise that we have to put up with whether we like it or not. It is an essential part of the sound of any note played on a piano, and it provides a partial answer to the most centipedal of all piano problems: the problem of the relation between a pianist's touch and the tone-quality he gets from the instrument.

A singer can sing a note, and while sustaining it, and making it (so far as we can tell) neither louder nor softer, can make very evident alterations in its tone-quality—most readily by changing from one vowel sound to another, for example, from "ah" to "ee." Similarly a violinist can play a note with his bow, and alter its tone-quality, loudness being constant, by moving the bow along the string toward or away from the bridge, or by altering the balance of pressure and velocity on the bow, and by other means. A woodwind or brass player can make such alterations by changing wind pressure and embouchure, to mention only two variables. These are ways of controlling the tone-qualities of instruments while playing them. The pianist has at his disposal nothing corresponding to these.

The reasons become obvious when we think about the manner in which these different kinds of performers come into bodily contact with their instruments. The singer's body *is* his instrument; the string player's instrument, like the wind player's, is constantly within his embrace while he plays it. In all three instances the body of the player both starts and sustains the sound, and does both *directly*.

The pianist's finger starts the sound but does not sustain it; and it starts the sound *indirectly*. The motion of his finger initiates a complicated series of mechanical motions, the end result of which is not a string in vibration but a hammer in free flight. When the hammer strikes the string it is not in contact with anything that is in contact with the finger. It is in this sense that I say of the pianist's finger that it starts the sound indirectly. And having started the sound the pianist can do nothing to alter its tone-quality.

Surely none of this is open to objection. But people will go to the stake in support of their answers to this next question: can the pianist, by altering his manner of pressing down the key, produce two or more notes of equal loudness but different tone-quality?

If we think about the manner in which the finger's motion is conveyed to the hammer by the action, only a negative answer to this question is possible. It does not matter whether a key is depressed by the finger of Arthur Rubinstein or by the tip of his umbrella: only one variable is controlled by the piano key and the manner in which it is depressed, and that is the velocity of the hammer at the instant it strikes the string. There are not two or more different ways of travelling at the same velocity along the same arc, as the hammer must do.

The velocity of the hammer, in its turn, controls *two* variables, but it controls neither independently of the other. These are loudness and tone-quality. For any given level of loudness there can be only one tone-quality, and any particular tone-quality can only be delivered at its precisely corresponding level of loudness. The same is not true of voice, strings or winds, on all of which some measure of independent control of either loudness or tone-quality is possible under normal conditions.[11]

A reviewer fell victim to the confusion over touch and tone in a comment published in 1963:

Of great help to him is the incomparable range and variety of his touch.

From the merest whisper, through *pianissimo, piano, mezzo-piano* and symmetrically up to *fortissimo* (which he never uses, of course, in Bach on the modern piano) Mr. Gould has one of the richest tonal palettes of any living pianist.[12]

It is obvious that this reviewer wanted to talk about "rich tonal palettes," which is the language of tone-quality. But he found himself talking about *pianissimo, piano*, etc. (the italics are his), which is the language of loudness, not of tone-quality.[13] This is a common error, and it is not a merely semantic one.

Among pianists and piano teachers of the top rank who have claimed that tone-quality can be independently controlled by alterations in finger touch, none was more greatly and justly admired for his "beautiful tone" than Josef Lhevinne. He claimed that if the key was touched with the soft pad of the fingertip the sound would ring and sing, whereas if it is touched by the bony tip the sound will be hard and metallic. A stiff wrist, he said, will cause bad tone because it cannot absorb shock as a loose wrist can.[14]

These are familiar precepts to many pianists. Although they are untrue if taken literally, they can nevertheless be effective as teaching devices, if only because they invite the student to listen to what he is doing on the piano. But Lhevinne goes further. He says that the soft and hard parts of the pianist's finger can be compared with a felt-tipped rod and a metal-tipped one striking a xylophone.[15] This is not only false, it is absurd. On a piano the same hammer strikes the same string no matter what we strike the key with, hard or soft. The felt and the metal will make different impact noises on the key, and these differences have some effect upon tone-quality, but not in the way Lhevinne says they do. Like the pianist's finger, they neither touch the string nor are they in contact with anything that touches the string when it is struck by the hammer.

There is a fairground test of manly strength in which the object is to bash a lever with a big mallet so that the lever will flick a metal slider with enough force to send it up a grooved board and ring a gong at the top. The picture is familiar: burly swain spits on palms, picks up mallet, takes a few ostentatious practice swings, and then with a grunt and a red face slams the mallet down on the lever. The tone-quality of the sound (provided he hits hard enough to strike the gong) is a matter of indifference to the swain, no doubt. But he has precisely the same control over it that the pianist has over the tone-quality of a string. No amount of technique (or saliva or body

English) on the part of either can control tone-quality independently of loudness.

About all this there is agreement among people who have seriously investigated hearing and sound. But to pianists and their listeners it is absurd: they know that pianists control tone-quality independently of loudness. Julius G. Báron, an American physicist, has rescued us from the absurdity.

As we have observed from our hypothetical experiments with audiotape, a note on a piano consists not merely of the sounds generated by the vibrating string and amplified by the sounding board. Báron says that it consists, in part, of this, but also of sounds "caused by interactions between parts of the piano mechanism and by the impact of the finger of the player upon the key and, indirectly, on the key bed."[16] All these sounds are included within what I have been calling chink, and these sounds can be varied without varying loudness. To illustrate this Báron points out the difference between percussive and nonpercussive tone-qualities, which he says is produced by the difference between pressing the key and striking it with the finger. He claims, rightly, that it is possible to strike a note in these two different ways with the loudness the same in each case. The difference in tone-quality will be a difference not in the manner of the string's vibrating, but rather in the manner of the chink's determining for us the character of the whole sound of the note from beginning to end. If we were to record two equally loud notes on tape, one percussive and the other nonpercussive, and clip out the chinks, we would not be able to tell them apart.

My conjecture, and the point of all this talk about chink, is that Gould is uncommonly (although unconsciously) aware of the effect of chink upon tone, and uncommonly interested in its artistic uses. He seeks a particularly incisive chink by means of which he can, with clean edges, delineate the contours of highly structured music. Equally he wants neat, quick damping at the termination of his notes, but also a degree of control over the speed of both chink and damping, so he can on occasion make "fluffy" sounds also. He wants to give shape to each individual sound envelope, including not merely the timbre of the vibrating strings, but the distinctive patterns of onset and termination, the *consonants* of individual musical notes.[17]

Gould displays astonishing control over these consonants in his piano playing (just as he does, incidentally, in his speech). This is why his extremely slow performances do not fall apart, and his extremely fast ones do not become muddled. But it is also at least in part the explanation of his beautiful piano tone. Above all, it explains his changeable and highly individual notions of what he wants from his piano.

CHAPTER 8

Creative Cheating

In the 1960s Glenn Gould was frequently referred to, by journalists and publicity people, as "the philosopher of recording." He does not speak of himself as a philosopher, but the expression "a new philosophy of recording" is his. It refers to what he saw as an emerging attitude toward recorded music and not to a philosophical system or discovery of his own. He has written numerous articles and scripts explaining how technological progress would make it possible for musical recording to advance from its early archival stage to a higher stage in which technology and technicians would participate in the creative process actively and in their own right.

In our European tradition, philosophical work is to a great extent done by the Socratic method of argument and counter-argument, by ongoing dialectical exchange. It is a contentiously cooperative activity. Since Gould is a solitary, and wants to be in complete control of all that he does, he is not in that tradition; he has no taste for dialectics. "I need spinal resilience," he says, "when I'm confronted with opinions not my own."

He is often flippant in his writings, but he is more sensitive to hostile criticism of them than of his recordings.[1] In his mid-twenties he told an interviewer that if he had not been a musician he would have been a writer. He said that part of the appeal of being a writer was that this vocation would allow him to set his own working hours.[2]

A recurrent philosophical theme in his writings is the relation between art and morality. This is ancient, very dark and difficult philosophical terrain. Gould's own ideas about it place him in contact with Plato, Aristotle, Kant, Schiller, Hegel and others. Although he does not quote them or mention them by name, we would be ill-advised to assume that he has not read them. And when an articulate person of artistic and moral stature speaks on such a topic, philosophers do well to listen.

According to Gould, artists have a moral mission and art has an unrealized potential for the betterment of humankind.[3] Human improvement can occur only as the result of modification in our attitudes as solitary, private individuals, and not as some kind of collective modification of our species, voluntary or not. Each person must accept the challenge of contemplatively creating his own "divinity."[4] "Divinity" here refers to the better part of individual human nature, which for Gould is the introspectively and ecstatically contemplative part; the worse part is that which abandons itself to herd impulse, as in the mindless, hysterical responses of crowds to spectacles and of populations to propaganda.

In 1974 Gould wrote:

I believe in the intrusion of technology because, essentially, that intrusion imposes upon art a notion of morality which transcends the idea of art itself. And before, as in the case of "morality," I use some other old-fashioned words, let me explain what I mean by that one. Morality, it seems to me, has never been on the side of the carnivore — at least, not when alternative life-styles are available. And evolution, which is really the biological rejection of inadequate moral systems—and, particularly, the evolution of man in response to his technology—has been anti-carnivorous to the extent that, step by step, it's enabled him to operate at increasing distances from, to be increasingly out of touch with, his animal response to confrontation.

A war, for instance, engaged in by computer-aimed missiles, is a slightly better, slightly less objectionable war, than one fought by clubs or spears. Not *much* better, and unquestionably more destructive, statistically, but better to the extent, at least, that, all things being equal, the adrenal response of the participants—we had better forget about the by-standers or the argument collapses — is less engaged by it. Well, Margaret Mead, if I read her rightly, disapproves of that distancing factor, of that sense of disengagement from biological limitation. But I do believe in it, and recordings, though they're rarely understood as such, are one of the very best metaphors we have for it.[5]

The argument collapses anyway: wars are not waged by weapons upon other weapons, but by people; they are waged for the purpose of destroying not the weapons only but the people of the opposite side.

Nevertheless, Gould's point is clear and it is an important one: that in addition to the hideousness of all warfare is the further (for him the ultimate) hideousness of frantic men with their blood up, smashing and slashing at the flesh of other men. There are many senses of the word "warfare," not all of them figurative. Artists are at war with one another in the sense that there is not enough public approval to go around: without technology, artists must risk their necks against the jealous rapacity of other artists in the marketplace, and against the rage of the fickle crowd in the arena. Gould is saying that for musicians the technology of recording is able to reduce the "adrenal" factor to a minimum.

At around this same time (1974) Gould seemed to be developing a new theme. It is hinted at in the quotation above where he says that technology "imposes upon art a notion of morality which transcends the idea of art itself." He has not yet explained this notion, but he expresses it more strongly and much more pessimistically in an article published earlier in the same year:

. . . I feel that art should be given the chance to phase itself out. I think that we must accept the fact that art is not inevitably benign, that it is potentially destructive. We should analyze the areas where it tends to do least harm, use them as a guideline, and build into art a component that will enable it to preside over its own obsolescence.[6]

From Gould's context it would seem that the destructiveness of art is in its competitive aspects, and "the areas where it tends to do least harm" are those areas in which the adrenal factor is mitigated by technology.

A hint of where Gould is going with this new line of thought is found in an article published in 1975:

Stravinsky claimed that the business of art is technique; I do not agree. Nor do I believe that the business of technology is the rule of science. . . . But I do believe that, once introduced into the circuitry of art, the technological presence must be encoded and decoded . . . in such a way that its presence is, in every respect, at the service of that spiritual good that ultimately will serve to banish art itself.[7]

Gould's moralizing usually relates to narrower but more accessible areas of human behaviour, particularly to the making and recording of music. For example, he readily accepts the accusation of people who think that to edit and splice a recorded musical performance is immoral: "They feel that there's a certain amount of cheating involved, and of course there is."[8]

Gould's story of the beginning of his love affair with the microphone provides an instance of another kind of cheating, or "creative dishonesty," as he calls it. He used the tone control on his own phonograph to alter the recorded sound of the bass-heavy studio piano on which he had broadcast a Mozart sonata:

> . . . I discovered that, by giving it a bass cut at 100 cycles or thereabouts and a treble boost at approximately 5000, the murky, unwieldy, bass-oriented studio piano, with which I had tried to deal earlier in the day, could be magically transformed. . . .
>
> . . . I had prevailed upon the most primitive technology to sponsor a suggestion of that which was not; my own contribution, as artist, was no longer the be-all and end-all of the project at hand, no longer a fait accompli. Technology had positioned itself between the attempt and the realization; the "charity of the machine," to quote the theologian Jean Le Moyne, had interposed itself between the frailty of nature and the vision of the idealised accomplishment. "Remarkable clarity — must have been an incredible piano," friends would say. "Believe me, you simply can't imagine," I would respond. I had learned the first lesson of technology: I had learned to be creatively dishonest.[9]

Our uneasiness with technology is understandable. In the early days of recording it was necessary to mutilate compositions drastically. They had to be cut to lengths which would fit a cylinder, and reorchestrated to suit the narrow band of frequencies to which early technology was restricted. As the apparatus improved, musicians welcomed the relief it gave from these limitations.

Musicians still have the bad old days in memory, even if only by ill repute. And they recall the good old days when technology made possible a return to "integrity" in recorded music, by which they mean "concert hall realism." Any move away from the latter seems like a move toward the dark days of the former.

Recorded speech gives rise to even greater suspicion and resentment than recorded music. It is easy to take a recording of someone's words and manipulate them so he can be heard saying the opposite, or even something he did not say at all. Nonsense can be edited to sound sensible, and the other way around. In broadcasting this is normal procedure. But it is also done in politics, and hence our suspicion and resentment. We would probably not object if only the speaker's mistakes and his throat-clearings[10] were deleted from the tape, but we have no reason to believe that editing is invariably used for such innocent purposes.

Another justified suspicion is that editing is used for the purpose of concealing, not just an occasional mishap, but a lack of competence on the part of the performer. He cannot play the piece properly, we suspect, so it becomes necessary to patch the performance. But this suspicion presupposes a definition of "competence" which may be inappropriate to the studio, however appropriate it may be to the concert hall. This is the definition in which competence includes the ability to play a work from beginning to end without hitch. But many a flawless concert performance has been as insipid as it was tidy. On the other hand, a performer in the recording studio might play a take which is full of life and detail, but has a few bad spots that would be disastrous in the concert hall. If they are such as can be repaired by an insert or a regeneration,[11] the result might be a better recording than could be made from a flawless but insipid straight-through performance.

There are three common objections to editing tape for such repairs: that splice points are audible; that we can hear differences between the original sounds and the inserted sounds; that splicing breaks the integrity and sweep of a performance. Gould knows about these objections and has dealt with them at length in his writings. It is possible, he points out, to remove every audible trace of click at splice points, and it is possible to match the sound of any piece of recorded material to the sound of any other. The technical means for doing these things have been in general use by audio technicians for almost twenty years.

Because people seemed unconvinced, in 1975 Gould published an article in which he reported an experiment he had conducted in order to resolve their doubts. In this experiment Gould played eight recorded pieces to eighteen listeners, and asked them to state how many splices they detected in each. Two of the pieces had no splices; one had thirty-four. These were the extremes; the numbers of splices varied in the other samples.

It is particularly significant that in one of the pieces having no splices the listeners thought they could detect a total of thirty-six splices. In the whole battery there were, in fact, sixty-six splices, but the highest score of correct identifications was only seven out of the sixty-six. Two listeners obtained this score, but one of them had to have more than twice the number of hearings required by the other, so they did not actually tie for first place. Oddly, the four highest scores went to listeners who could not read music. Among the listeners participating in the experiment were two radio producers, people who spend their working lives supervising the recording and editing of music on tape, and listening to the results. Both scored zero, having failed to locate correctly *any* of the sixty-six splices.

Gould makes no undue claims for the design of his experiment and its results, but because of it we should now hesitate before claiming that all splices are audible, as either clicks or mismatches, or that musicians are likely to be more sensitive than nonmusicians to edited breaks in the grand line of a performance.

The latter is the third of the objections to splicing mentioned above. It presupposes the existence of, as one pianist puts it, "the sense of a long line stretching across the whole piece," which "can rarely be achieved unless the playing continues from beginning to end without stopping."[12] To this argument Gould replies:

. . . splicing doesn't damage lines; good splices build good lines, and it shouldn't much matter if one uses a splice every two seconds or none for an hour so long as the result *appears* to be a coherent whole.[13]

This point raises a large theoretical question: what is the difference between *appearing* to be a coherent whole and *being* a coherent whole? The question is a crucial philosophical challenge to Glenn Gould's New Philosophy. Two imaginary situations will illustrate the distinction.

An automobile that lacks an engine will, nevertheless, *appear* to be a coherent whole to the casual passersby, but it will not *be* a coherent whole. Its appearance will be distinct from its being, as will quickly become evident to anyone who tries to drive it away.

Our second imaginary situation involves film-making, with which Gould himself often makes comparisons. On the back lot of a motion picture studio we might find a street with, among other structures, a saloon, a bank, a saddlery and a funeral parlour, each with a hitching post in front. From certain vantage points we might not be able to see that these are façades, supported out of sight at the back by crude, sloping timbers. But we would not be tempted to hitch our horse and enter any of these buildings in the hope of doing our banking or buying refreshment, because we would know the rules and could not be deceived about actualities underlying "mere" appearances. The appearances are sustained not by actuality but by sloping timbers.

A piece of music in performance is more like the movie set than it is like the automobile without an engine. It exists *as* and *for* appearance; the music *is* its own appearance. There is no actuality underlying it. Its coherence comes from the ways in which musical appearances in general are related among themselves, each to every other, each to the whole of a piece, and the whole to each of its apparent parts. It is entirely phenomenal, entirely separate from any noumenal ground. Musical coherence, like mathematical coherence, is abstracted from actuality, not based upon it. Music, unlike the automobile without an engine, cannot appear to be coherent while actually being incoherent; neither can it appear to be incoherent while actually being coherent. Its appearance and its actuality are one and the same. Otherwise expressed: music *actually appears*, and its appearance is the kind of actuality it has.

One piece of music might be more or less coherent than another. And one performance of a piece might be more or less coherent than another performance of it. Coherence is a mark of success and incoherence is a mark of failure in performance—failure to discriminate among the several elements and to synthesize or interrelate those elements coherently.

For people who oppose the New Philosophy position, to "interrelate elements coherently" means to unify the musical elements under a single vital impulse, to combine them into a kind of organism. To dissect the performance is to wipe out the life that is in it. "Life" in this sense is an actuality-principle. For Gould, however, to interrelate elements coherently means to analyse and dissect, to reveal the backbone of the music by the very manner of performing it, of actualizing it in audible appearance.

Gould's most persuasive justification of creative cheating was published in an interview article of 1962, when he was still giving concerts.

GOULD: . . . I love recording because if something lovely does happen, there is a sense of permanence, and if it doesn't happen, one has a second chance to achieve an ideal.

INTERVIEWER: Then you have no objection to splicing tapes from several performances into one?

GOULD: I can honestly say that I use splicing very little. I record many whole movements straight through. But I can also say that I have no scruples about splicing. I see nothing wrong in making a performance out of two hundred splices, as long as the desired result is there. I resent the feeling that it is fraudulent to put together an ideal performance mechanically. If the ideal performance can be achieved by the greatest amount of illusion and fakery, more power to those who do it.[14]

A person could accept all this and still wonder about *ecstasy*, which according to Gould is the only proper quest of the artist: can it be recorded? Can it be spliced? We raised these two questions in Chapter 4, where they seemed on the surface to be merely rhetorical questions requiring negative answers if any. But Gould's answers would be in the affirmative, and he would borrow, as he often does, from the techniques of the motion picture to justify and explain himself:

Let us assume that . . . some artists really do underestimate their own editorial potential, really do believe that art must always be the result of some inexorable forward thrust, some sustained animus, some ecstatic high, and cannot conceive that the function of the artist could also entail the ability to summon, on command, the emotional tenor of any moment, in any score, at any time — that one should be free to "shoot" a Beethoven sonata or a Bach fugue in or out of sequence, intercut almost without restriction, apply postproduction techniques as required, and that the composer, the performer and, above all, the listener will be better served thereby.[15]

Gould would concede that it is possible for performers to unify their performances under "some inexorable forward thrust, some sustained animus, some ecstatic high." He is, in fact, happy when a performance of his own develops in that way. But he maintains that it is not the *only* way. "By taking advantage of the post-taping afterthought . . . one can very often transcend the limitations that performance imposes upon the imagination." These are the words in which he stated the moral of his anecdote about the recording he made of the A Minor Fugue from Book I of *The Well-Tempered Clavier* by J.S. Bach. In this recording he was able, by means of intercuts on tape, to produce contrasts which would have been impossible in a concert performance. These contrasts would have been not only impossible but unimaginable without knowledge of the editing possibilities of audiotape.

He does not claim that any edited version must be better than any straight-through version; he says only that the possibilities open to the performer at the editing stage should always be kept in mind, and that a recording artist ought to be both competent and willing to choose between the one and the other.

In a motion picture an actor might be seen leaping from his horse and striding up to the saloon door in a towering rage. The next cut might show the saloon's interior with the door flying open and the actor striding in, still in a towering rage. The two sets, street and interior, might have been miles apart; the two scenes might not have been shot in sequence; yet on film the actor's rage is perceived as one, not as two different rages. But he would not have been expected to sustain his rage from the filming of the one to the filming of the other. An actor can lash himself into a rage for the five seconds it takes to leap from his horse and stride up to the door. At some other time and place he can lash himself into a rage for the five seconds it takes to burst into the interior set and stand glowering. From these two exercises in "the ability to summon, on command, the emotional tenor of any moment," the film editor can create the "appearance" of a man in a towering rage making a single move from the outside to the inside of the saloon. Gould asks why a musical performer should be accused of fraud when he does the same.

Someone might reply that the actor lashes himself into a fake rage, a "merely" apparent rage, and that a better actor would display a genuine rage. The film-makers should use a genuine saloon with cameras both outside and inside the saloon to capture the "line" of the actor's performance. To this Gould might answer that *everything* we see on a motion picture screen is an appearance only, so the differences between a fake rage and a genuine one are swallowed up in the technology; that this straight-through or "actual" method of filming the scene leaves too much to chance; that appearances can be made more "realistic" by good editing than they can by the best acting.

An actor's rage is a matter of technique. It is always and only an apparent rage. If he were in a genuine rage he would not be sufficiently in control of his body to work at all. Similarly, the pianist's ecstatic high, whether he maintains it for the entire length of a piece, or for just a portion, is significant only insofar as it "appears." Its genuineness, whatever that might be, is of no aesthetic significance for the listener.

Gould can be seen slipping in and out of his ecstatic high in the films and videotapes which show him playing the piano, sometimes in small excerpts intended to illustrate a point in his commentary. The shift from talking to playing requires a kind of blackout, an invocatory silence; the return to speaking from playing leaves him damp and panting. These transitions are smooth but not effortless.

Some performers find it easier than others to make these shifts. But for all performers such slipping in and out of ecstasy is available as a means, in conjunction with the technology of recorded sound, to expand the creative imagination beyond the traditional possibilities of performance.

CHAPTER 9

Radio
As
Music

Many of Glenn Gould's admirers are not yet acquainted with his so-called "contrapuntal radio documentaries"; most people who are acquainted are baffled by them, with good reason. Nevertheless, these works have for a decade been Gould's main artistic preoccupation. They, and not his many piano recordings, are for him the culmination of the New Philosophy, and his most ambitious efforts at creative cheating have gone into the making of them. In these works he pushes to extremes every claim he has made about art and technology, and every device he has experimented with in his piano recordings. The New Philosophy stands or falls with the Gould contrapuntal radio documentaries.

They belong to a genre of which he can be said to be the inventor and, thus far, the only practitioner. He makes them originally for CBC radio, but two of them are available on disc: "The Idea of North" and "The Latecomers." These are the first two parts of what Gould calls *The Solitude Trilogy*; the third and most recent is "The Quiet in the Land." All three deal with persons or groups of people who accept isolation or who choose to stand apart from the cultural mainstream. Other works by Gould in this genre are a radio portrait of Stokowski and one of Casals, and "Schoenberg: the First Hundred Years." A piece on Richard Strauss is in preparation.

The earlier Gould documentaries, including the first two of the *Solitude* trilogy, were made in the CBC's studios in Toronto. More recently he has been making them in his own studio which is equipped with the most advanced apparatus for processing recorded sound in the New Philosophy manner. It provides him with the facilities he needs to work in his own way and in his own time. The CBC has always been exceedingly supportive, but when he is absorbed in a project he becomes single-minded: "hectic" is a weak description of the situation in the CBC studios on those days when Gould was trying to make four hands do the work of eight, and to make the equipment perform in ways for which it was never intended. The technical facilities and routines of the CBC became inadequate for him, excellent though they were, so he moved out. Of course he continues in close contact with the CBC, making radio and television shows, talking and playing, as he has been doing since the 1950s.

The Gould contrapuntal radio documentaries are not easily described. According to Robert Hurwitz in *The New York Times*, listening to one of them is "comparable to sitting on the IRT during rush hour, reading a newspaper, while picking up snatches of two or three conversations as a portable radio blasts in the background, and the car rattles down the track."[1] On a first hearing of one of these works the listener is struck by the fact that, for sizable portions of it, two or more voices are heard simultaneously, along with various sound effects and musical fragments. Is Gould joking?

At the beginning of "The Idea of North," for example, a woman is heard mumbling about snow, seals, polar bears and half-frozen lakes. The listener turns up the volume in an effort to make out what she is saying. Another voice enters over, and then another, all talking at once. Soon nobody is mumbling and the listener has to turn down the volume, not knowing that this opening segment of three minutes' duration is a drawn-out crescendo from *ppp* to *fff*, with the voices of one woman and two men interwoven into something like a Baroque trio sonata. The apparent confusion culminates in Glenn Gould introducing himself and his program, while the trio fades out and train noises fade in, representing departure from Winnipeg for Fort Churchill, Manitoba.

On a second hearing the listener will know better, and will not be deceived into thinking that there is something wrong with the signal or with his set at the beginning. And so it goes. With each new hearing one learns more of the rules of the piece, and allows it to reveal its many details, layer upon layer, as one would do with a fugue by J.S. Bach.

Gould insists that these works are music. In 1970 he said in a television interview:

The whole idea of what music is has changed so much in the last five years. I feel something quite remarkable happening because I think that much of the new music has a lot to do with the spoken word, with the rhythms and patterns, the rise and fall and inclination, the ordering of phrase and regulation of cadence in human speech.

I've been doing radio documentaries—taking, let us say, an interview like this one to the studio, on tape, and pulling on this phrase, and accentuating that one, and throwing some reverb in, and adding a compressor here and a filter there—it's *unrealistic* to think of that as anything but composition. It really is, in fact, composition. I think our whole notion of what music is has forever merged with all the sounds that are around us, everything that the environment makes available.

I think that the renaissance contrapuntalists were the first practical men, as composers. They were the first people who recognized that it was possible and feasible and *realistic* to expect the ear to be aware of many simultaneous relationships, to follow their diverse courses, and to be involved in all of them—not to expect a particular precedence accorded to any one of them, not to expect any bowing or scraping on the part of the two or three remaining voices to the one that was uppermost or lowermost or cantusfirmusmost or whatever.

I think that these were the first *realistic* people, in the sense that they understood some aspects at least of this environmental compôte which was to become music, and which is now, perhaps for the first time, truly becoming music.[2]

From this excerpt we can form some idea of Gould's techniques in his documentaries. He is making tape collages, or what we might call "com-positions," using prerecorded audio materials of many kinds, but emphasizing the spoken word; he is mixing these materials polyphonically. For him the end result is "realistic." As we saw in the preceding chapter, Gould's view is that "actuality" is the chance-ridden given, or what he here refers to as "all the sounds that are around us, everything that the environment makes available," so far as these can be collected in raw form on audiotape. "Realism" is what the artist makes of all these by processing and mixing them in the studio.

His clearest statement to date of this distinction between actuality and realism has been made in a film not yet released to the public:

I think we ought to distinguish between realism and actuality. I think one can create a realistic environment and still maintain editorial control, whereas true actuality inevitably suggests some sort of aleatoric approach.[3]

By "aleatoric" Gould means the chance element in events which are not mediated by technology. He applies the term to events in the natural environment, and also to events in the human environment which have not been modulated and manipulated (on, for example, film, videotape or audiotape). These are actual events. Any such event, and any element or combination of such events, can be removed or modified or replaced, or mixed with other events and elements, in any proportions, under editorial control in a studio such as his own, or in editing facilities such as can be found in the motion picture and recording industries. He would say that the result is realistic.

Gould also insists that his documentaries are drama, and in the credits for some of them are the words "written by Glenn Gould." But they are hybrids of music, drama and several other strains, including essay, journalism, anthropology, ethics, social commentary, contemporary history. Their techniques owe more to the motion picture than to any other source, and they share the dramatic aims of the motion picture as well.

Gould emphasizes the dramatic element, and describes some of the techniques, in a 1968 interview:

What we've tried to do . . . is to create what I have grown rather fond of calling "contrapuntal radio," which is a term that I've picked up from a fondness for contrapuntal music, and tried, rather arbitrarily, to attach to another medium, where it has not belonged in the past. It's amazing to me that it has not, because there's no particular reason, it seems to me, why one shouldn't be able to comprehend, clearly and concisely, two or three simultaneous conversations.

Some of our most aware experiences are gleaned from sitting in subways, in dining-cars on trains, in hotel lobbies — simultaneously listening to several conversations, switching our point of view from one to another— picking out strands that fascinate us.

I've just made an hour of radio which had some success, and a lot of critics, of course; we found all sorts of ill-favour with people who were rather traditionally-minded about the experience of radio.

The basis of it was that we tried to have situations arise cogently from within the framework of the program in which two or three voices could be overlapped, in which they would be heard talking — simultaneously, but from different points of view—about the same subject. We also tried to treat these voices as though they belonged to characters in a play, though all the material was gained from interviews. It was documentary material, treated in a sense as drama. It was, in fact, a documentary which thought of itself as a play. It was a program about the Canadian North, ostensibly. What it was really about, as a friend of mine kindly said, was "the dark night of the human soul." It was a very dour essay on the effects of isolation upon mankind.

The five people we used as characters in this play-documentary were all people who had experienced isolation in some very special way, and had things to say about it. By the time we were about half-way through that hour, we had a fair notion as to which aspect of isolation had attracted each of them; so, in the second half, we began superimposing conversations or phrases, because by this time our characters had become archetypes and we no longer needed their precise words to identify them and their position. We needed only the sound of each of their voices and the texture of that sound mixing with other voices to do this.[4]

The work is, of course, "The Idea of North." The five characters can be heard as if conversing in various combinations, responding to each other in the ordinary way. But in his liner notes to the disc of this documentary Gould says:

Our five guests were, of course, interviewed separately. They did not, at any time during the making of "North," have occasion to meet, and whichever drama-like juxtapositions came about were achieved through some careful after-the-fact work with the razor-blade on tape, and not through any direct confrontation among our characters.[5]

These dramatic confrontations, then, did not take place between "actual" people, but were assembled from bits of prerecorded tape; they are "realistic" in Gould's special sense of that word. He cuts and sorts the raw spoken materials and mixes them into entirely new configurations, having altered them in many ways. Some he makes louder, some softer, some closer, some more distant, with gradations of these and other dimensions in which the sound (the *appearance*) of the completed product can be shaped. In these ways he creates patterns of increasing and decreasing emotional tension, suspense, and other dramatic devices.

There is a scene in my documentary about Newfoundland — "The Latecomers"—which would appear to be taking place between, I suppose, a man and a wife, certainly a lady and gentleman who are engaged in rather intimate conversation. The scene is set very simply — the gentleman is slightly to the left of centre ("The Latecomers" . . . is in stereo, of course) the lady slightly to the right. There is an open space between them, as it appears, through which one hears water—the sea being the basso-continuo for "The Latecomers." . . . Anyway, we came to think of it as our "Virginia Woolf" scene—in Albee's sense—in that the relationship which appeared to exist between them developed some rather interesting overtones. Now, these were overtones, of course, which were manufactured by the razor-blade. To the best of my knowledge, these two people had never met — certainly, the dialogue represented in that scene never took place, as dialogue — and yet, I have a strange feeling, that had they met, it would have.[6]

Gould says that the editing of "The Latecomers" required almost 400 hours of work. Of the fourteen "characters" he interviewed for this piece, one presented difficulties that were particularly dramatic:

We needed him very badly. He was a delightful man, very articulate and very perceptive, but he had a habit of saying "um" and "uh" and "sort of" and "kind of" constantly — so constantly, in fact, that you got absolutely sick of the repetitions. I mean, every third word was separated by an "um" and an "uh." . . .

Well, we spent — this is no exaggeration — We spent three long weekends — Saturday, Sunday and Monday, eight hours per day — doing nothing but removing "ums" and "uhs," "sort ofs" and "kind ofs," and righting the odd syntactical fluff in his material.

Gould estimates that in this character's speech he made four edits in each line of the typewritten transcript. And since there were fourteen pages of transcript with thirty lines of double-spaced type on each, he calculated (as a "conservative guess") "that there were 1600 edits in that man's speech alone in order to make him sound lucid and fluid, which he now does. We made a new character out of him." A "real" character, Gould might say:

You see, I don't really care how you do it. I don't think it's a moral issue. I don't think that kind of judgement enters in it. If it takes 1,600 splices, that's fine.[7]

Many of Gould's dramatic encounters are not dialogues but crowd scenes, "counterpoint" in many voices. As we have already noticed, Gould believes that people ought to be able to follow several lines of information at any one time. He does not mix the voices in his crowd scenes casually.

If you examine any of the really contrapuntal scenes in my radio pieces, you'll find that every line stacks up against the line opposite, and either contradicts it or supplements it, but uses, in any case, the same basic terminology—a set of numbers, similar or identical terms, or whatever.[8]

"The Quiet in the Land" contains some of the most felicitous of these techniques, including several "imitations" in the strict musical sense, where words in one voice are echoed by another voice in a carefully measured interval of time, in another register and tone-quality. In this work Gould seems to have solved problems of combining complexity with clarity which were unsolved in earlier documentaries.

An interviewer once asked Gould about the origins of his contrapuntal radio documentaries. Their composer replied:

I suppose they began around 1945 or '46 when I used to listen to the inevitable "Sunday Night Stage" something-or-others for which, in those days, Andrew Allan & Co. were responsible. I was fascinated with radio. A lot of that kind of ostensibly theatrical radio was also, in a very real sense, documentary-making of a rather high order. At any rate, the distinctions between drama and documentary were quite often, it seemed to me, happily and successfully set aside.[9]

Gould here refers to what many of us look back on as the great days of Canadian broadcasting. Beginning in 1944, and for almost a decade, the Toronto studios of the CBC produced a series of weekly radio plays throughout the winter seasons, many of them written specially for the series, with a close-knit company of actors, writers, directors and technicians who rose to prominence while bringing radio drama to a level of excellence which may never be surpassed. Some of the plays written for this "Stage" series were based on Canadian history, some of it recent, hence Gould's suggestion that they combined the theatrical with the documentary.

Most of these plays, and in the early days of the series all of them, were broadcast "live." The listener at home heard not a tape or disc played on the radio, but the actual voices, sound effects and music. The voice you heard was uttering those words at the moment you heard them; the door you heard shutting was being shut by the sound-effects man at the moment you heard it. This was what Gould would have called "actuality."

Nowadays a radio drama is put together from tape-recorded takes which can be selected, edited and processed in the New Philosophy manner, much as a motion picture might be, or a commercial musical recording. The producer of a radio drama has more freedom and flexibility than were available in the old "Stage" days. He can delete or rearrange the words of a speech; he can combine, as dialogue, speeches which were not uttered by actors face-to-face. He can record all his music cues and sound effects separately, and mix them at his convenience and under editorial control. This is "realism."

The old "Stage" radio plays were innovative showpieces for youthful talent, and their spirit lives on in Glenn Gould. Technology has made life safer and duller for people who make radio plays. No longer do they go on the air facing the risks that go with live performance — a mistimed cue, a bell instead of a car horn, a scatological spoonerism, a fanfare instead of a muted string tremolando, an actor breaking up under the strain, an operator hitting the wrong switch in a panic. Gould runs deliberate risks with the technology itself, and stretches it sometimes to the breaking point. We may, for example, fail to sort out his busier crowd scenes; a juxtaposition of effects may be unintentionally funny; an elaborate structure may collapse of its own weight and complexity.

"The Idea of North" was first broadcast in December 1967 by the CBC as part of its celebration of Canada's centennial year. It is the earliest full-blown Gouldian contrapuntal radio documentary, but it does not mark a creative departure for Gould, since for at least the five previous years he had been making broadcasts which consisted of fragments of interviews "voice over" with fragments of the music being talked about. In these are many passages in which the voice is more "alongside" the music than "over" it, with the result that neither the words nor the music can be followed. This can be irritating, because the music is always interesting and important, as are the words of the people speaking. Gould breezily accepts this and urges us to develop what he considers our untapped potential for following more than one line of information at any one time. He overestimates us, misguided perhaps by his own capacities, which are prodigious, as he has revealed in several different ways, particularly in his recordings of polyphonic music at the keyboard. B.H. Haggin wrote:

. . . both his intellectual power and his technical mastery are evident in the amazing way in which he maintains this sustained life not just in one but in all the interweaving strands of the contrapuntal textures in the Partita No. 6 and the Fugues in E Major and F-sharp Major from Book 2 of The Well-Tempered Clavier. I can't recall another pianist achieving anything like this playing of counterpoint, or achieving everything else in these performances that makes them so extraordinary.[10]

Joachim Kaiser was equally gratified.

Polyphony presents no difficulties whatsoever to this magnificent pianist; the independence and freedom of his hands is astonishing; the art with which the parts are precisely held and shaded staggering.[11]

Harold C. Schonberg says of Josef Hofmann that "he seemed to have a brain built into each of his velvet fingertips."[12] This figure serves equally well for Gould. Sometimes while playing homophonic music Gould will create a kind of counterpoint by selectively accentuating notes and forcing them to stand out, connected together as if they belonged to an independent and additional melodic voice not provided by the composer. Joachim Kaiser noticed a particularly inspired example of this in Gould's recording of the Intermezzos by

Brahms.[13] It is particularly noticeable in Gould's recordings of certain arid passages in Mozart[14] where he invents motives which add interest and complexity to music which for him is otherwise too simple and undemanding.

In ways that most of us are not, Gould appears to be a multi-channel information-processing machine. Richard Kostelanetz commented upon this.

. . . he simply connects himself into a variety of inputs and they feed into him. . . . Gould watches a lot of television, exploits his hi-fi set, reads several newspapers . . . carries a radio with him all the time, and at home sometimes listens to both the AM and FM simultaneously. "Quite mysteriously, I discovered that I could better learn Schoenberg's difficult piano score, *Opus 23*, if I listened to them both at once, the FM to hear music and the AM to hear the news. I want to stay in touch." Gould can learn a Beethoven score while carrying on a conversation; and he often reads one of the many magazines to which he subscribes while listening attentively to someone on the telephone. Afterward, he will remember details from both inputs. . . .[15]

In a film made in 1975 Gould says:

Crazy as it sounds, I always write with at least two competing audio sources —usually one TV program and one radio program in—I was going to say— the background, but I think middle-ground might be more accurate. And if I go to a restaurant, I automatically find myself disentangling three or four conversations from tables nearby.[16]

These accounts, like others we have encountered before, suggest Gould is able to divide or partition himself, to have one part at work on one task and another part on another, both at the same time. In the anecdote of The Last Resort he directed one level of attention to a dull and easy left-hand piano part while another attended to the technical problem that had arisen in his right hand. In one of his more famous keyboard mannerisms one hand seems to be conducting the other in passages where one is for the moment free, as if each hand were operated by a separate intelligence. (This mannerism, if that is the right word, can be seen in almost any of his films or TV shows.)

He is what we might call a polyperson in yet another sense. He is a one-man repertory company of fictitious characters, people of different types, accents and ethnic origins. They turn up in some of his writings, in radio skits and occasionally on television. His Mozart finales display much the same thing. They are like the Act I finales of Mozart's comic operas, with the several characters rushing around the stage singing earnestly. Gould sustains a distinct dramatic personality for each musical line or motive throughout all the inter-changes and ramifications. This I think he could not do without himself entering into each character (or motive, episode or line), and into all of them at once. I can think of no other pianist who does this.

Glenn Gould's contrapuntal radio documentaries are less widely known than might be expected, considering his international re-nown as an innovative recording artist. They have been broadcast outside Canada, but not extensively, and there has been very little published criticism of them.

There are two major difficulties with these works. As I have already mentioned, most of us are less competent than Gould to handle several lines of information at one time. It is no use urging us to employ some untapped potential, because the problem is not entirely one of rusty or untrained capacity to respond perceptually. In part the problem is what people who study hearing would call "masking": one channel covers or conceals another. In a brass fortissimo we cannot hear the bassoon; indeed, the bassoonist often cannot hear himself. In a room full of stacked paintings we can by no amount of extra visual effort see the paintings or parts of paintings which are underneath others. We have to separate them physically.

The other difficulty is that radio is normally a one-time medium, at least so far as the listener is concerned. What he misses on first hearing he will not have another chance to hear except in unusual circumstances. "The Idea of North" has been broadcast in Canada more than twenty times, but of course not always in the same region or on the same network; and a listener who wanted to hear it again would be hard-put to discover where and when to expect it. The rebroadcasts are scheduled months or years apart, which makes it impossible to remember details from one hearing to the next. And the amount of detail is formidable. Take the music cues alone. Gould selects, cuts and combines these with as much attention to theme and key relationships as a good composer does in writing a piece of conventional music, and with as much skill, but so elaborately as to make them imperceptible to anyone except himself. So he then writes articles and scripts to explain these and other complexities to would-be listeners. There is nothing wrong with this — Gould's lengthy explanations are like T.S. Eliot's famous notes to his poems: they are not external to the works of art but are integral parts of them.

Gould reminds one of those mediaeval craftsmen who took great pains with details behind posts and at the back of choir stalls where no human eye would see them, convinced that their work was nevertheless seen by the eye of God. Surely the total of 1,600 edits in the speech of just one character out of fourteen in an hour-long broadcast is a case in point.

Gould acknowledges that he tends toward "busy-ness." He says that as counterpoint his radio documentaries are more like Reger's music than Bach's in this respect.[17] In his own defence he wrote in the liner notes for *The Idea of North*:

> . . . there are, in the prologue and the various scenes of which "North" consists, a number of techniques which I would be inclined to identify as musically derived. The prologue, indeed, is a sort of trio-sonata. . . . And there are other, perhaps more complex, occasions which simulate musical techniques as well. One such is the scene devoted to the subject of the Eskimo which takes place, apparently, in a dining-car aboard a train—the train being our basso-continuo throughout most of the programme—and in which Miss Schroeder, Mr. Vallee, Mr. Lotz and Mr. Phillips are more or less simultaneously occupied in conversation†—the resultant distractions making the listener's rôle not unlike that of a dining-car steward intent upon giving equal service to all.
>
> The point about these scenes, I think, is that they test, in a sense, the degree to which one can listen simultaneously to more than one conversation or vocal impression. It's perfectly true that, in that dining-car scene, not every word is going to be audible, but then by no means every syllable in the final fugue from Verdi's *Falstaff* is either, when it comes to that. Yet few opera composers have been deterred from utilizing trios, quartets or quintets by the knowledge that only a portion of the words they set to music will be accessible to the listener—most composers being concerned primarily about the totality of the structure, the play of consonance and dissonance between the voices—and, quite apart from the fact that I do believe most of us are capable of a much more substantial information-intake than we give ourselves credit for, I would like to think that these scenes can be listened to in very much the same way that you'd attend the *Falstaff* fugue.

Gould's analogy of the dining car steward is a weak one. The dining car steward must be sufficiently attentive to what the diners are saying that he can involve himself here and there when remarks are made (though not to him directly) about such matters as the temperature of the soup or the speed of the service. This is what psychologists call "cocktail effect," a special instance in which the nature of the job controls the steward's auditory scanning and selection of information from the compote. This control is purposive and

---

† It must be remembered that the voices of these people were recorded at separate times. The people did not "actually" meet or talk together.

practical. But nothing of the kind controls the scanning and selection done by the listener to music, of which the role is neither purposive nor practical. It is ecstatic, if we accept Gould's opinion. But the contrapuntal radio documentaries lend themselves to neither ecstasy, nor purpose, nor practice. They are pure *play*, sometimes fascinating, sometimes beautiful, sometimes edifying, sometimes distracting — but never boring.

This is not to deny that they are art. There is play in all art and art in all play, and some art (like play) makes up its rules as it goes along. Gould's art in these works is of this kind, and it more resembles Schoenberg's art than Bach's in this respect. And it more resembles film than music. But play or not, Gould is most definitely not joking.†

---

† CBS Records released in 1977 a disc by Gould of piano pieces by Jan Sibelius. This release is particularly momentous as the first by any performer of classical music in which the mixing process is described in some detail and acknowledged as itself a contributory art. The techniques described in the liner notes are those of the Gould contrapuntal radio documentaries; Gould has in fact been gradually introducing them into his piano recordings for some time, but this is the first in which they are identified and featured.

In 1975 he volunteered the information that *The Solitude Trilogy* is an autobiographical statement, or at least that it is as close to an autobiographical statement as he expects ever to come on radio. And since radio is his favourite medium we may have to settle for this.

CHAPTER 10

Talking Nonsense
On Anything
Anywhere

Paul Myers wrote: ". . . I believe that all Glenn Gould's performances deserve special recognition and understanding. I can think
of no other pianist with whom he can be compared, and it would,
perhaps, be fairer to state that he belongs in a special musical
category of his own."[1] But to be nothing more than a pianist,
however unique, has never been Gould's intention. The musical
public, however, does not accept this; B.H. Haggin expressed it for
many people when he wrote that Glenn Gould ". . . prefers talking
nonsense on anything anywhere to playing marvellously in the
concert hall."[2]

Glenn Gould as pianist (or keyboardist) has produced a formidable catalogue of recordings and has had a short but brilliant career as
a concert artist. On these the greater part of his reputation rests.

As composer he has produced a string quartet, a choral fugue,
two cadenzas, numerous unpublished pieces and much more. He
considers the contrapuntal radio documentaries to be musical compositions, which they are by the criteria of the 1960's avant garde.
He also considers that in his recorded and concert performances he
has participated in the composing or re-composing of the music he
played.

As author he has produced the "nonsense" mentioned by Haggin
in the petulant remark quoted above. Haggin's criticisms of Gould's
recordings and concerts include some of the most perceptive that

have been written and some of the most favourable. But his worry about Gould's written and spoken utterances became evident in his report on two lectures given by Gould at Hunter College in New York on January 31 and March 3, 1964. The lectures were in a series entitled "The Piano Sonata," and were advertised as "lecture-recitals." Haggin did not know that Gould was within a few weeks of the final concert of his career (March 28 of that same year); probably nobody knew this, not even Gould himself, which in retrospect adds poignancy to Haggin's account.

"Glenn Gould's two lectures in the Hunter College piano series last winter revealed him as, in some ways, a Canadian counterpart of Donald Tovey . . . Gould . . . spoke out of an awesome knowledge of particular works of all periods. . . ."[3] But it worried Haggin ". . . that Gould carried his interest in the structural harmonic element of the music [in this case the first movement of Beethoven's Opus 109] to the point of regarding it as primary and as more important than the thematic melodic element," and remarked that "this attitude had been evident in some of his recent recorded performances — notably the one of Mozart's Concerto K.491."[4] Elsewhere Haggin wrote of this performance: "the piano part [is] delivered with a bold and powerful sculpturing of phrase, a purposeful energy in every note of fast runs and figurations, a sustained tension and momentum, that I never before heard in the playing of this music, and that made it one of the greatest performances I have ever heard."[5]

But of the Hunter College lectures Haggin wrote:

Another thing to worry about is Gould's apparently increasing disinclination to play music in public and his preference for writing and talking about it. The audience that filled the hall for his first lecture was there because of its experiences with his power to illuminate music with his playing; but most of the audience did not find his statements at the lecture illuminating because these statements — representing his knowledge of the music they referred to — did not connect in the minds of his hearers with the similar knowledge of the music needed to make the statements meaningful to them, and because Gould did not sufficiently provide them with this knowledge by playing the music on the piano.[6]

Raymond Ericson reported on the first lecture in *The New York Times*:

It was obvious that some listeners would have preferred to hear Mr. Gould make music and not talk. After he had played just a few measures early in the evening, he was greeted with prolonged applause. To this he merely shook his head, indicating that he was intent on giving his lecture. He did not stop for an intermission, and several persons walked out because they had apparently expected more music.[7]

Nine years later I wrote to Hunter College asking if I might see any documentation they possessed dealing with Gould's lectures there. The reply is an intriguing epilogue to this story: that they had carefully looked into it but found no information regarding his having lectured there.[8]

Nothing more clearly illustrates the prevailing reluctance to accept Glenn Gould as author than the almost total neglect of his writings about the music of Arnold Schoenberg, which in number of titles (and perhaps of words) exceed the published works on Schoenberg by any other writer in the English language. Even with their many repetitions deleted, Gould's essays and scripts would make a sizable volume; and if they had been written by almost anyone but Gould they would by now have been discussed at length and in a lively manner by critics and scholars.

In 1966 Yehudi Menuhin said on CBC television that Gould knows more about Schoenberg, and perhaps has a more genuine understanding of his music, than anyone else.[9]† Gould's earliest writing on Schoenberg of which we have evidence was a set of notes for a concert at the Royal Conservatory in 1952 commemorating the first anniversary of the composer's death. In addition to this his writings on Schoenberg include a monograph, an article in a quarterly journal, thirteen scripts for radio and four for television (partly or entirely devoted to Schoenberg), one film, six essays for liner notes, two public lectures, and a talk disc.‡

It appears from the Foreword to the 1964 monograph *Arnold Schoenberg: A Perspective* that Gould had a more pleasant experience lecturing at the University of Cincinnati than he did at Hunter College:

This public lecture, delivered to a capacity audience in the University of Cincinnati's Wilson Auditorium, by the world renowned Canadian pianist Glenn Gould, can hardly be expected, in its present form, to recreate the excitement of the event itself, since the genial magic of Gould's lecture manner cannot be put on paper. Perhaps it can be suggested by saying that Gould the lecturer is an extension of Gould the interpreter, and those

---

† In his autobiography Menuhin wrote: "Perhaps no one in the world knows as much about Schoenberg as Glenn does, or more than he does about the recording and broadcasting of music." Yehudi Menuhin, *Unfinished Journey* (London: Macdonald and Janes, 1976), p. 333. See also Peter Cossé, "Seine Waffe ist der Geige," *fono forum* 3 (1977), 212-15.

‡ *See* Appendix — Writings by Gould on Arnold Schoenberg.

qualities of lucidity and warmth, style and wit, that shine through his performer's art, animate his speaking as well and make his lecture style as formidable as his musical performance.[10]

In *The Music Index* is listed only one review of this monograph: Robert Baksa's in *Music Journal*. Baksa said that "the text is the work of a brilliant musical mind and well worth reading."[11]

The many writings by Gould on Schoenberg, whatever their merit, have gone largely unnoticed. But let Gould make one historical blunder in his writings, as in 1960 he did in his article "Bodky on Bach," and there is glee in the common-room. Musicologists no doubt agreed in spirit with Abram Chasins, who around this same time wrote that he found Gould's "widely publicized scholarship to be greatly exaggerated."[12]

"Bodky on Bach" appeared in the *Saturday Review* of November 26, 1960. It is a review of Erwin Bodky's *The Interpretation of Bach's Keyboard Works*. In the opening paragraph Gould says:

It hardly seems possible that the same man who urges the Bach student to develop his interpretation through analysis of the internal evidence of a composition can, a few chapters later, seriously discuss the integral connection between the 14-note subject of the C major fugue from Volume I of "The Well-Tempered Clavier" and the fact that the alphabet positions of the letters in the name of Bach total the number 14, and further that by adding the initials J.S. we can produce the inverted number 41 (my own addition stubbornly yields 43).[13]

Unfortunately it is well established that Bach made deliberate play in his music with numerical symbols, including the cryptical use of numbers 14 and 41 as his own signature. And Gould's problem with the number 41 was a consequence of his not knowing that in the old German alphabet "I" and "J" are not two different letters but two forms of the same letter, the ninth in the alphabet. If in this alphabet we assign 1 to A, 2 to B, 3 to C, and so on, I and J will be 9, S will be 18, and J.S. BACH will add up to 41, as Bodky said; this is the way Bach would have added.

A later issue of *Saturday Review* included two smug letters to the editor putting Gould straight; we may suppose there were others.[14]

The remarkable thing about the "Bodky on Bach" episode is not that it occurred, but that in all his many writings Gould has made remarkably few such obvious errors. Many professional scholars have done worse. But for those who insist that the shoemaker should stick to his last and Glenn Gould to his piano it was proof that, although he plays marvellously, his verbal utterances are likely to be nonsense.

If Gould says that Mozart's music lacks harmonic adventurousness (as one of the reasons for his lack of enthusiasm for much of it), these people will cry "nonsense!" They would not do so if the same were said by Alfred Einstein[15] or Donald Francis Tovey,[16] which (in different ways) it was.

On the other hand, one cannot deny that Gould puts barriers in the way of our taking him as seriously as we might: his facetiousness, his clowning, his early ponderousness and obscurity, his vaulting arguments, his outrageous exaggerations. Not everyone will agree that Istvan Anhalt's Fantasia for Piano ". . . is one of the finest piano works of its period" (1954),[17] or that Fartein Valen's Sonata Number 2, Opus 38, contains ". . . one of the most exalting moments in music. . . . I think it's one of the great piano sonatas of the twentieth century."[18] I do not disparage the music of Anhalt or Valen when I say that their names are not household words among the musical public. And Bizet's *Variations Chromatiques*, even in Gould's astonishing recorded performance, scarcely lives up to his evaluation of it as "one of the very few masterpieces for solo piano to emerge from the third quarter of the 19th century. . . ."[19] Gould's enthusiasm is attractive, and should earn a respectful hearing for the works he praises; but we can sometimes be excused for wondering how seriously he intends himself to be taken.

On a more general and theoretical level, Gould has a central thesis which he intends us to take very seriously indeed, although few people have yet done so.

He did not invent this thesis, but as recording artist he has done more to implement it innovatively in practice than has any other musician, excepting perhaps one or two in popular music. As writer he has elaborated it more extensively than anyone, and there is little clowning, facetiousness or exaggeration in his writings about it. It is for him so obviously true and valid that he scarcely thinks it worth formulating explicitly.

His thesis is that recorded music is an autonomous art, an art having its own conventions, techniques, history, mythology, morale and criteria. Recorded music is to concert music as film is to the dramatic stage: a younger cousin, not an offspring and not a dependent.

Gould's recordings test his thesis to the limit and beyond. Many of his writings were produced partly or mainly to justify his (as they seemed to us) extravagant and eccentric interpretations in these recordings. In all this Gould is reacting against the Old Philosophy notion that a recording is a concert in amber, and against critics who expect a recording to be something it is not, or need not be: a substitute for a live performance. A recording is no more a substitute for a live performance than a film is a substitute for a stage play.

We keep asking the wrong question: What is it that we value in a live musical performance that must inevitably be lost in a recording of it? The right question is this: What is it that we value in a recording that we cannot have in a live performance? A musical recording is a work of art in its own right, and not a shadow or reflection of something else. Hence we should ask not what does the technology keep from us, but rather what does the technology present to us that a live performance cannot?

Gould has shown that we cannot accuse technology (when properly used) of intruding destructively in musical recordings. If, for example, we cannot locate the splices when we listen to the record, then we may not claim that they are destructive.

He has argued in his writings, and in his recordings has repeatedly demonstrated, that for certain kinds of music it is possible for a recording to provide more lucidity and coherence than can be obtained in the concert hall, and that for these kinds of music this is desirable. The technology of recording, he says, has widened the artistic horizons of composers, performers and listeners, and has introduced new possibilities for the artistic imagination. His own recordings are not "testaments" or "definitive statements." They are parts of his continuing search after ways to make artistic use of recorded music as an autonomous art. This is why a Gould recording is, as Joachim Kaiser says, "a physical and acoustical experiment."[20]

Every Gould recording, like every Gould essay, script, film, documentary and composition, is part of his Promethean effort to share with us the ecstatic awareness of his own many-dimensional, tonal, imaginative perspectives. Gould is the oldtime sage in our epigraph from Diderot at the beginning of this book, in whom are united the philosopher, the poet and the musician. We diminish him when we confine him to one or another, and we diminish ourselves.

Epilogue

Nothing about Glenn Gould is as perplexing as the wrath he arouses in some people. They are convinced that his singing, gestures and grimaces are affectations. His antics, including his more eccentric performances on disc, have been called a threat to the great romantic tradition of virtuoso piano playing. He has no *right*, it is implied, to prevent our hearing him in live concerts and recitals playing the pieces we want to hear. As for his seclusion, it is just another of his affectations.

These and other complaints I have read or heard, and I marvel at the earnestness and the heat of them. It all began, I suppose, in the 1950s, when the media were trying to exploit this unconventional young genius. He was great copy. Then they noticed that he was not so crazy, and had all along been good-naturedly exploiting them. No story he told was consistent with any other. And the answers he gave to interviewers' questions − predictable questions about his childhood and home life − were given shape and content by his lively imagination. All this may account for the wrath of the press and of some reviewers. For the rest, it is surely neither remarkable nor reprehensible that a man should strive to discover the conditions under which he works best, and having discovered them choose to work under those conditions.

So, while experts rant ("But it's not *Mozart!*"), and while reviewers insinuate that Gould plays the way he does because he is unable to do otherwise (that is, "better"), a large and devoted following of sensitive people is listening to Glenn Gould and understanding the whole point of what he is doing.

A performance for Gould is not a contest but a love affair with the music. A performer, he believes, should not perform in order to be hailed as the greatest since X or Y, much better than Z, and so on; he should not even perform in order to surpass his own previous performances. He should, by performing a piece of music, create the one-time, unique work of art that is that particular performance of the piece. This is not a commitment to the task of delivering to the audience a perfect performance of the work. It is rather a commitment to creating, here and now, a new work of art that is unlike any other performance of the piece, possible or imagined, past or future. It is a mental involvement in the possibilities of this unique unfolding of the music, as if it were newly composed.

For the listener, no less than for the performer, Gould's view is significant. Obviously not all listeners are artists, nor are they equally capable of listening artistically. But Gould invites us to listen to music without being on display, without exposing ourselves to other people's evaluations of our taste and judgment. He invites us to listen without comparing one pianist's recording of a piece with those by a dozen others, without comparing a performing edition of a piece with its Urtext. By cutting through a lot of cultural snobbery among listeners, and a lot of theoretical and historical irrelevancies among critics, he runs the risk of attracting our resentment. But he also opens to us a range of alternatives in musical awareness to which we might otherwise be oblivious.

The proper quest of both artist and listener, Gould tells us, is "ecstasy," that introspective awareness of our "personhood," of the humanity within each that embraces all. He claims that the technology of recording has revealed limitless possibilities for more intimate yet more widespread communion from self to self than could ever be possible in the arena. He makes good on this claim in each of his recordings by revealing his own innermost self confidingly and without inhibition. No politician or movie star, despite the gossip magazines, is as accessible and transparent to the public as Glenn Gould in his recordings and writings. He is an enigma only to those who refuse to hear.

Meanwhile, he lives and works in Toronto, isolated from it, a voluntary exile in his home town, the "greatest glory"† of its musical life.

A strange glory! If you are in Toronto, you will not hear him talk or play, or see him at a cocktail party or reception, or in the audience at a concert, as you might expect to do with the musical glories of other cities. In fact, few local music lovers are even aware that he lives in their midst. He has achieved the anonymity he craved when he stood in the international limelight during the 1950s and early '60s.

Yet many professional musicians now living in Toronto have encountered him in one way or another, as have many technical and production people in radio and television. From their consensus emerges a description of Gould as a spontaneous, considerate person, full of humour and intellectual curiosity, receptive to new musical and technological ideas from all sources, and ready to try anything.

Although he has never taken pupils, a few musicians, early in their careers, have come into brief but memorable contact with him. A young Canadian pianist at the rehearsal for his debut with the Toronto Symphony encountered problems with the Massey Hall piano and froze; someone had the bright idea of telephoning Gould to ask if he would talk to the young pianist and help get his mind off the difficulties. Gould consented, and the two spent the afternoon in relaxed piano-talk. That evening the debutant played happily and beautifully at his concert. On another occasion a gifted young woman, recently settled in Toronto, was pleasantly surprised to be asked to play with Gould in a television production. She and the other players presented themselves at the studio for the taping; Gould arrived last, with his floppy cap over his eyes and his overcoat collar turned up. He sat on his battered folding chair and out of the folds of his coat extracted a newspaper from which he read a funny story to put the other musicians at ease, and then took them brilliantly through some difficult music by Webern. There are many such vignettes.

It is evident that the life of Glenn Gould is a work in progress, a work done with unflagging zest. In his radio documentary on Leopold Stokowski Gould said of the maestro (then almost ninety), that he was "very much a man of the future." Of Glenn Gould (who is now at about half that age) the same can even more aptly be said.

---

†From the citation read by the President of the University of Toronto on the occasion of the conferring of Gould's honorary degree, June 1, 1964.

Appendix

I *Glenn Gould from Ten to Twenty: A Chronology*

1942 — Began studies at the Royal Conservatory of Music of Toronto.

1944 — February. Competed victoriously in the First Kiwanis Music Festival.

1945 — June. Passed associateship examination as soloist in performance (piano) at the Royal Conservatory.

— September. Entered Malvern Collegiate Institute.

— December 12. Concert debut. Played organ at Eaton Auditorium.

1946 — May 8. Orchestral debut. Played first movement of Beethoven's Concerto No. 4 with Royal Conservatory Orchestra, conducted by Ettore Mazzoleni, in Massey Hall.

— June. Passed associateship examinations in musical theory at the Royal Conservatory.

— October 28. Awarded diploma, Associate of the Royal Conservatory of Music of Toronto.

1947 — January 14. First performance with a professional orchestra. Played Beethoven's Concerto No. 4 (complete) with the Toronto Symphony Orchestra, conducted by Bernard Heinze.

— April. First public solo piano recital. A student recital at the Royal Conservatory.

— October 20. First public solo piano recital as a professional artist, in Eaton Auditorium.

1948 — Composed his first major work, a piano sonata.

1950 — December 24. First network radio broadcast recital, on CBC.

1951 — January. Performed two of his own compositions in a concert at the Royal Conservatory.

— Terminated studies at Malvern Collegiate Institute.

1952 — Discontinued piano lessons with Alberto Guerrero.

— September 8. The first pianist to be televised by the CBC. The occasion was the opening of CBLT in Toronto.

II Eighteenth Century Mechanical Instruments

Music from machinery did not begin with Thomas Alva Edison's phonograph in the 1870s, as we might think it did. A hundred years before Edison the technology of mechanical musical instruments had developed to a high level. The eighteenth century musical clock is a manifestation of this, and it tells us a few things about the New Philosophy. In one of its varieties it was an ornamental timepiece which told the hour not by striking chimes but by blowing tunes on organ pipes, a different tune for each hour of the day. The clock's tripping mechanism actuated a bellows and a rotating cylinder or barrel. Stuck into the barrel were pins and bridges which, as they rotated, engaged the playing mechanism of the organ pipes. The arrangement of pins was a simple translation from staff notation of the piece to be played.

Haydn, Mozart, and Beethoven wrote pieces for these barrels. Haydn wrote thirty or more, none of particular worth. Mozart wrote three. They are mature works and among his greatest creations:[†] Adagio and Allegro for a Mechanical Organ in F Minor, K.594; Fantasia for a Mechanical Organ in F Minor, K.608; Andante for a Small Mechanical Organ in F, K.616.

The difference between Haydn's and Mozart's pieces for musical clock or mechanical organ is of special interest to us.

Haydn's compositions for musical clocks are related to his works for the piano. . . . They point to . . . all those short pianoforte pieces that were instrumental in building up nineteenth-century keyboard music."[‡]

In other words, Haydn wrote piano pieces which were pinned on the barrel of musical clocks. Mozart, on the other hand, wrote pieces which were not conceived in terms of the piano or any other instrument, which were written instead with the capabilities of the mechanical organ in mind. They cannot be played on the piano without faking. As Einstein says, Mozart's K.616 ". . . contains little passages of mechanical velocity that Mozart would have written quite differently for the piano."[§] The other two, K.594 and K.608, can be played at the piano with four hands quite satisfactorily, or at the organ with pedals in a thinned-out version. But none of the three is a piece of piano music adapted to the machine; all are pieces conceived and worked out specifically in terms of the machine's own capabilities. They ignore the limitations of the manual keyboard, not

---

[†] G. de Saint-Foix, *The Symphonies of Mozart*, trans. Leslie Orrey (London: Dennis Dobson, 1947), p. 162.

[‡] Karl Geiringer, *Haydn: A Creative Life in Music* (London: George Allen & Unwin, 1947), pp. 275-6.

[§] Alfred Einstein, *Mozart: His Character, His Work*, trans. Arthur Mendel and Nathan Broder (New York: Oxford University Press, 1965), pp. 268-9. See also the essay "Mozart's Compositions for Mechanical Organ" in A. Hyatt King, *Mozart in Retrospect*, rev. ed. (London: Oxford University Press, 1970), pp. 198-215.

only in velocity, but in stretch, in crossing of parts, and in many of the distinctive keyboard hurdles.

In this comparison between Haydn and Mozart, Mozart is a New, and Haydn is an Old Philosophy figure. Beethoven was both Old and New: some of his compositions for mechanical organs were originally written by him for conventional instruments; some were written specifically for the barrel. The difference is evident. In the latter the music is outside the capabilities of all but the most accomplished pianists, and it breaks away from the established technical limitations, exploiting possibilities which, but for the technology, would be denied both composers and performers of keyboard music. The New Philosophy makes playable the unplayable, and thinkable the unthinkable.

III *Ecstasy and Authenticity*

John Beckwith raised the question of authenticity in an article published in 1960:

Gould is not only a persuasive Bach player but a well-read one; and this makes me wonder why he does not adopt the organ or harpsichord for his Bach performances, rather than the unauthentic piano.†

Of course Gould has not been silent about this:

After I had recorded all forty-eight Preludes and Fugues of Bach's *Well-Tempered Clavier*, and on the piano indeed, I could scarcely avoid the question of my choice of instruments. Throughout the twentieth century, the debate has dragged on over how far the piano, specifically the grand piano, is able to satisfy the requirements of this music. Many people say: "If Bach had had a grand piano, he would have used it." The counter-argument is based upon the position that Bach, ignoring artistic progress, moved within the whole vast realm of sounds with which he was intimately familiar.

Obviously, Bach's style of composing bears the mark of his aversion to writing for any determinate keyboard instrument — and it is, in fact, more than doubtful that he would have changed his sense of essential up-to-dateness if someone had added to the catalogue of his household instruments the most modern, quick-repeating concert grand of Mr. Steinway.‡

This is a compelling argument against the purist's view that Bach's music is more authentically, and hence better, played on harpsichord than on piano. It is an argument based upon Bach's sublime instrumental indifference. It does not matter which instrument Bach himself would have preferred to play these pieces upon, supposing he had a preference and that both harpsichord and modern grand piano were available to him. All that matters aesthetically is how the instrument is played in relation to the music itself, here and now. By whatever means the performer can best get into a "close relationship" to the music — into a state of ecstatic communion with it — by that means the performer can best realize the aesthetic value of the piece. Gould has said:

The performer has to have faith that he is doing, even blindly, the right thing, that he may be finding interpretive possibilities not wholly realized even by the composer.§

Gould's most revealing statement of his own position in the theory and practice of criticism in the arts is this:

Let's assume that someone were to improvise at the piano a sonata in the style of Haydn and to pass it off, at first, as a genuine work of that composer. The value

---

† John Beckwith, "Notes on a Recording Career," *The Canadian Forum* 40, no. 480 (January 1961), p. 219.
‡ *Erstmals in Deutscher sprache* (disc), CBS, GG 1 (1972), author's translation. In the disc *Glenn Gould: Concert Dropout*, Gould makes it clear that this argument does not work as well for certain less "instrumentally indifferent" keyboard works of J.S. Bach.
§ Asbell, "Glenn Gould," p. 93.

that the unsuspecting listener would assign to this opus (let's assume it was brilliantly done and most admirably Haydnesque) would very much depend upon the degree of chicanery of which the improviser was capable. So long as he was able to convince the audience that this work was indeed that of Haydn, it would be accorded a value commensurate with Haydn's reputation.

But now let us imagine that the improviser decided to inform the listener that this was not in fact a work of Haydn, though it very much resembled Haydn, but was in fact a work by Mendelssohn. The reaction to this bit of news would run something along the lines of — "Well, a pleasant trifle — obviously old-fashioned, but certainly shows command of an earlier style" — in other words, bottom-drawer Mendelssohn.

But one last examination of this hypothetical piece: let us assume that, instead of attributing it to Haydn or to any later composer, the improviser were to insist that it was a long-forgotten and newly discovered work of none other than Antonio Vivaldi, a composer who was, by seventy-five years, Haydn's senior. I venture to say that, with that condition in mind, this work would be greeted as one of the true revelations of musical history — a work that would be accepted as proof of the farsightedness of this great master, who managed in this one incredible leap to bridge the years that separate the Italian baroque from the Austrian rococo, and our poor piece would be deemed worthy of the most august programs.†

Gould calls this kind of judgment "the van Meegeren syndrome" ‡ and has great contempt for it:

The determination of the value of a work of art according to the information available about it is a most delinquent form of aesthetic appraisal. Indeed, it strives to avoid appraisal on any ground other than that which has been prepared by previous appraisals. §

Gould is here saying that the aesthetic value of a work of art is a result, not of what went into the making of the work and our understanding of this, but rather of the unique, private, ecstatic occasion of contemplating it. Aestheticians call this the anti-intentionalist position; it is consistent with Gould's New Philosophy of recording, which rejects the view that the composer's intentions for the piece are final or authoritative. His position also rejects the view that any performer's intentions on any occasion of performing a work are final, authoritative and binding. At every stage in the complex of technical processes — selection and placement of microphones, playing the instrument, recording the raw takes, editing, mixing, pressing, choice of pick-up, of amplifiers, of loudspeakers, placement of loudspeakers, adjustment of tone, balance, and loudness — the decisions of the composer and of the performer are subject to overruling in further artistic decisions, to revision and alteration in keeping with the possibilities and the limitations of the available apparatus.

---

† Glenn Gould, "Strauss and the Electronic Future," *Saturday Review* 47 (May 30, 1964), p. 58. From here Gould goes on to argue against "originality" as an aesthetical category, but comes to grief on a double negative.

‡ Hans van Meegeren was a famous Dutch forger of the present century whose "Vermeers" were duly authenticated and sold for immense sums. Gould says van Meegeren is one of his private heroes, and writes about him and the syndrome in "The Prospects of Recording," *High Fidelity Magazine* 16, no. 4 (April 1966), p. 54.

§ Ibid., pp. 54-5.

IV Ecstasy on Demand: Richard Strauss

Gould says that ecstasy is the only proper quest of the artist. In a passage which I cannot hope to square with the main exposition of this book, he says that ecstasy can be *simulated* by an artist. Here are the embarrassing words:

Richard Strauss turns on ecstasy rather easily, just as [Franz] Schmidt will turn on profundity; and by that I simply mean that the music *sounds* ecstatic, whether indeed it is or not.

He was a very petit-bourgeois figure, you know; we've seen many prints of him in his little Lester Pearson bow-tie. . . . But out of this petit-bourgeois figure comes music of what seems to me a transcendental ecstasy . . . it seems so readily available; one likes to think of a Beethovenian figure, occasionally working through to this state; but, for Strauss, there is no question of working through to ecstasy: it's always *there*. It's what happens when he puts notes to paper, it seems. . . . I think that, in Strauss's case, however, there are indeed genuinely ecstatic moments. I think that, in all the early tone poems and in the best of the operas . . . one has a feeling of transcendence that is absolutely extraordinary.†

My embarrassment is not with the notion of simulated or apparent ecstasy. It is with the idea that it should be possible to distinguish, by listening to the music of Richard Strauss, between simulated ecstasy and genuine ecstasy. In Chapter 8 I argue, following a suggestion from Gould, that this distinction cannot be made in the case of a musical work of art; that the ecstasy which *appears* to us (i.e., is simulated or made *apparent*) is the real and only ecstasy. The New Philosophy could not withstand an argument which demonstrated that there is genuine as well as apparent ecstasy, and that both kinds are distinguishable in music. Gould's point in Chapter 8 will be that one can turn what he calls the "ecstatic high" on and off, upon demand, for the purpose of making taped inserts for splicing into a final edited version of a recorded piece.

---

†*Conversations with Glenn Gould: Strauss* (film), BBC (1966).

V Writings by Gould on Arnold Schoenberg

1953 — liner notes to Hallmark RS3. The music is the Berg Sonata but the comments are mainly on Schoenberg.

1956 — article, "The Dodecaphonists' Dilemma" in *The Canadian Music Journal*.

1959 — liner notes to Columbia ML 5336, Three Piano Pieces, Op. 11.

1962 — two-hour CBC broadcast, "Arnold Schoenberg: the Man Who Changed Music." (Includes interviews with Aaron Copland, Goddard Lieberson, Dr. Peter F. Ostwald, Winthrop Sargeant and Gertrud Schoenberg.)
— liner notes to Columbia ML 5739, Piano Concerto, Op. 42.

1963 — second lecture in Gould's three inaugural MacMillan Lectures at the University of Toronto (July 9).

1964 — monograph, *Arnold Schoenberg: A Perspective*. Print version of a lecture given by Gould in the Corbett Music Lectures Series at the University of Cincinnati in April 1963.

1966 — CBC telecast (May 18) with Yehudi Menuhin.
— liner notes to Columbia M2S 736, Schoenberg's Piano Music.
— talk disc *Schoenberg*, Columbia MPS 8 (*Audition*, quarterly sound magazine of the Columbia Masterworks Club.)
— BBC film, *Conversations with Glenn Gould: Schoenberg*.

1967 — liner notes to Columbia MS 7036, Fantasy for Violin and Piano, Op. 47; and MS 7037, "Ode to Napoleon."
— liner notes to Columbia MS 7039, Concerto for Piano and Orchestra, Op. 42; Concerto for Violin and Orchestra, Op. 36.

1969 — broadcast on Schoenberg in the CBC series, "The Art of Glenn Gould."

1970 — liner notes to Columbia MS 7098, Schoenberg's Piano Music.

1974 — a series of ten one-hour CBC broadcasts on Schoenberg in honour of the hundredth anniversary of his birth.
— a segment on Schoenberg in the CBC telecast by Gould, "The Age of Ecstasy."
— contrapuntal radio documentary "Schoenberg: the First Hundred Years."

1975 — a segment on Schoenberg in the CBC telecast by Gould, "New Faces, Old Forms."
— a segment on Schoenberg in the CBC telecast by Gould, "The Flight from Order."

1978 — article, "Portrait of a Cantankerous Composer," in *The Globe and Mail*, March 18, 1978.

Notes

The following abbreviations have been used in the Notes: CBC for Canadian Broadcasting Corporation and BBC for British Broadcasting Corporation. The terms "broadcast" and "telecast" have been used to signify "radio broadcast" and "television broadcast" respectively.

Notes to Chapter 1

1. Glenn Gould, "Yehudi Menuhin: Musician of the Year," *High Fidelity/Musical America* 16, no. 13 (December 1966), p. 8. Anyone who has written for print publication and also for radio and television knows that these are two quite different kinds of writing. In the present book I quote from Glenn Gould's writings, some originally intended for print and some for other media. I have tried to bring them into stylistic harmony with one another, mainly by means of minor changes in punctuation, some of them suggested by Mr. Gould himself. He has in no other way participated in the writing of the book.

2. Bernard Asbell, "Glenn Gould," *Horizon* 4, no. 3 (January 1962), p. 91. Florence Greig Gould, mother of Glenn Gould, died in 1975. Her maiden name is spelled "Greig," unlike the composer's ("Grieg").

3. Vincent Tovell, *At Home with Glenn Gould* (disc), Radio Canada Transcription E-156, CBC (1959).

4. *Glenn Gould: On the Record* (film), National Film Board of Canada (1960).

5. Dennis Braithwaite, "Glenn Gould," *Toronto Daily Star*, March 28, 1959.

6. Ibid.

7. Alfred Bester, "The Zany Genius of Glenn Gould," *Holiday* 35, no. 4 (April 1964), p. 150.

8. Ibid., p. 151. For a marvellous account of what it was like to grow up in Toronto's Beach district, next door to Glenn Gould, see Robert Fulford, "Beach Boy," in *The Toronto Book*, ed. William Kilbourn (Toronto: Macmillan of Canada, 1976), pp. 89-98.

9. Tovell, *At Home with Glenn Gould*.

10. *Toronto Daily Star*, February 21, 1946.

11. Toronto *Globe and Mail*, February 17, 1944.

12. *Toronto Daily Star*, February 17, 1944.

13. John Beckwith, "Alberto Guerrero, 1886-1959," *Canadian Music Journal* 4, no. 2 (Winter 1960), p. 34.

14. Fulford, "Beach Boy," pp. 92-3.

15. Ibid., p. 90.

16. Tovell, *At Home with Glenn Gould*.

17. Glenn Gould, liner notes to *Glenn Gould's First Recordings of Grieg and Bizet* (disc), Columbia, M 32040 (1973).

18. Jonathan Cott, *Forever Young* (New York: Random House, 1977), p. 42.

19. Glenn Gould, "Stokowski: a Portrait for Radio" (broadcast), CBC (February 2, 1971).

20. Gould frequently compares recording music with film-making.

Chapter 8 deals at some length with this comparison.

21. Tovell, *At Home with Glenn Gould*.

22. Toronto *Telegram*, December 13, 1945.

23. Glenn Gould, "His Country's 'Most Experienced Hermit' Chooses a Desert-Island Discography," *High Fidelity Magazine* 20, no. 6 (June 1970), pp. 29, 32.

24. Allen Sangster, Toronto *Globe and Mail*, May 10, 1946.

25. *Toronto Daily Star*, May 9, 1946.

26. Toronto *Telegram*, May 9, 1946.

27. *Current Biography, 1960*, article "Glenn Gould," says erroneously that this concert took place in 1957 and that the conductor was Sir Ernest MacMillan.

28. Toronto *Globe and Mail*, January 15, 1947.

29. Toronto *Telegram*, January 15, 1947.

30. *Toronto Daily Star*, January 15, 1947.

31. Tovell, *At Home with Glenn Gould*.

32. Ibid.

33. Toronto *Telegram*, October 21, 1947.

34. Toronto *Globe and Mail*, October 21, 1947.

35. *Toronto Daily Star*, October 21, 1947.

36. *CBC Times* 3, no. 23, p. 7.

37. Ezra Schabas and Stuart Nall, *Musical Courier* 150, no. 6 (November 15, 1954), p. 35.

38. *Washington Post*, January 3, 1955.

39. *New York Times*, January 12, 1955.

40. John Briggs, *Musical Courier* 153, no. 3 (February 1, 1955), p. 86.

41. Reprinted in the liner notes to the rechannelled version of *The Goldberg Variations*, Columbia, MS 7096.

42. Harold Rutland, "Impressions of Glenn Gould," *Musical Times* 100, no. 1397 (July 1959), p. 388.

Notes to Chapter 2

1. *Glenn Gould: Concert Dropout* (disc), Columbia, BS 15 (1968).

2. Vincent Tovell, *At Home with Glenn Gould* (disc), Radio Canada Transcription E-156, CBC (1959).

3. Ned Rorem, *Music and People* (New York: George Braziller, 1968), p. 5.

4. *Conversations with Glenn Gould: Bach* (film), BBC (1966).

5. Glenn Gould, "Rubinstein," *Look*, March 9, 1971, pp. 53-4.

6. Claude Debussy, *Monsieur Croche the Dilettante Hater*, in *Three Classics in the Aesthetics of Music* (New York: Dover Publications, 1962), p. 22.

7. Alfred Bester, "The Zany Genius of Glenn Gould," *Holiday* 35, no. 4 (April 1964), p. 152.

8. *Glenn Gould: Concert Dropout*. R.G. Collingwood has an expression for this kind of listening to music: "licensed eavesdropping." See his *The Principles of Art* (Oxford: Clarendon Press, 1938), p. 322.

9. Glenn Gould, "The Prospects of Recording," *High Fidelity Magazine* 16, no. 4 (April 1966), pp. 46-63.

10. Ibid., p. 59.

11. *Glenn Gould: Concert Dropout*.

12. Ibid.

13. Gould, "The Prospects of Recording," p. 47.

14. *Conversations with Glenn Gould: Beethoven* (film), BBC (1966).

15. Glenn Gould, "The record of the decade, according to a critic who should know, is Bach played on, of all things, a Moog synthesizer?" *Saturday Night* 83, no. 12 (December 1968), p. 52.

16. Walter Carlos explains these techniques in *Glenn Gould on the Moog Synthesizer*, available on reel or cassette tape from CBC Learning Systems (Catalogue No. 326L).

17. Ivan Berger, "A Console for Would-be Conductors," *High Fidelity Magazine* 26, no. 5 (May 1976), pp. 50-1.

18. Mark F. Davis, "Mahler in a Hanger, or What Ambient Information Will Mean to You," *High Fidelity Magazine* 26, no. 5 (May 1976), pp. 52-4.

Notes to Chapter 3

1. Roland Gelatt, *The Fabulous Phonograph* (Philadelphia and New York: J.B. Lippincott Company, 1954-5), pp. 38-9. This is perhaps a myth. Leonard Marcus says that there is no evidence that Hofmann made a recording for Edison in 1888 while visiting the inventor in his New Jersey laboratory. But there is evidence that Edison sent Hofmann, at the pianist's request, a recording machine. Hofmann made a recording of a small piece of his own composition and sent it to Edison in 1891. "According to a letter Hofmann sent in 1953 to Roland Gelatt, former editor of *High Fidelity*, Edison in his reply dubbed it 'the very first regular piano record'." See Leonard Marcus, "Recordings Before Edison," *High Fidelity Magazine* 27, no. 1 (January 1977), p. 67.

2. Josef Hofmann invented mechanisms and modifications for, among other things, pianos and automobiles. There is no evidence that Glenn Gould possesses remarkable mechanical abilities. But see *Der Spiegel*, May 6, 1968, for a ridiculous assertion that Gould built an outboard motor.

3. *Glenn Gould: Off the Record* (film), National Film Board of Canada (1960).

4. Betty Lee, "The Odd, Restless Way of Glenn Gould," Toronto *Globe Magazine*, December 1, 1962, p. 11.

5. Glenn Gould, "Rubinstein," *Look*, March 9, 1971, p. 54.

6. Glenn Gould, "Stokowski: a Portrait for Radio" (broadcast), CBC (February 2, 1971).

7. Glenn Gould, "The Prospects of Recording," *High Fidelity Magazine* 16, no. 4 (April 1966), p. 49.

8. Broadcast, CBC (April 30, 1967).

9. An early version is quoted and discussed in Chapter 5.

10. "The Well-Tempered Listener" (telecast), CBC (March 22, 1970).

11. Glenn Gould, "Address to a Graduation," *Bulletin of the Royal Conservatory of Music of Toronto* (Christmas 1964), not paginated.

12. Broadcast, CBC (April 30, 1967).

13. These are Gould's words. He has used them in "An Epistle to the Parisians: Music and Technology, Part I," *Piano Quarterly*, no. 88 (Winter 1974-5), p. 7, and on several other occasions.

14. Broadcast, CBC (April 30, 1967).

15. Joseph Roddy, "Apollonian," *The New Yorker* 36, no. 13 (May 14, 1960), p. 52.

16. Gould, "The Prospects of Recording," pp. 52-3.

17. Gelatt, *The Fabulous Phonograph*, p. 52.

18. Ibid., p. 28.

19. A. Clutton-Brock, "The Psychology of the Gramophone," *Gramophone* 1, no. 9 (February 1924), p. 173. Half a century later Christopher Stone wrote: "Arthur Clutton Brock [sic] wrote his last article before his death for our magazine, and he pleaded with all the sensitiveness of his nature and the charm of his writing for the acceptance of the gramophone record as producing a new quality of music, a quality of fairy music, very lovely in its way, and with some advantages over the music of concert halls and drawing rooms which we had known all our lives." Christopher Stone, "Musicians and Mechanical Music," *The Gramophone Jubilee Book*, ed. R. Wimbush (Harrow, Middlesex: General Gramophone Publications, 1973), p. 81.

20. Gould, "The Prospects of Recording," p. 59.

21. Glenn Gould, "An Argument for Music in the Electronic Age," University of Toronto *Varsity Graduate* 11, no. 3 (December 1965), pp. 118-19.

22. *Glenn Gould: Concert Dropout* (disc), Columbia, BS 15 (1968). Gould often says that a concert is a poor substitute for a recording. Incidentally, John McClure was a producer at Columbia Records at the time of this interview.

23. Broadcast, CBC (April 30, 1967).

24. Ibid.

25. Donald Francis Tovey, *A Companion to "The Art of Fugue"* (London: Oxford University Press, 1931), p. 6.

26. Gould, "The Prospects of Recording," p. 51.

27. *Conversations with Glenn Gould: Bach* (film), BBC (1966).

28. Ibid.

29. *Glenn Gould: Concert Dropout*.

30. Paul Myers, "Glenn Gould," *Gramophone* 50, no. 597 (February 1973), p. 1,478.

Notes to Chapter 4

1. *Glenn Gould: Off the Record* (film), National Film Board of Canada (1960). These neighbours were a Mr. and Mrs. Doolittle, who lived in a cottage next to the Goulds'. Isabel Doolittle plays country dances on the violin.

2. Joseph Roddy, "Apollonian," *The New Yorker* 36, no. 13 (May 14, 1960), p. 69.

3. Anthony Storr, *The Dynamics of Creation* (London: Secker and Warburg, 1972), p. 57.

4. Joachim Kaiser, *Great Pianists of Our Time*, trans. David Wooldridge and George Unwin (London: George Allen & Unwin, 1971), pp. 18-19.

5. *Glenn Gould: Concert Dropout* (disc), Columbia, BS 15 (1968).

6. Alfred Bester, "The Zany Genius of Glenn Gould," *Holiday* 35, no. 4 (April 1964), p. 152.

7. Ibid., p. 156.

8. Glenn Gould, "Address to a Graduation," *Bulletin of the Royal Conservatory of Music of Toronto* (Christmas 1964), not paginated.

9. Bester, "Zany Genius," p. 156.

10. Glenn Gould, "His Country's 'Most Experienced Hermit' Chooses a Desert-Island Discography," *High Fidelity Magazine* 20, no. 6 (June 1970), pp. 29-32.

11. Glenn Gould, liner notes to *The Idea of North* (disc), CBC, PR-8 (1971).

12. ". . . are the absurdly competitive extravaganzas of our operatic colleagues not the product of, or, maybe, the antidote to, the vulgar artistic hostility of those sun-baked societies who have built an operatic tradition in which their primal instinct for gladiatorial combat has found a more gracious but thinly disguised sublimation?" Glenn Gould, "Let's Ban Applause!" *Musical America* 82, (February 1962), p. 11.

13. Glenn Gould, "Glenn Gould Interviews Glenn Gould about Glenn Gould," *High Fidelity Magazine* 24, no. 2 (February 1974), p. 77.

14. Richard Kostelanetz, *Master Minds* (New York: Macmillan, 1967), pp. 18-35 passim.

15. Bester, "Zany Genius," p. 156.

16. Glenn Gould, "The Age of Ecstasy" (telecast), CBC (February 20, 1974).

17. Immanuel Kant, *Critique of Judgment*, trans. J.H. Bernard (New York: Hafner Publishing Co., 1951), p. 116. Kant continues: "On the other hand, to fly from men from misanthropy, because we bear ill-will to them, or from anthropophoby (shyness), because we fear them as foes, is partly hateful, partly contemptible." I quote this because someone might protest its absence. I would have quoted it in the main text if I had thought it applicable to Gould.

18. Bester, "Zany Genius," p. 154.

19. I have used the year 1971 because it is the latest for which statistics are available dealing with both music festivals and the examination system of the Royal Conservatory.

20. Geoffrey Payzant, "The Competitive Music Festivals," *Canadian Music Journal* 4, no. 3 (Spring 1960), p. 36.

21. Statistics Canada, *Music Competition Festivals*, Catalogue 81-588 Occasional (Ottawa: Statistics Canada, 1973).

22. Glenn Gould, "We, Who Are About to Be Disqualified, Salute You!" *High Fidelity/Musical America* 16, no. 12 (December 1966), p. 23.

23. Ibid. These four paragraphs are selected from throughout the article.

24. Bernard Asbell, "Glenn Gould," *Horizon* 4, no. 3 (January 1962), p. 89.

25. Ibid., p. 90.

26. "The Scene" (broadcast), CBC (October 7, 1972).

27. Gould, "Glenn Gould Interviews Glenn Gould," p. 78.

28. Ibid.

29. *Glenn Gould on the Moog Synthesizer* (tape), CBC Learning Systems, catalogue no. 326L (1972).

30. Bernard Gavoty, *Arthur Rubinstein*, trans. F.E. Richardson (Geneva: René Kister, 1956), p. 22.

31. Ernst Bacon, *Notes on the Piano* (Seattle and London: University of Washington Press, 1968), p. 101.

32. A strong case can be made for the view that any innovation or any genuine invention occurs in the mind of a solitary person. But even the most brilliantly inventive musician must rely upon a large number of collaborators if his inventive performance or composition is to be heard. And these collaborators must compete for their jobs as singers, instrumentalists, audio technicians, producers, and the like. Very little "opting" is open to them.

33. Gould, "Let's Ban Applause," p. 11.

34. Karl H. Wörner, *Stockhausen: Life and Work*, trans. Bill Hopkins (London: Faber & Faber, 1973), p. 66.

35. Asbell, "Glenn Gould," p. 90.

36. Compare Igor Stravinsky, *Poetics of Music in the Form of Six Lessons*, trans. Arthur Knodel and Ingolf Dahl (New York: Vintage Books, 1947), p. 131.

37. Glenn Gould, "The record of the decade, according to a critic who should know, is Bach played on, of all things, a Moog synthesizer!," *Toronto Saturday Night* 83, no. 12 (December 1968), pp. 52, 54.

38. Jean Le Moyne, *Convergences*, trans. Philip Stratford (Toronto: Ryerson Press, 1966).

39. Ibid., p. 248. Also, "I have always been struck by Mozart's lightness, by his frivolity. His voluminous work contains an enormous quantity of prattle" (p. 249).

40. Pierre de Grandpré, *Histoire de la littérature francaise du Québec*, vol. 4 (Montreal: Beauchemin, 1967), p. 284.

41. Lewis Mumford, *Art and Technics* (New York: Columbia University Press, 1952), p. 6.

42. *Glenn Gould, Concert Dropout*.

43. Glenn Gould, "The Search for Petula Clark," *High Fidelity Magazine* 17, no. 11 (November 1968), p. 68.

44. Broadcast, CBC (July 15, 1969). There is no piano concerto by Louis-Moreau Gottschalk. But in 1963 Boosey & Hawkes (New York) published a version of Gottschalk's *Grand tarantelle* with solo piano part edited by Eugene List and the second piano part orchestrated by Hershy Kay. Perhaps Gould was thinking of this.

45. Ibid.

46. *Conversations with Glenn Gould: Beethoven* (film), BBC (1966).

47. Bester, "Zany Genius," p. 153.

48. Broadcast, CBC (July 15, 1969). "Let us have no concertos, in which this delicate instrument is dragged before the crowd and has to fight a duel with the orchestra. All beautiful compositions notwithstanding, the piano is no concerto-instrument." Oscar Bie, *A History of the Pianoforte and Pianoforte Players*, trans. E.E. Kellett and E.W. Naylor (London: J.A. Dent & Sons, 1899), p. 326.

Notes to Chapter 5

1. Peter F. Ostwald, *The Semiotics of Human Sound* (The Hague: Mouton, 1973), p. 72.

2. Joseph Roddy, "Apollonian," *The New Yorker* 36, no. 13 (May 14, 1960), p. 74.

3. Anthony Storr, *The Dynamics of Creation* (London: Secker & Warburg, 1972), p. 92.

4. Glenn Gould, "Anti Alea," included in Broadcast, CBC (July 22, 1969).

5. Broadcast, "Ideas" Series, CBC (November 23, 1966).

6. Storr, *The Dynamics of Creation*, p. 93.

7. Vincent Tovell, *At Home with Glenn Gould* (disc), Radio Canada Transcription E 156, CBC (1959).

8. Bernard Asbell, "Glenn Gould," *Horizon* 4, no. 3 (January 1962), p. 93.

9. Glenn Gould, "The Anatomy of Fugue" (broadcast), CBC (March 4, 1963). Gould also made a film version. It is described in *The New Yorker* 39, no. 42 (December 7, 1963), pp. 47-9.

10. Glenn Gould, "So You Want to Write a Fugue?" (New York: G. Schirmer, 1964), pp. 23-30.

11. Storr, *Dynamics*, p. 110.

12. Ibid., p. 97.

13. Roddy, "Apollonian," p. 82. Oscar Levant in his concert-giving days was much more ritualistic than Gould. Certain pieces could be played before others but not after; he always wore in concert a wristwatch given to him by George Gershwin; he always touched, before a concert, a pair of gloves given to him by a girl. Oscar Levant, *The Memoirs of an Amnesiac* (New York: G.P. Putnam's Sons, 1965), p. 17.

14. Asbell, "Glenn Gould," p. 91.

15. Artur Schnabel, *My Life and Music* (London: Longmans, Green and Co., 1961), p. 11.

16. Ibid., p. 25.

17. Ibid., p. 124.

18. Ibid., p. 26.

19. Artur Schnabel, *Music and the Line of Most Resistance* (New York: Da Capo Press, 1969), pp. 59-60.

20. Ibid., p. 19.

21. Ibid., pp. 19-20.

22. Ibid., p. 21.

23. Ibid., p. 22.

24. Ibid., p. 68.

25. Ibid., p. 63.

26. William Mason, *Memories of a Musical Life* (New York: Century Co., 1902), p. 116.

27. Schnabel, *Music and the Line*, pp. 75-6.

28. Roddy, "Apollonian," p. 64.

29. *Glenn Gould: Concert Dropout* (disc), Columbia, BS 15 (1968).

30. Broadcast, CBC (July 23, 1970).

31. Tovell, *At Home with Glenn Gould.*

32. Glenn Gould, liner notes to Columbia disc M 30825 (Byrd, Gibbons).

33. Glenn Gould, Introduction, *Bach's Well-Tempered Clavier* 1 (New York: Amsco Music Publishing Company, 1972), p. iii.

34. Ibid., p. vii.

35. Glenn Gould, liner notes to *Arnold Schoenberg* (disc), Columbia, MS 7098 (1970).

36. Asbell, "Glenn Gould," p. 91.

37. Joachim Kaiser, *Grosse Pianisten in unserer Zeit*, rev. ed. (Munich: R. Piper & Co., 1972), pp. 183-4.

38. Glenn Gould, "Address to a Graduation," *Bulletin of the Royal Conservatory of Music of Toronto* (Christmas 1964), no pagination.

Notes to Chapter 6

1. *The Oxford Dictionary of Quotations*, 2d ed. (London: Oxford University Press, 1953), p. 166.

2. In the Columbia disc *Glenn Gould: Concert Dropout*, the interviewer asks Gould about his singing while he plays—what function does it serve? Gould replies: "That's very difficult, and it's one of those centipedal questions — you know, Schoenberg once said that he would not willingly be asked by any of his composition students exactly why such-and-such a process served him well, because the question made him feel like that centipede who was asked in which order it moved its hundred legs, and afterwards he could move no legs at all — there's something impotent-making about that question. I'm rather afraid of it." *Glenn Gould: Concert Dropout* (disc), Columbia, BS 15 (1968).

3. Arthur Koestler, *The Act of Creation* (London: Hutchinson, 1964), p. 76.

4. Jonathan Cott, *Forever Young* (New York: Random House, 1977), pp. 37-8.

5. Ibid., p. 36.

6. Ibid., pp. 33-6; Bernard Asbell, "Glenn Gould," *Horizon* 4, no. 3 (January 1962), pp. 92-3; *Glenn Gould: Concert Dropout.*

7. Cott, *Forever Young*, p. 33.

8. Alfred Bester, "The Zany Genius of Glenn Gould," *Holiday* 35, no. 4 (April 1964), p. 153.

9. A. Hyatt King, *Mozart in Retrospect*, rev. ed. (London, Oxford University Press, 1970), p. 231; Reginald R. Gerig, *Famous Pianists and Their Technique* (Washington and New York: Robert B. Luce, 1974), pp. 83-4, 96, 207.

10. *Diapason*, 53, no. 6 (May 1962), p. 31.

11. Arnold Schultz, "Contest Standards — Are They Logical?" *Piano Teacher* 5, no. 5 (May-June 1963), p. 6.

12. Asbell, "Glenn Gould," p. 91.

13. Claude Debussy, *Monsieur Croche the Dilettante Hater*, in *Three Classics in the Aesthetics of Music* (New York: Dover Publications, 1962), p. 7.

14. Richard Kostelanetz, *Master Minds* (New York: Macmillan, 1967), p. 31.

15. See also *Life* 40, no. 11 (March 12, 1956), p. 107.

16. Vincent Tovell, *At Home with Glenn Gould* (disc), Radio Canada Transcription E-156, CBC (1959).

17. Glenn Gould, "An Argument for Richard Strauss," *High Fidelity Magazine* 12, no. 3 (March, 1962), p. 49.

18. *Atlantic Monthly* 210, no. 3 (September 1962) p. 114; *Library Journal* 87, no. 1 (October 1, 1962), p. 3, 430; *Hi Fi Stereo Review* 9, no. 3 (September 1962), p. 69; *High Fidelity Magazine* 12, no. 8 (August 1962), p. 73; *Audio* 47, no. 1 (January 1963), p. 48; *Gramophone* 40, no. 473 (October 1962), p. 200; *Records in Review*, 1972 ed. (Great Barrington, Mass.: Wyeth Press, 1972), p. 42. In a CBC broadcast (June 1963) John Beckwith said: "Gould's approach seems downright unmusical, and the image it evokes for me is of the trained seal who beeps out 'God save the Queen' on a set of car horns." *The American Organist* said that Biggs is better and so is Flentrop, disposing of Gould and Casavant with one stroke. *American Organist* 45, no. 9 (September 1962), pp. 21-2.

19. "At first his playing on the organ at All Saints' was 'just for fun,' but eventually he was persuaded to record a couple of works by Bach. So far this is all that has been done. But it won't stop there. 'I hope to do one recording session a year,' Mr. Gould said. 'That is all I have time for.' " *Stratford* (Ontario) *Beacon-Herald*, July 28, 1962. "I am also thinking of making a recording next year of Mendelssohn organ sonatas, which will be a shock to everybody. I adore Mendelssohn." Glenn Gould in *Asbell*, "Glenn Gould," p. 92.

20. Cott, *Forever Young*, p. 43.

21. This instrument was installed in 1937. It is described in William Harrison Barnes, *The Contemporary American Organ*, 5th ed. (New York: J. Fischer & Bro., 1952), pp. 252-3.

22. Sometimes the bass, or structurally lowest, voice in a fugue is silent or crosses above a higher voice. It continues to be the "real bass" even when such situations cause another voice (e.g., the tenor) to become temporarily the grammatical bass of the music. Structure is weakened when this temporary bass is given the sound peculiar to the real bass, as happens if the temporary bass line is played on organ pedals.

23. For a variety of views on the question of whether *The Art of the Fugue* is keyboard music or not, see: Jacques Chailley, *L'Art de la fugue de J.-S. Bach* (Paris: Alphonse Leduc, 1971), pp. 5-7; A.E.F. Dickinson, *Bach's Fugal Works* (London: Sir Isaac Pitman & Sons, 1956), pp. 116-7; Gustav M. Leonhardt, *The Art of Fugue* (The Hague: Martinus Nijhoff, 1952), pp. 7-34; Donald Francis Tovey, *A Companion to "The Art of Fugue"* (London: Oxford University Press, 1931), pp. 72-5.

24. Roland Gelatt, "Music Makers," *High Fidelity Magazine* 12, no. 13 (March 1962), p. 67.

25. "The actual size of the span of an octave in these older instruments was usually about 6-1/3 inches (16 cm.), hence somewhat small when compared with the roughly 6-1/2 inches (16.6 cm.) of the modern piano." Hans Neupert, *Harpsichord Manual*, 2d ed., trans. F.E. Kirby, (Kassel: Barenreiter, 1968), p. 22.

26. Cott, *Forever Young*, pp. 43-4.

27. Ibid., p. 51.

28. Ibid., pp. 43-4.

29. Gelatt, "Music Makers," p. 67.

30. John Beckwith, "Stratford," *Canadian Music Journal* 6, no. 1 (Autumn 1961), p. 23.

31. *Glenn Gould: Concert Dropout.*

32. Cott, *Forever Young*, p. 34.

33. Asbell, "Glenn Gould," p. 92.

34. *Glenn Gould: Concert Dropout.*

Notes to Chapter 7

1. Jock Carroll, " 'I don't think I'm at all eccentric,' says Glenn Gould," *Weekend Magazine* 6, no. 27 (July 7, 1956), p. 11.

2. *Glenn Gould: Concert Dropout* (disc), Columbia, BS 15 (1968).

3. Ibid.

4. Bernard Asbell, "Glenn Gould," *Horizon* 4, no. 3 (January 1962), p. 92.

5. "Assimilatability" is my coinage, but it is suggested by Gould in this quotation: ". . . certain action characteristics were just so unassimilatable in relation to the piano that was my standard and the basis of my judgment." *Glenn Gould: Concert Dropout.*

6. Strictly speaking, of course, not the harpsichord but the clavichord ranks highest in tactile grab and immediacy. But it is exclusively an intimate domestic instrument, relatively rare; and I am here concerned with instruments which are commonly before the public in concert and on disc, and on which Glenn Gould can be heard.

7. Michael Polanyi, *Personal Knowledge* (Chicago: University of Chicago Press, 1958), pp. 55-6.

8. Compare Polanyi's account here with Arthur Koestler's explanation of the centipede paradox in Chapter 6 above.

9. Polanyi, *Personal Knowledge*, p. 59.

10. For readers to whom all this is new and suspect, a helpful summary can be found in Robert Erickson, *Sound Structure in Music* (Berkeley: University of California Press, 1975), pp. 59-68.

11. I am here trying to keep the vocabulary simple and consistent. For instance, I use "loudness" for both loudness and intensity of sound, although in strict usage "loudness" is a property of an auditory percept and "intensity" is a property of an emission of acoustical energy. Also I speak of a hammer striking a string, although not all hammers strike only one string. And neither "timbre" nor "tone-quality" precisely covers what we are talking about here; yet "tone-quality" accords with the quotations presented in this chapter. I am not alone in having difficulties with the technical vocabulary of the physics and psychology of musical sound.

12. Robert Sabin, "Glenn Gould: a Poet and a Seeker," *American Record Guide* 30, no. 4 (December 1963), p. 292.

13. I know only one remark by Glenn Gould concerning "tone-colour." It appears in the film *Conversations with Glenn Gould: Beethoven*, BBC (1966). Here Gould clearly is talking not about tone-colour but about loudness, as is Sabin in the passage quoted (see Note 12 above).

14. Josef Lhevinne, *Basic Principles in Pianoforte Playing* (New York: Dover Publications, 1972), pp. 18-19.

15. Ibid., p. 14.

16. Julius G. Baron, "Physical Basis of Piano Touch," *Journal of the Acoustical Society of America* 30, no. 2 (February 1958), p. 151.

17. The word *consonant* (*con-sonant*) should be here taken in a composite sense including both "sounding with" and "sounding by means of."

Notes to Chapter 8

1. Jock Carroll, " 'I don't think I'm at all eccentric,' says Glenn Gould," Toronto *Weekend Magazine* 6, no. 27 (July 7, 1956), p. 10.

2. Vincent Tovell, *At Home with Glenn Gould* (disc), Radio Canada Transcription E-156, CBC (1959).

3. Luia Saiko, "Glenn Gould: Artist with a Mission," *Hamilton* (Ontario) *Spectator*, June 4, 1958.

4. See Chapter 4, Note 33.

5. Glenn Gould, "An Epistle to the Parisians: Music and Technology, Part I," *Piano Quarterly* 23, no. 88 (Winter 1974-5), p. 18.

6. Glenn Gould, "Glenn Gould interviews Glenn Gould about Glenn Gould," *High Fidelity Magazine* 24, no. 2 (February 1974), p. 77.

7. Glenn Gould, "The Grass is Always Greener in the Outtakes," *High Fidelity Magazine* 25, no. 8 (August 1975), p. 54.

8. *Glenn Gould: Concert Dropout* (disc), Columbia, BS 15 (1968).

9. Gould, "Epistle," p. 17.

10. The article "Epistle" by Gould originally appeared, in French, as the liner notes to CBS disc 76371 released in France in 1974. I do not know who translated Gould's English into French for this disc. It was not an enviable task. Gould says that if an actor were to record Hamlet's words as "To be or—like, uh—not to be," there could be no objection to

editing out the "like, uh" noises. In the French version, "like, uh" is rendered "euh, beeen."

11. Gould provides a helpful glossary in his article "Greener." The following definitions are quoted from p. 57.

Insert: A recorded performance usually designed to supplement a take; frequently of brief duration but, on occasion, extending throughout the major portion of a work and defined by the fact that it does not include the opening of said work.

Regeneration: the dubbing from one tape machine to another of material that appears with identical note values at two or more spots in a work; usually of brief duration but occasionally, if ill-advisedly, used for da capos, double-bar repeats, etc.

12. Gould, "Greener," p. 54, quoting Stephen Bishop.

13. Gould, "Epistle," p. 18.

14. Bernard Asbell, "Glenn Gould," *Horizon* 4, no. 3 (January 1962), p. 90. Note that the word "ideal" is used here in its colloquial sense of "the best possible."

15. Gould, "Greener," p. 55.

Notes to Chapter 9

1. Robert Hurwitz, "The Glenn Gould Contrapuntal Radio Show," *New York Times*, January 5, 1975. See also: Robert Lewis Shayon, "TV-Radio," *Saturday Review* 54, no. 7 (February 13, 1971), p. 43; Richard Kostelanetz, "Text-Sound Art: A Survey, Part II," *Performing Arts Journal* 2, no. 3 (Winter 1978), pp. 71-83.

2. "The Well-Tempered Listener" (telecast), CBC (March 22, 1970). Gould frequently uses the word "compote"; at one stage I considered using it instead of my own "com-position" for purposes of this chapter.

3. *Radio as Music* (film), CBC (1975).

4. *Glenn Gould: Concert Dropout* (disc), Columbia, BS 15 (1968).

5. Glenn Gould, liner notes to *The Idea of North* (disc), CBC, PR-8 (1971).

6. John Jessop, "Radio as Music: Glenn Gould in Conversation with John Jessop," *The Canada Music Book/Les Cahiers Canadiens de musique*, no. 2 (Spring-Summer, 1971), p. 17.

7. Glenn Gould, "Rubinstein," *Look*, March 9, 1971, p. 58.

8. *Radio as Music*.

9. Jessop, "Radio as Music," p. 13.

10. B.H. Haggin, *Music Observed* (New York: Oxford University Press, 1964), p. 216.

11. Joachim Kaiser, *Great Pianists of Our Time*, trans. David Wooldridge and George Unwin (London: George Allen & Unwin, 1971), pp. 147-8.

12. Harold C. Schonberg, *The Great Pianists* (New York: Simon and Schuster, 1963), p. 366.

13. Kaiser, *Great Pianists*, pp. 144-5.

14. *Canadian Composer*, March 1969, pp. 40-1.

15. Richard Kostelanetz, *Master Minds* (New York: Macmillan, 1967), p. 20.

16. *Radio as Music*.
17. Ibid.

Notes to Chapter 10

1. Paul Myers, "Glenn Gould," *Gramophone* 50, no. 597 (February 1973), p. 1,478.
2. B.H. Haggin, A *Decade of Music* (New York: Horizon Press, 1973), p. 216.
3. B.H. Haggin, "Music and Ballet Chronicle," *Hudson Review* 17, no. 3 (Autumn 1964), p. 440.
4. Ibid., p. 441.
5. B.H. Haggin, *Music Observed* (New York: Oxford University Press, 1964), p. 248.
6. B.H. Haggin, "Music and Ballet Chronicle," pp. 441-2.
7. Raymond Ericson, "Lecture Is Given by Glenn Gould," *New York Times*, February 1, 1964, p. 13. Gould gave the same lectures at the Gardner Museum in Boston on February 2 and March 8 of this same year. He was not panned in Boston.
8. Gould repeats his Hunter College remarks about Op. 109, with piano illustrations, in the film *Conversations with Glenn Gould: Beethoven*, BBC (1966).
9. Telecast, CBC (May 18, 1966).
10. Glenn Gould, *Arnold Schoenberg: A Perspective* (Cincinnati: University of Cincinnati, 1964), p. v.
11. *Music Journal* 23, no. 4 (April 1965), p. 83.
12. Abram Chasins, *Speaking of Pianists*, 2d ed. (New York: Alfred A. Knopf, 1961), pp. 300-1.
13. Glenn Gould, "Bodky on Bach," *Saturday Review* 43, no. 48. (November 26, 1960), pp. 48-50.
14. *Saturday Review* 43, no. 53 (December 31, 1960), pp. 47-8.
15. Alfred Einstein, *Mozart: His Character, His Work*, trans. Arthur Mendel and Nathan Broder (New York: Oxford University Press, 1965), pp. 157-163.
16. Donald Francis Tovey, *Essays in Musical Analysis* 1 (London: Oxford University Press, 1935), p. 8.
17. Glenn Gould, liner notes to Columbia discs M 32110046 and M 32110045, Anhalt *et al*. Gould said of Fantasy No. 1 by Oskar Morawetz: "I think it's one of the very finest things of its genre . . . there's a lot of Prokoviev in this piece . . . but this, I think is better than anything Prokoviev ever wrote for piano. . . ." Tovell, *At Home with Glenn Gould* (disc) Radio Canada Transcription E-156, CBC (1959).
18. Broadcast, CBC (July 18, 1972).
19. Glenn Gould, liner notes to *Grieg and Bizet* (disc), Columbia M 32040.
20. Joachim Kaiser, *Grosse pianisten in unserer Zeit*, rev. ed. (Munich: R. Piper & Co., 1972), p. 183.

Bibliography

This bibliography includes articles by Glenn Gould that have appeared in various periodicals. It does not include scripts for radio, television, film, or disc, or his program notes or liner notes. The items are listed chronologically by year of publication.

"The Dodecaphonists' Dilemma." *Canadian Music Journal* 1 (Autumn 1956), pp. 20-29.

"Bodky on Bach." *Saturday Review* 43 (November 26, 1960), pp. 48, 55.

"Let's Ban Applause!" *Musical America* 82 (February 1962), pp. 10-11, 38-9.

"An Argument for Richard Strauss." *High Fidelity Magazine* 12 (March 1962), pp. 46-9, 110-11.

Arnold Schoenberg: A Perspective. Cincinnati: University of Cincinnati, 1964.

"Strauss and the Electronic Future." *Saturday Review* 47 (May 30, 1964), pp. 58-9, 72.

"Address to a Graduation." *Bulletin of the Royal Conservatory of Music of Toronto* (Christmas 1964), not paginated.

"An Argument for Music in the Electronic Age." University of Toronto *Varsity Graduate* 11 (December 1964), pp. 26-7, 114-27.

"Dialogue on the Prospects of Recordings." University of Toronto *Varsity Graduate* 11 (April 1965), pp. 50-62.

"The Ives Fourth." *High Fidelity/Musical America* 15 (July 1965), pp. 96-7.

"The Prospects of Recording." *High Fidelity Magazine* 16 (April 1966), pp. 46-63.

"Yehudi Menuhin: Musician of the Year." *High Fidelity/Musical America* 16 (December 1966), pp. 7-9.

"We, Who Are About to be Disqualified, Salute You!" *High Fidelity/Musical America* 16 (December 1966), pp. MA-23-24, 30.

"The Search for Petula Clark." *High Fidelity/Musical America* 17 (November 1967), pp. 67-71.

"The record of the decade, according to a critic who should know, is Bach played on, of all things, a Moog Synthesizer?" *Saturday Night* 83 (December 1968), pp. 52, 54.

" 'Oh, for Heaven's Sake, Cynthia, There Must Be Something Else On'!" *High Fidelity/Musical America* 19 (April 1969), pp. MA-13.

"Should We Dig Up the Rare Romantics? No. They're Only a Fad." *New York Times*, November 23, 1969.

"His Country's 'Most Experienced Hermit' Chooses a Desert-Island Discography." *High Fidelity Magazine* 20 (June 1970), pp. 29, 32.

"Admit It, Mr. Gould, You Do Have Doubts about Beethoven." Toronto *Globe and Mail Magazine* (June 6, 1970), pp. 6-9.

"Liszt's Lament? Beethoven's Bagatelle? Or Rosemary's Babies?" *High Fidelity Magazine* 20 (December 1970), pp. 87-90.

"Rubinstein." *Look* (March 9, 1971), pp. 53-58.

"Gould Quizzed." *American Guild of Organists and Royal Canadian College of Organists Magazine* (November 1971), pp. 31-2.

Introduction, *Bach's Well-Tempered Clavier* 1. New York: Amsco Music Publishing Company, 1972.

"Glenn Gould Interviews Himself about Beethoven." *Piano Quarterly* 21 (Fall 1972), pp. 2-5.

"Hindemith: Kommt seine Zeit (wieder)?" Trans. Peter Mueller, *Hindemith-Jahrbuch* 1973/III, pp. 131-136.

"Data Bank on the Upward Scuttling Mahler." Toronto *Globe and Mail*, November 10, 1973.

"Glenn Gould Interviews Glenn Gould about Glenn Gould." *High Fidelity Magazine* 24 (February 1974), pp. 72-8.

"Data Bank on the Upward Scuttling Mahler." *Piano Quarterly* 22 (Spring 1974), pp. 19-21.

"Today, Simply Politics and Prejudices in Musical America Circa 1970 . . . but for Time Capsule Scholars It's Babbit vs. Flat Foot Floozie." Toronto *Globe and Mail*, July 20, 1974.

"Conference at Port Chilkoot." *Piano Quarterly* 22 (Summer 1974), pp. 25-8.

"The Future and Flat-Foot Floogie." *Piano Quarterly* 22 (Fall 1974), pp. 11, 12, 14.

"An Epistle to the Parisians: Music and Technology, Part 1." *Piano Quarterly* 23 (Winter 1974-5), pp. 17-19.

"Glenn Gould Talks Back." *Toronto Star*, February 15, 1975.

"Krenek, the Prolific, Is Probably Best Known to the Public at Large as—Ernst Who?" Toronto *Globe and Mail*, July 19, 1975.

"The Grass Is Always Greener in the Outtakes." *High Fidelity Magazine* 25 (August 1975), pp. 54-9.

"A Festschrift for 'Ernst Who'???" *Piano Quarterly* 24 (Winter 1975-6), pp. 16-18.

"Streisand as Schwarzkopf." *High Fidelity Magazine* 26 (May 1976), pp. 73-75.

"Bach to Bach (and Belly to Belly)." Toronto *Globe and Mail*, May 29, 1976.

"Fact, Fancy or Psycho-history: Notes from the P.D.Q. Underground." *Piano Quarterly* 24 (Summer 1976), pp. 40-43.

"On Mozart and Related Matters: A Conversation with Bruno Monsaingeon." *Piano Quarterly* 24 (Fall 1976), pp. 12-19.

"Boulez by Joan Peyser." *The New Republic* 175, no. 26 (December 25, 1976), pp. 23-25.

"Portrait of a Cantankerous Composer," *The Globe and Mail*, March 18, 1978.

Articles under the Pseudonym Dr. Herbert von Hochmeister

"The CBC, Camera-Wise." *High Fidelity/Musical America* 15 (March, 1965), pp. 86P-87P.

"Of Time and Time Beaters." *High Fidelity/Musical America* 15 (August, 1965), pp. 136-7.

"L'Esprit de jeunesse, et de corps, et d'art." *High Fidelity/Musical America* 15 (December, 1965), pp. 188-90.

Published Compositions

Cadenzas to the Concerto No. 1 in C Major for Piano and Orchestra by Beethoven, Op. 15 (Great Neck, New York: Barger & Barclay, 1958).

"So You Want to Write a Fugue?" For four-part chorus of mixed voices with piano or string quartet accompaniment (New York: G. Schirmer, 1964).

String Quartet, Op. 1 (Great Neck, New York: Barger & Barclay, 1956).

Filmography

Conversations with Glenn Gould, BBC (1966). In English. Four films, black and white, each 40 min.: 1. *Bach*, 2. *Beethoven*, 3. *Schoenberg*, 4. *Strauss*.

Glenn Gould, National Film Board of Canada (1960). In English. Two films, black and white, each 30 min.: 1. *Off the Record*, 2. *On the Record*. (Documentary profile of Gould.)

Glenn Gould, National Film Board of Canada (1960). In French. Black and white, 22 min. 45 sec. (Documentary profile of Gould.)

Slaughterhouse Five, Universal Pictures (1972). Directed by George Roy Hill. In English. Colour, 104 min. (Music performed, arranged, and some of it composed by Gould.)

Spheres, National Film Board of Canada (1969). By Norman McLaren and Rene Jodoin. Colour, 7 min. 28 sec. (Animation, with music of Bach played by Gould on the piano.)

The Terminal Man, Warner Brothers (1974). Directed by Michael Hodges. In English. Colour, 104 min. (The music consists of Gould playing the *Goldberg Variations*.)

Discography

All titles listed are on 33-1/3 rpm phonodiscs. All record releases are Columbia Records unless otherwise indicated. In Columbia releases of certain periods, the letter prefix "MS" indicates stereo, and "ML" indicates mono.

All items are listed by composers alphabetically; works by one composer are listed alphabetically by title in English. Sometimes there are variants in the title of the same work as printed on different recordings. Examples: Berg, Sonata Opus 1 and Berg, Sonata; Morawetz, Fantaisie and Morawetz, Fantasy in D Minor. The titles as given on the recordings in question have been used here.

The year of recording (in boldface type) is followed by the year of release (in roman text type). Year of release applies to the first release in North America only. Releases elsewhere, and re-releases in North America, are not included. In many Gould discs the material has been recorded at different times, months or even years apart. The year of recording, as given in this Discography, merely indicates that in the year mentioned Gould included among his activities the recording of part or the whole of the work listed.

Bach's *The Well-Tempered Clavier* Volumes I and II are listed as WTC-I and WTC-II respectively.

The short form "trans." indicates transcribed.

Musical performances by Gould are on piano except J.S. Bach, *The Art of the Fugue*, Fugues 1-9 (organ) and G.F. Handel, Suites 1-4 (harpsichord).

Musical Performances by Gould

ANHALT, I.
Fantasia for Piano. Columbia Masterworks 32110046 (stereo), 32110045 (mono) (**1967**, 1967).

BACH, J.S.
Art of the Fugue, Fugues 1-9. MS 6338, ML 5738 (**1962**, 1962).

Concerto No. 1 in D Minor. Columbia Symphony, Bernstein. ML 5211 (**1957**, 1957).

Concerto No. 2 in E Major. Columbia Symphony, Golschmann. MS 7294 (**1969**, 1969).

Concerto No. 3 in D Major. Columbia Symphony, Golschmann. MS 7001, ML 6401 (**1967**, 1967).

Concerto No. 4 in A Major. Columbia Symphony, Golschmann. MS 7294 (**1969**, 1969).

Concerto No. 5 in F Minor. Columbia Symphony, Golschmann. MS 6017, ML 5298 (**1958**, 1958).

Concerto No. 7 in G Minor. Columbia Symphony, Golschmann. MS 7001, ML 6401 (**1967**, 1967).

English Suites 1-6. M2 34578 (**1971, 1973-6**, 1977).

French Suites 1-4. M 32347 (**1972-3**, 1973).

French Suites 5, 6. M 32853 (**1971, 1973**, 1974).

Fugue in E Major from WTC-II. ML 5186 (**1957**, 1957).

Fugue in F-sharp Minor from WTC-II. ML 5186 (**1957**, 1957).

Goldberg Variations. ML 5060 (**1955**, 1956).

Inventions and Sinfonias. MS 6622, ML 6022 (**1963-4**, 1964).

Italian Concerto. MS 6141, ML 5472 (**1959**, 1960).

Overture in the French Style. M 32853 (**1973**, 1974).

Partitas Nos. 1, 2. MS 6141, ML 5472 (**1959**, 1960).

Partitas Nos. 3, 4. MS 6498, ML 5898 (**1962-3**, 1963).

Partita No. 5. CBC International Service Program 120 (**1954**, 1954).

Partitas Nos. 5, 6. ML 5186 (**1957**, 1957).

Sinfonias. (See Inventions and Sinfonias.)

Sonatas (three) for Viola da Gamba and Harpsichord. Leonard Rose, cello. M 32934 (**1973-4**, 1974).

Sonatas (six) for Violin and Harpsichord. Jaime Laredo, violin. M2 34226 (**1975-6**, 1976).

Toccata No. 7 in E Minor. MS 6498, ML 5898 (**1963**, 1963).

WTC-I, Preludes and Fugues 1-8. MS 6408, ML 5808 (**1962**, 1963).

WTC-I Preludes and Fugues 9-16. MS 6538, ML 5938 (**1963**, 1964).

WTC-I, Preludes and Fugues 17-24. MS 6776, ML 6176 (**1965**, 1965).

WTC-II, Preludes and Fugues 1-8. MS 7099 (**1966-7**, 1968).

WTC-II, Preludes and Fugues 9-16. MS 7409 (**1969**, 1970).

WTC-II, Preludes and Fugues 17-24. M 30537 (**1971**, 1971).

BEETHOVEN, L. v.
Bagatelles, Op. 33, Op. 126. M 33265 (**1974**, 1975).

Concerto No. 1 in C Major. Columbia Symphony, Golschmann. MS 6017, ML 5298 (**1958**, 1958).

Concerto No. 2 in B-flat Major. Columbia Symphony, Bernstein. ML 5211 (**1957**, 1957).

Concerto No. 3 in C Minor. Columbia Symphony, Bernstein. MS 6096, ML 5418 (**1959**, 1960).

Concerto No. 4 in C Major. New York Philharmonic, Bernstein. MS 6262, ML 5662 (**1961**, 1961).

Concerto No. 5 in E-flat Major. American Symphony, Stokowski. MS 6888, ML 6288 (**1966**, 1966).

Sonata No. 5 in C Minor, Op. 10, No. 1. MS 6686, ML 6086 (**1964**, 1965).

Sonata No. 6 in F Major, Op. 10, No. 2. MS 6686, ML 6086 (**1964**, 1965).

Sonata No. 7 in D Minor, Op. 10, No. 3. MS 6686, ML 6086 (**1964**, 1965).

Sonata No. 8 in C Minor, Op. 13 (*Pathétique*). MS 6945, ML 6345 (**1966**, 1967).

Sonata No. 9 in E Major, Op. 14, No. 1. MS 6945, ML 6345 (**1966**, 1967).

Sonata No. 10 in G Major, Op. 14, No. 2. MS 6945, ML 6345 (**1966**, 1967).

Sonata No. 14 in C-sharp Minor, Op. 27, No. 2 (*Moonlight*). MS 7413. (**1967**, 1970).

Sonata No. 16 in G Major, Op. 31, No. 1. M 32349 (**1971, 1973**, 1973).

Sonata No. 17 in D Minor, Op. 31, No. 2 (*Tempest*). M 32349 (**1967, 1971**, 1973).

Sonata No. 18 in E-flat Major, Op. 31, No. 3. M 32349 (**1967**, 1973).

Sonata No. 23 in F Minor, Op. 57 (*Appassionata*). MS 7413 (**1967**, 1970).

Sonata No. 30 in E Major, Op. 109. ML 5130 (**1956**, 1956).

Sonata No. 31 in A-flat Major, Op. 110. ML 5130 (**1956**, 1956).

Sonata No. 32 in C Minor, Op. 111. ML 5130 (**1956**, 1956).

Symphony No. 5 in C Minor, trans. Liszt. MS 7095 (**1967-8**, 1968).

Thirty-two Variations in C Minor. M 30080 (**1966**, 1970).

Variations in E-flat Major, Op. 35. M 30080 (**1967, 1970**, 1970).

Variations in F Major, Op. 34. M 30080 (**1967**, 1970).

BERG, A.
Sonata Opus 1. Hallmark RS 3 (**1953**, 1953).
Sonata. ML 5336 (**1958**, 1959).

BIZET, G.
Premier Nocturne. M 32040 (**1972**, 1973).

Variations Chromatiques. M 32040 (**1971**, 1973).

BRAHMS, J.
Intermezzos (ten). MS 6237, ML 5637 (**1960**, 1961).
Quintet in F Minor. Montreal String Quartet. CBC Transcription Service Program 140 (**1957**, 1957).

BYRD, W.
First Pavan and Galliard (**1967**), Sixth Pavan and Galliard (**1967**), A Voluntary (**1967**), Hughe Ashton's Ground (**1971**), Sellinger's Round (**1971**). M 30825 (1971).

GIBBONS, O.
Allemande, or Italian Ground (**1968**), Fantasy in C (**1968**), Salisbury Pavan and Galliard (**1969**). M 30825 (1971).

GOULD, G.
"So You Want to Write a Fugue?". GG-101. Quartet of voices with string quartet accompaniment. (**1963**, 1964).

String Quartet, Op. 1. Montreal String Quartet. CBC International Service Program No. 142. (**1956**).

String Quartet, Op. 1. Symphonia Quartet. MS 6178, ML 5578 (**1960**, 1960).

GRIEG, E.
Sonata No. 7 in E Minor. M 32040 (**1971**, 1973).

HANDEL, G.F.
Suites 1-4. M 31512. (**1972**, 1972).

HAYDN, J.
Sonata No. 3 in E-flat Major (1789-90). ML 5274 (**1958**, 1958).

HETU, J.
Variations for Piano. Columbia Masterworks 32110046 (stereo), 32110045 (mono) (**1967**, 1967).

HINDEMITH, P.
Piano Sonatas (three). M 32350 (**1966-7, 1973**, 1973).

Sonatas (four) for Brass and Piano. Various soloists. M2 33971 (**1975-6**, 1976).

KRENEK, E.
Sonata No. 3. ML 5336 (**1958**, 1959).

MORAWETZ, O.

Fantaisie. CBC International Service Program 120 (**1954**, 1969).

Fantasy in D Minor. Columbia Masterworks 32110046 (stereo), 32110045 (mono) (**1966**, 1967).

MOZART, W.A.

Concerto No. 24 in C Minor, K.491. CBC Symphony, Susskind. Columbia MS 6339, ML 5739 (**1961**, 1962).

Fantasia in C Minor, K.475. (See Fantasia and Sonata in C Minor, K.475/457.)

Fantasia in D Minor, K.397. M 32348 (**1972**, 1973).

Fantasia and Fugue in C Major, K.394. ML 5274 (**1958**, 1958).

Fantasia and Sonata (No. 14) in C Minor, K.475/457. M 33515 (K.475, **1966-7**; K.457, **1973-4**; 1975).

Sonata No. 1 in C Major, K.279. MS 7097 (**1967**, 1968).

Sonata No. 2 in F Major, K.280. MS 7097 (**1967**, 1968).

Sonata No. 3 in B-flat Major, K.281. MS 7097 (**1967**, 1968).

Sonata No. 4 in E-flat Major, K.282. MS 7097 (**1967**, 1968).

Sonata No. 5 in G Major, K.283. MS 7097 (**1967**, 1968).

Sonata No. 6 in D Major, K.284. MS 7274 (**1968**, 1969).

Sonata No. 7 in C Major, K.309. MS 7274 (**1968**, 1969).

Sonata No. 8 in A Major, K.310. M 31073 (**1969**, 1972).

Sonata No. 9 in D Major, K.311. MS 7274 (**1968**, 1969).

Sonata No. 10 in C Major, K.330. ML 5274 (**1958**, 1958).

Sonata No. 10 in C Major, K.330. M 31073 (**1970**, 1972).

Sonata No. 11 in A Major, K.331. M 32348 (**1965, 1970**, 1973).

Sonata No. 12 in F Major, K.332. M 31073 (**1965-6**, 1972).

Sonata No. 13 in B-flat Major, K.333. M 31073 (**1970**, 1972).

Sonata No. 14 in C Minor, K.457. (See Fantasia and Sonata in C Minor, K.475/457.).

Sonata No. 15 in C Major, K.545. M 32348 (**1967**, 1973).

Sonata No. 16 in B-flat Major, K.570. M 33515 (**1974**, 1975).

Sonata No. 17 in D Major, K.576. M 33515 (**1974**, 1975).

Sonata in F Major with Rondo, K.533/K.494. M 32348 (**1972-3**, 1973).

PROKOVIEV, S.

Sonata No. 7 in B-flat Major, Op. 83. MS 7173 (**1967**, 1969).

"The Winter Fairy" (from *Cinderella*), trans. M. Fichtengoltz. Albert Pratz, violin. Hallmark RS-3. (**1953**, 1953).

SCHOENBERG, A.
Fantasy for Violin and Piano, Op. 47. Israel Baker, violin. MS 7036, ML 6436 (**1964**, 1967).

Five Piano Pieces, Op. 23. MS 6817, ML 6217 (**1965**, 1966).

Ode to Napoleon Buonaparte, Op. 41. Juilliard Quartet; John Horton, speaker. MS 7037, ML 6437 (**1965**, 1967).

Piano Concerto, Op. 42. CBC Symphony, Craft. MS 6339, ML 5739 (**1961**, 1962).

Piano Pieces, Op. 33 a/b. MS 6817, ML 6217 (**1965**, 1966).

Six Little Piano Pieces, Op. 19. MS 6817, ML 6217. (**1964-5**, 1966).

Songs, Op. 1, 2, 15. Donald Gramm, bass-baritone; Ellen Faull, soprano; Helen Vanni, mezzo-soprano. MS 6816, ML 6216 (**1964-5**, 1966).

Songs, Op. 3, 6, 12, 14, 48, Op. Posth. Donald Gramm, bass-baritone; Cornelis Opthof, baritone; Helen Vanni, mezzo-soprano. M 31312 (**1964-5, 1968, 1970-1**, 1972).

Suite for Piano, Op. 25. MS 6817, ML 6217 (**1964**, 1966).

Three Piano Pieces, Op. 11. ML 5336 (**1958**, 1959).

SCHUMANN, R.
Quartet in E-flat Major for Piano and Strings. Juilliard Quartet. MS 7325 (**1968**, 1969).

SCRIABIN, A.
Sonata No. 3. MS 7173 (**1968**, 1969).

SHOSTAKOVITCH, D.
Three Fantastic Dances, trans. H. Glickman. Albert Pratz, violin. Hallmark RS-3 (**1953**, 1953).

SIBELIUS, J.
Three Sonatinas, Op. 67; *Kyllikki*, Three Lyric Pieces for Piano, Op. 41. M 34555 (**1977**, 1977; mixed 1977).

STRAUSS, R.
Enoch Arden. Claude Rains, speaker. MS 6341, ML 5741. (**1961**, 1962).

TANEIEFF, S.
"The Birth of the Harp," trans. A. Hartmann. Albert Pratz, violin. Hallmark RS-3 (**1953**, 1953).

WAGNER, R.
Three transcriptions by Gould: *Die Meistersinger*, "Prelude"; "Dawn and Siegfried's Rhine Journey" from *Die Götterdämmerung*; *Siegfried Idyll*. M 32351 (**1973**, 1973).

Recorded Interviews with Gould

At Home with Glenn Gould. Interview with Vincent Tovell. Radio Canada Transcription E-156, CBC (**1959**, 1959).

Glenn Gould: Concert Dropout. Interview with John McClure. BS-15 (**1968**, bonus disc released 1968 with MS 7095).

Radio Documentaries by Gould

The Idea of North. CBC Publications Disc PR-8 (**1967-8**, 1971).

The Latecomers. CBC Publications Disc PR-9 (**1968-9**, 1971).

Glenn Gould on the Moog Synthesizer (recorded 1968). Reel or cassette only. CBC Learning Systems Catalogue No. 326L (released 1972).

Acknowledgements

Grateful acknowledgement is made to the following for permission to use the copyrighted material indicated below. Every reasonable care has been taken to correctly acknowledge copyright ownership. The author and publisher would welcome information that will enable them to rectify any errors or omissions in succeeding printings.

AMERICAN HERITAGE: for excerpts from Bernard Asbell, "Glenn Gould," ©1962 American Heritage Publishing Co., Inc. Reprinted by permission from *Horizon* Magazine (January 1962).

GEORGE BRAZILLER, INC. and NED ROREM: for excerpt from Ned Rorem, *Music and People*.

BRITISH BROADCASTING CORPORATION and HUMPHREY BURTON: for excerpts from "Conversations with Glenn Gould."

THE CANADA MUSIC BOOK/LES CAHIERS CANADIENS DE MUSIQUE and JOHN JESSOP: for excerpts from John Jessop, "Radio as Music," *The Canadian Music Book/Les Cahiers Canadiens de musique* (Spring-Summer 1971).

CANADIAN BROADCASTING CORPORATION: for a variety of items as indicated in the Notes.

CBS RECORDS: for a variety of items as indicated in the Notes.

ENCYCLOPEDIA OF MUSIC IN CANADA: for Discography and Filmography.

ROBERT FULFORD: for excerpt from Robert Fulford, "Beach Boy," *The Toronto Book*, ed. William Kilbourn (Toronto: Macmillan Company of Canada, 1976).

ROLAND GELATT and MACMILLAN PUBLISHING COMPANY: for excerpts from Roland Gelatt, *The Fabulous Phonograph, 1877-1977*. Copyright © 1954, 1955, 1965, 1977 by Roland Gelatt.

GENERAL GRAMOPHONE PUBLICATIONS LIMITED: for excerpts from Christopher Stone, "Musicians and Mechanical Music," *The Gramophone Jubilee Year Book*; A. Clutton-Brock, "The Psychology of the Gramophone," *The Gramophone* 1 (February 1924); Paul Myers, "Glenn Gould," *The Gramophone* 50 (February 1973).

GLOBE AND MAIL, TORONTO: for excerpts from a February 17, 1944 article, and articles by Allen Sangster (May 10, 1946), Pearl McCarthy (January 15, 1947), Colin Sabiston (October 21, 1947). Also for an excerpt from

Betty Lee, "The Odd, Restless Way of Glenn Gould," *Globe Magazine* (December 1, 1962).

B.H. HAGGIN: for excerpts from B.H. Haggin, *The Hudson Review*, Autumn 1964, copyright 1964 by B.H. Haggin; *Music Observed*, Oxford University Press, 1964, reissued as *35 Years of Music* by Horizon Press, 1974, copyright 1964, 1974 by the author; *A Decade of Music*, Horizon Press, 1973, copyright by the author.

HIGH FIDELITY/MUSICAL AMERICA: for excerpts from Glenn Gould, "Let's Ban Applause," *Musical America* (February 1962); "The Prospects of Recording," *High Fidelity* (April 1966); "We Who Are About to Be Disqualified, Salute You," *Musical America* (December 1966); "Yehudi Menuhin: Musician of the Year," *Musical America* (December 1966); "The Search for Petula Clark," *High Fidelity* (November 1968); "His Country's 'Most Experienced Hermit' Chooses a Desert-Island Discography," *High Fidelity* (June 1970); "Glenn Gould Interviews Glenn Gould about Glenn Gould," *High Fidelity* (August 1975). Also for excerpts from Roland Gelatt, "Music Makers," *High Fidelity* (March 1962) and Leonard Marcus, "Recordings before Edison," *High Fidelity* (January 1977).

ARTHUR KOESTLER and MACMILLAN PUBLISHING COMPANY: for excerpts from Arthur Koestler, *The Act of Creation*. Copyright © Arthur Koestler 1964, 1969.

RICHARD KOSTELANETZ and MACMILLAN PUBLISHING COMPANY: for excerpts from Richard Kostelanetz, *Master Minds*. Copyright © 1967 by Richard Kostelanetz.

YEHUDI MENUHIN: for excerpt from Yehudi Menuhin, *Unfinished Journey* (London: Macdonald and Janes, 1976).

JEAN LE MOYNE: for excerpts from a CBC interview.

LEWIS MUMFORD: for excerpt from Lewis Mumford, *Art and Technics* (New York: Columbia University Press, 1952).

NATIONAL FILM BOARD OF CANADA: for excerpts from *Glenn Gould: On the Record* and *Glenn Gould: Off the Record*.

THE NEW YORK TIMES: for excerpts from articles by John Briggs (January 12, 1955), Raymond Erickson (February 1, 1964) and Robert Hurwitz (January 5, 1975). © 1955/64/75 by The New York Times Company. Reprinted by permission.

HAROLD RUTLAND and NOVELLO AND COMPANY LIMITED: for excerpt from Harold Rutland, "Impressions of Glenn Gould," *Musical Times* (July 1959).

THE PIANO QUARTERLY: for excerpts from Glenn Gould, "An Epistle to the Parisians," *The Piano Quarterly* (Winter 1974-5).

PRINCETON UNIVERSITY PRESS: for excerpts from Artur Schnabel, *Music and the Line of Most Resistance*, copyright 1942 by Princeton University Press. Reprinted by permission of Princeton University Press.

RANDOM HOUSE, INC.: for excerpt from Jonathan Cott, *Forever Young*. Copyright © 1974 by Straight Arrow Press, Inc. Copyright © 1977 by Rolling Stone Press. Reprinted from *Forever Young*, by Jonathan Cott, by permission of Random House, Inc.

SATURDAY REVIEW: for excerpts from Glenn Gould, "Bodky on Bach," *Saturday Review* (November 26, 1960); "Strauss and the Electronic Future," *Saturday Review* (May 30, 1964).

COLIN SMYTHE LIMITED, BUCKINGHAMSHIRE, ENGLAND and ST. MARTIN'S PRESS INC., NEW YORK: for excerpts from Artur Schnabel, *My Life and Music*.

ANTHONY STORR and MARTIN SECKER & WARBURG: for excerpts from Anthony Storr, *The Dynamics of Creation*. Copyright © 1972 by Anthony Storr. Reprinted by permission of A.D. Peters & Co. Ltd.

SUMMY-BIRCHARD COMPANY: for excerpt from an article by John Briggs, *Musical Courier* (February 1955).

THE TORONTO STAR: for excerpts from articles by Augustus Bridle (February 17, 1944; May 9, 1946; January 15, 1947; October 21, 1947) and Dennis Braithwaite (March 28, 1959). Reprinted with permission — The Toronto Star.

THE TORONTO SUN SYNDICATE: for excerpts from articles by Edward W. Wodson, *The Telegram* (December 13, 1945; March 9, 1946; January 15, 1947; October 21, 1947). Courtesy of: The Toronto Sun Syndicate re: The Telegram.

TRAVEL/HOLIDAY MAGAZINE: for excerpts from Alfred Bester, "The Zany Genius of Glenn Gould," *Holiday* (April 1964). Reproduced with permission from *Travel/Holiday* Magazine, Floral Park, New York.

THE UNIVERSITY OF CHICAGO PRESS: for excerpts from Michael Polanyi, *Personal Knowledge*, © Copyright 1958 and 1962 by Michael Polanyi.

UNIVERSITY OF CINCINNATI: for excerpt from Glenn Gould, "Arnold Schoenberg: A Perspective," *University of Cincinnati Occasional Papers No. 3* (1964).

THE VARSITY GRADUATE: for excerpt from Glenn Gould, "An Argument for Music in the Electronic Age," University of Toronto *Varsity Graduate* (December 1964).

THE WASHINGTON POST: for excerpts from a review by Paul Hume (January 3, 1955).

Index

152; and the New Composer, 27; and the New Listener, 26, 29-32; and the New Performer, 26-27; New York debut of, 14; on non-repetitiveness of musical performance, 59, 67-68; and "non-take-twoness," 28, 75; and the North, 54-56; orchestral debut of, 9, 150; as organist, 3-4, 8, 45, 95-101, 112-113; philosophy of recording of, 34-50, 98, 101, 119, 124-126, 128, 129; as polyphonist, 135-136, 138; and psycho-analysis, 73-75, 75n; as recording artist, 14-16, 33-35, 47-50; and recording technology, 20, 35-37, 121-124; romanticism of, 62; Schnabel's influence on, 6, 9, 77-81; on Schoenberg, 44-45, 83, 142, 143; and sense of tactilia, 94, 102-104, 107; singing of, 5, 81, 89; and solitude, 5, 12, 51-57, 64, 66, 119; solo recital debut of, 11; Soviet Union tour of, 17; and Steinway CD 318, 104-108, 113; on Stokowski, 7, 34; on Strauss, 97; String Quartet, 16-17; on Switched-on Bach, 29, 69; and tactile immediacy, 109-110; and tape editing, 39, 124-127, 133; on teaching, 53; on technology as mediator, 56, 61, 69-71, 122; and the Tel Aviv piano, 93-94; and tone-quality, 109, 117-118; as transcriber, 85-87; vacuum cleaner anecdote of, 35-36, 87-88, 91; on Wagner, 87-88; on The Well-Tempered Clavier, 83-84; as writer, 35, 140-141, 142-144. Performances: Bach's The Art of the Fugue, 17, 19; Bach's Concerto in D Minor, 17; Bach's Partita No. 4 in D Major, 19; Bach's Partita No. 5 in G Major, 13, 24; Bach's Three-part Inventions (Sinfonias), 13, 17; Beethoven's Concerto No. 2, 17; Beethoven's Concerto No. 3, 17; Beethoven's Concerto No. 4, 10, 16, 18; Beethoven's Sonata, Opus 109, 13, 17, 90; Beethoven's Sonata, Opus 110, 19; Berg's Sonata, 13, 17; Brahms' Concerto in D Minor, 72; Chopin's Sonata No. 3 in B Minor, Opus 58, 82n; Krenek's Third Sonata, 19; Mahler's Second Symphony, 17; Scarlatti, 11; Sweelinck, 13; Webern's Variations, Opus 27, 13. Radio Broadcasts: "The Idea of North," 128, 129, 131-132, 135, 137; "The Latecomers," 128, 132; "The Quiet in the Land," 128, 133; "Schoenberg: The First Hundred Years," 128; The Solitude Trilogy, 128, 139n. Recordings: Bach's The Art of the Fugue, Fugues 1-9, 46, 96, 98, 99-101; Bach's Partita No. 5, 24; Bach's Two and Three-Part Inventions, 106-107, 113; Beethoven's Fifth Symphony, 74, 85-86; Beethoven's Sonatas, Opus 109/110/111, 16; Brahms' Intermezzos, 135; Emperor Concerto, 49, 72; Goldberg Variations, 15, 16, 37, 38; Handel: Suites for Harpsichord, Nos. 1-4, 101, 102; The Well-Tempered Clavier, 38-39, 126. Writings: Arnold Schoenberg: A Perspective, 142; "Bodky on Bach," 143; "The Prospects of Recording," 29, 32; "The Search for Petula Clark," 71

Gould, Russell Herbert, 1
Grieg, Edvard, 1, 71
Guerrero, Alberto, 3, 5, 6, 12, 53, 152
Guy, Elizabeth Benson, 10
Haggin, B.H., 135, 140, 141
Hambourg, Mark, 77, 78
Hamilton Symphony Orchestra, 12
Harpsichord, 110, 112
Harpsi-piano, 104
Haydn, Franz Joseph, 153, 155
Heinze, Bernard, 10, 152
Hess, Myra, 13, 23
High Fidelity Magazine, 31, 96
Hindemith, Paul, 37, 53
Hofmann, Josef, ix, 2, 33, 135
Holiday, 3
Homburger, Walter, 12, 15, 17
Horowitz, Vladimir, 62
Hume, Paul, 13-14
Hunter College (New York), 19, 141, 142
Hurwitz, Robert, 129
"The Idea of North" (radio broadcast), 128, 129, 131-132, 135, 137
The Idea of North (recording), 54, 138
Idealism, musical, 80-88, 97-98
Intentions of the artist, 154
Israel, 18, 93
Ives, Charles, 53
Kaiser, Joachim, 52, 65, 135, 145
Kant, Immanuel, 57

Tape editing, 39, 43, 49-50; appearing vs being in, 125-127; and coherence, 124-125

Tchaikovsky, Peter Ilyich, 84

Technology, and action at a distance, 56; and art, 120-121, 145; and "the charity of the machine," 51, 56, 61, 63, 69-71, 120-121, 122; and music, 35-36, 69. See also Recording technology

Tel Aviv, 93

Tone-quality, 109, 117-118

Toronto, 1, 55; "Beach" neighbourhood of, 6

Toronto Conservatory of Music. See Royal Conservatory of Music of Toronto

Toronto Daily Star, 10

Toronto Evening Telegram, 8

Toronto Symphony, 10, 12, 152

Tovell, Vincent, 82

Tovey, Donald Francis, 46, 72

Town Hall (New York), 14

Transcription of music, 84-87

Tureck, Rosalyn, 7, 13, 102

University of Cincinnati, 19, 142

University of Toronto, 19

University of Wisconsin, 19

Unspecified open score, 6, 80, 83-84, 98

Uptergrove (Ontario), 1, 2, 12, 51, 55, 93

Utilitarianism, 70

Uxbridge (Ontario), 1

Valen, Fartein, 144; Sonata No. 2, Opus 38, 144

Vancouver Symphony Orchestra, 12

van Meegeren, Hans. See Meegeren, Hans van

Vienna, 17

Vivaldi, Antonio, 156

von Karajan, Herbert. See Karajan, Herbert von

Wagner, Richard, 85, 86-87. Works: Die Götterdämmerung, 85; Die Meistersinger, 85; Lohengrin Prelude, 86; Rienzi, 86; Siegfried Idyll, 85, 86; Tannhäuser Overture 86; Tristan und Isolde, 7

Webern, Anton, 8, 13. Works: Opus 5, 8; Variations, Opus 27, 13

The Well-Tempered Clavier, 4, 38-39, 83-84, 126

Wellesley College, 19

"Whimsical Nonsense," 7

Willan, Healey, 96

Williamson Road Public School, 2, 51

Wodson, Edward W., 8-9, 10, 11